INTIFADA

INTIFADA

THE PALESTINIAN UPRISING

DON PERETZ
SUNY–Binghamton

WESTVIEW PRESS
BOULDER ◆ SAN FRANCISCO ◆ LONDON

Published in 1990 in the United States of America by Westview Press, Inc., 5500 Central Avenue, Boulder, Colorado 80301, and in the United Kingdom by Westview Press, Inc., 13 Brunswick Centre, London WC1N 1AF, England

Library of Congress Cataloging-in-Publication Data
Peretz, Don, 1922–
   Intifada: the Palestinian uprising/Don Peretz.
     p. cm.
   Includes bibliographical references.
   ISBN 0-8133-0859-3—ISBN 0-8133-0860-7 (pbk.)
   1. West Bank—History—Palestinian Uprising, 1987–   . 2. Gaza Strip—
History—Palestinian Uprising, 1987–   . I. Title.
DS110.W47P46 1990
956.95'3044—dc20   89-25076
                                                                                                  CIP

Printed and bound in the United States of America

 The paper used in this publication meets the requirements of the American National Standard for Permanence of Paper for Printed Library Materials Z39.48-1984.

10   9   8   7   6   5   4   3   2   1

CONTENTS

ILLUSTRATIONS

PREFACE

This book is intended as an overview of the uprising—the Intifada—of the Palestinian Arabs in the West Bank and Gaza, territories occupied by Israel since the June 1967 war. In the two years since the Intifada began during December 1987, it has acquired unusual international importance and visibility and has led to a number of significant changes in the policies of the principal actors involved, especially Israel, the United States, the Palestine Liberation Organization, and the Palestinian inhabitants of the occupied territories. The Intifada has altered, in many ways, the dimensions of the Arab-Israeli conflict by rearranging the order of political and diplomatic priorities of those involved and by thrusting the conflict to the forefront of international attention. This book describes the background, origins, and causes of the uprising and its impact on the actors; it also examines the prospects for coping with it.

I am obligated to my wife, Dr. Maya Peretz, for her assistance in preparing the manuscript and in helping to meet the publisher's deadlines, which sprang upon us more quickly than anticipated. Thanks also go to Deena Hurwitz, to *Palestine Perspectives*, and to the UNRWA Liaison Office in New York for the photos used. Finally, I wish to express my appreciation to the Rockefeller Foundation for the time I spent at its Study Center in Bellagio, Italy, during the final editing stage of this book.

Don Peretz

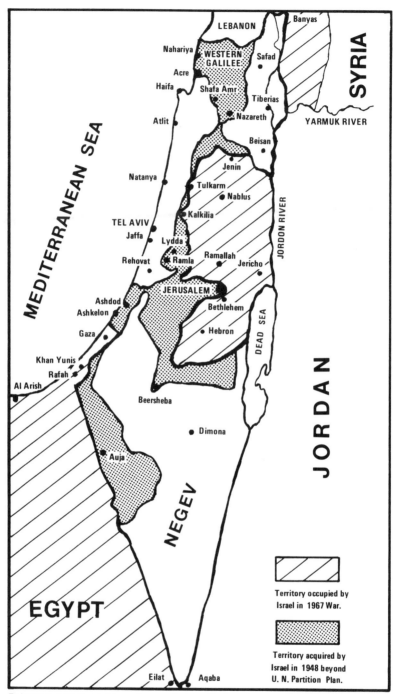

Palestine, Israel, and Israeli-occupied territories. *Source:* Don Peretz, *The Government and Politics of Israel,* 2nd ed. (Boulder, Colo.: Westview Press, 1983).

1

ORIGINS OF THE INTIFADA

The Palestine uprising, or Intifada, that erupted in Gaza and the West Bank during December 1987 was the latest manifestation of the 70-year-old Arab-Israeli conflict. The roots of the struggle can be traced to the nineteenth century, which witnessed the rise of Arab nationalism and of Zionism, the movement to establish a Jewish national home in Palestine. Both movements were influenced by modern European nationalism, but each had its own distinctive characteristics.

Arab nationalism was in part a reaction against the Ottoman government, which had controlled Palestine and other Arabic-speaking areas of the Eastern Mediterranean since the sixteenth century. In the early twentieth century, the Ottomans attempted to make the Turkish language and culture dominant in their empire, a course of action opposed by Arab nationalists who wanted to revivify their own tradition.

Jewish nationalism—in part a reaction to European anti-Semitism, in part an attempt to revive the Hebrew language and culture—sought to unite the Jews of the world in support of a home in Palestine, which, according to the Old Testament, was the land of their ancestral origin. The organized Jewish national movement was called Zionism; its goal, a return to Zion (after Mount Zion in Jerusalem). By the end of World War I, the Jews constituted about 10 percent of Palestine's population; more than 90 percent were Muslim and Christian Arabs.

After Turkey's defeat by the Allied Powers in World War I, the new League of Nations divided the former Arab provinces of the Ottoman Empire into mandates assigned to Great Britain and France. Britain received the mandate for Palestine and remained in control until 1948. During the war, the British had promised to aid both Arab nationalists and Zionists in the achievement of their goals in exchange for assistance, promises that were difficult if not impossible to reconcile in Palestine. Arab nationalists in the country opposed establishment of the Jewish national home there and demanded independence like the other neighboring Arab countries. The Zionists wanted Palestine to become a Jewish state and insisted that the British help them by permitting large-scale Jewish immigration, settlement, and development of the country. Despite continued conflict among the Arabs, British, and Jews during the mandate, the Zionists greatly expanded their presence, increasing the Jewish population by ten times, from 60,000 to 600,000—a growth from a tenth to a third of Palestine's population.

During World War II, liquidation by Nazi Germany of nearly 90 percent of European Jewry underscored the urgency of emigration from the continent. Zionists became more militant in their demands that the British open the gates of Palestine to Jewish refugees and increasingly impatient to establish the Jewish state. By the end of the war, Great Britain, weary of conflicts throughout its far-flung empire, decided to give up the mandate and turned the problem over to the newly formed United Nations. In November 1947, the UN General Assembly recommended partition of Palestine into Jewish and Arab states and an international zone encompassing Jerusalem and the surrounding areas. The Zionists accepted the partition proposal; but the Arabs of Palestine, supported by other Arab states, opposed it, and civil war broke out between the Jewish and Arab inhabitants. When the mandate ended, in May 1948, surrounding Arab states joined the fighting against the new nation of Israel declared on May 14, 1948, as the last British troops left the country.

Between 1947 and 1949, as a result of the first Arab-Israeli war, most Arabs left their homes in areas controlled by Israel. They became refugees in the surrounding Arab countries. During the next forty years, four more wars were fought between Israel and these states, in 1956, 1967, 1973, and 1982. In 1967, Israel defeated Egypt, Syria, and Jordan, thereby acquiring additional territory—the Sinai Peninsula and the Gaza Strip from Egypt, Arab East Jerusalem and the West Bank from Jordan, and the Golan Heights from Syria. Sinai was returned as part of the 1979 peace treaty with Egypt; however, Gaza, the Golan area, East Jerusalem, and the West Bank have been occupied by Israel since 1967. In Gaza and the West Bank there are several hundred thousand refugees who fled from Israel during the first war in 1947–1949 in addition to the indigenous Palestinian Arab population who remained in their homes. These nearly 2 million Arabs, both refugees and indigenous inhabitants, consider Palestine their homeland. And there are another approximately 2 million Palestinians scattered among surrounding countries (Jordan, Lebanon, Syria, the Arabian Peninsula) as well as beyond the Middle East, who continue to identify with their homeland and with their compatriots living under Israeli occupation.

After the Arab defeat in the 1967 war, a new phase of Palestinian Arab nationalism began. Several new guerrilla organizations and other Palestinian groups were formed, most eventually becoming part of the Palestine Liberation Organization (PLO), established in 1964. The PLO underwent a metamorphosis after the 1967 war. Both the United Nations and the prevailing international consensus acknowledged it as the representative of the Palestinian people. Since 1967, the PLO and its various affiliated factions have become the organization that most Palestinians regard as their spokesman. Although the PLO did not initiate the Intifada, it soon played an important role in the organization of the latter and in maintaining contact between Palestinians under occupation and the outside world.

Israel has refused either to recognize the PLO or to enter direct negotiations with it. While the stated reason is the organization's "terrorist" activity, even more important is the fact that relations with the PLO would be tantamount to recognizing the national rights of the Palestinians. Many Israelis are reluctant to validate Palestinian nationalism because they fear it would undermine their own claims to the country. Even before 1967 there were Israeli nationalists who believed that all of mandatory Palestine belonged by right to the Jewish people. After Israel conquered the territories in 1967, a strong movement emerged calling for annexation of the West Bank and Gaza (Golan and East Jerusalem were annexed by 1982). As a principal goal of the large Likud party has been to annex the territories, its leaders have been more reluctant than those in Labor, the other large party, to make territorial concessions for peace. Former Likud Prime Minister Menachem Begin was willing to return Sinai to Egypt as part of the peace settlement, but he and his Likud colleagues regard the West Bank and Gaza as part of the historical Land of Israel; therefore, they refuse to consider the possibility of departure from these territories.

Differences between Likud and Labor over the future of the territories have been a major obstacle to changing the status quo of continuous occupation—and it is the occupation that, after twenty years, led to the Intifada. The uprising soon attracted world attention. In 1988, it dominated events in Israel and the occupied territories, becoming the focus of media coverage of the Arab-Israel conflict and the Middle East. Repercussions of the Intifada were widespread, affecting not only the policies of Israel but also those of the Arab world, Western European nations, and the United States.

Within the West Bank and Gaza, the Intifada had far-reaching influences on the political, economic, social, and even cultural life of the Palestinian Arab population. As a result, fundamental changes began to appear in most aspects of daily life—in the power structure of the community;

in relations between men and women, youth and their elders, Christians and Muslims, and urban and rural settlements, and among the various regional centers of the West Bank and Gaza. It is probably still too early to determine whether these changing relationships will become permanent or to what extent they will have a truly revolutionary impact on Palestinian society. But it seems likely that the "shaking up" of this society has been so traumatic that many aspects of the change that occurred during 1988 will be long-lasting. (In Arabic, Intifada means "to shake off.")

The outward manifestations of the Intifada were not new or unique during the twenty years of Israeli occupation. On many occasions since 1967, there have been eruptions of discontent among the Palestinians and countermeasures taken by occupation forces to repress them. The years since 1967 have been replete with incidents involving stone throwing, Molotov cocktails, strikes, demonstrations, refusal to pay taxes, large-scale arrests, imprisonment without trial, deportations, punitive destruction of homes and property, beating, and the use of tear gas and live ammunition against crowds. What, then, is new or unique about the events that began in December 1987, and why have they become the focus of so much local and international concern?

The major purpose of this book is to examine the Intifada in the context of regional and international events; to place the uprising in the time-frame of past, present, and future; to determine why it is unique; and to discover its significance in the contemporary history of the Middle East.

ORIGINS OF CIVIL RESISTANCE

Within weeks of the conquest and occupation of the West Bank and Gaza, Israel initiated policies intended to integrate the territories into its security system and economic infrastructure. It was clear from the nature of Israeli investments in military facilities, the road network, and water and electricity supplies that the occupation would be prolonged beyond a mere matter of weeks or months. Although the legal framework of the previous Jordanian authority was maintained in the West Bank, within three weeks of occupation the Israeli Knesset amended its own basic legislation, the Law and Administration Ordinance, empowering "the Government to extend Israeli law, jurisdiction and public administration over the entire area of Eretz Israel [former mandatory Palestine]."[1] This law was accompanied by legislation empowering the minister of interior to enlarge by proclamation any municipal corporation designed under the Law and Administration Ordinance. On the following day, June 28, 1967, the borders of Jerusalem were extended and Israeli legislation was applied to the enlarged capital under the terms of the new laws.

Since the occupation began, Israeli law has been extended only to East Jerusalem and the Golan Heights, not to the West Bank and the Gaza region. However, Israelis who favor annexation have exerted strong pressure on the government to take advantage of the legislation that is in place and to apply Israeli law to all the occupied territories—a step tantamount to annexation. Instead, the West Bank and Gaza have been ruled under a system of military government initiated in June 1967. There are separate military government administrators for the West Bank and Gaza, but both are responsible to the minister of defense. In each area the military governor is vested with the authority held by the ruler prior to occupation—in the West Bank, with the authority of the previous Jordanian government, and in Gaza, with that of the former Egyptian administrators. The military governors have total executive and legislative power, which enables them to make new laws, cancel old ones, and suspend or annul existing ones.[2] They are responsible only to the minister of defense, not to any other public authority or body. Legislation and actions of the military government are not subject to review or supervision (although in some respects the Supreme Court of Israel has very limited authority over military law), and the minister of defense may be called to account in the Knesset for the actions of his subordinates. The general practice of military government is to maintain the Jordanian or Egyptian legal system that existed prior to the occupation. Since 1967, however, Israeli commanders have modified the previous legislation by unilaterally issuing some 1,500 new military orders governing all aspects of life including education, agriculture, land and water rights, taxation, and social welfare, as well as security and military matters. Changes in pre-occupation legislation have been so extensive that for all practical purposes, a new Israeli legal and administrative structure imposed on the old evolved during the last two decades.

While the international consensus frequently perceives Israeli policies and their implementation to be in violation of the 1949 Fourth Geneva Convention dealing with occupied territories, Israel maintains that it has not contravened international law because it does not recognize Gaza and the West Bank as occupied territories. According to Israeli perception, neither Jordan nor Egypt has legal claims within the area of former mandatory Palestine; indeed, Israel is seen as having proprietary rights (both legal and moral) to all of Palestine, which is regarded as Eretz Israel even by political factions opposed to outright annexation. Most Israelis base their claims on Israel's ancient borders and on the borders set during the British mandatory period from 1920 to 1948. From the official Israeli view, this common perception thus vitiates any rights of the Palestinian Arabs to establish an independent political entity within the borders of former mandatory Palestine because all the country belongs to the Jewish people.

This fundamental difference in perceptions of "national rights"—in reality a continuation of the seventy-year conflict between the Zionist and Palestinian Arab nationalist movements for control of former mandatory Palestine—is the root cause of tensions leading to the Intifada of 1988. Israel's conquest of all of mandatory Palestine in 1967 forced the issue to a head by confronting Palestinians with a new reality— the reality of total Israeli control of "their" land and of approximately half the total population that identifies itself as Palestinian. In the period from the establishment of Israel in 1948 to 1967, only a small number of Palestinians, the Arab citizen minority of Israel, were subject to the authority of the Jewish State. The Arab defeat in the 1967 war, followed by the extension of Israel's rule over all of Palestine and over approximately one and a half million additional Palestinians, was a major factor in the resurgence of Palestinian nationalism, demands for self-determination, and emergence of the Palestinian resistance movement.

From the beginning in 1967, the resistance movement had two forms: paramilitary and civil. Israel quickly ended most significant paramilitary activity within areas under its control, and since 1967 such armed resistance has been carried out by the various Palestinian commando or guerrilla organizations operating outside of the occupied territories. Most of these organizations are affiliated with the PLO; all are labeled by Israel as terrorist organizations. These diverse paramilitary factions periodically stage incursions into Israel and the occupied territories; but in terms of damage to or losses by Israel, they are more of a nuisance than a serious military threat. From the Palestinian perspective, their value has been in consciousness raising and propaganda.

Far more serious has been the rise and persistence of civil resistance. From the early days, there has been widespread opposition to Israeli occupation and to the policies for its implementation. Within weeks of the war, several Palestinian notables, mostly spokesmen for Jordan, were deported for leading protests against the occupation and unification of Jerusalem.[3] The first deportee, in September 1967, was Sheikh Abd al-Hamid al-Sayih, president of the Jerusalem Sharia Court and a leader of the Muslim community. Former mayor of Jordanian East Jerusalem, Ruhi al-Khatib, was deported in March 1968 after being charged with inciting the population to strike and with spreading false information about Israeli policies. Deportation of Palestinians charged with disrupting security or public order has remained a constant form of punishment throughout the occupation period. An estimated 2,000 residents have been forcibly deported since 1967.[4]

UNRWA distributes food to children at Agency schools in the Gaza Strip. UNRWA photo by Zaven Mazakian.

Sparked by Israel's unification of Jerusalem, widespread public opposition to the occupation began in July 1967 and quickly spread throughout the territories. Other issues causing protests were military censorship of school texts and punitive demolition of Arab houses; but most important of all was the protest against the occupation itself. A pattern of civic resistance soon developed that persisted for the next twenty years, consisting of strikes by merchants, businesses, and schools, demonstrations by marchers, the display of Palestinian flags or national colors, and the chanting of slogans calling for independence. High school and university students were often in the vanguard, shouting slogans that identified them with the guerrillas labeled as terrorists by Israelis. These demonstrations often degenerated into stone throwing, spitting, and insults aimed at the Israeli troops.

Israeli reaction has followed a consistent pattern as well, gradually escalating over the years until it reached the levels of 1988. Initially, attempts were made to quell demonstrations through such conventional police tactics as the use of water hoses, clubs, and tear gas; then warning shots were fired; and, finally, the demonstrators were directly shot at. When demonstrations persisted, curfews were imposed on neighborhoods, refugee camps, or whole towns and cities. Since 1967, schools and universities have been periodically closed by the military, which charged that they were the focal points of the disturbances. Both men and women students were among those arrested as "ring leaders" of the resistance. Many were held without trial, and many were deported.

Israeli tactics for dealing with civil resistance to the occupation have scarcely altered in twenty years, although the intensity of one or another method might have changed. The strikes and demonstrations have had little impact within Israel itself, even though "the Israel government came to view them as a threat to its own security, in large part because it believed that local terrorists were recruited from among those who first had been involved in such political protest activities. Thus Israel took an increasingly severe line on demonstrations, which in turn fanned the resistance of the West Bank population and added to the likelihood of violent action during the demonstrations."[5]

The military authorities have had several rationales for dealing severely with civil resistance. Initially, they maintained that use of harsh measures would discourage youths from participating in demonstrations or other forms of protest; that the imposition of fines and curfews or the closing of shops would cause such economic stress that community elders and leaders would deter or contain anti-occupation activities; and that the arrest, imprisonment, or deportation of "troublemakers" would diminish if not eliminate the number of political protests. Little faith was put in attempts to win over the population through "good works," for as ex-Defense Minister Dayan observed: "To be fair, the main source of unrest is that they don't want to see us here, they don't like the occupation." Attempts to "manage" or "manipulate"[6] civil unrest were made through various tactics, including the use by intelligence services of informers to create divisiveness within the Palestinian community, the instigation or rekindling of family and tribal feuds, and, in 1982, the establishment of Village Leagues.

The twenty-year-long attempts to cope with civil resistance certainly failed to eliminate it. Some might argue that the resistance was contained and would have totally undermined Israeli control of the territories had military tactics been less severe, but indications are that the contrary is true, that the measures used intensified and extended opposition to the occupation. This is evidenced by the rise in new generations of leaders to replace those who were deported over the years. As Palestinian "notables" were deported, new leaders emerged, and as they were imprisoned or deported, still others replaced them; consequently, the number of those in prison or deported has not decreased but instead has grown over the years. It seems that the larger the number of those punished, the greater the increase in the number of dissidents; hence the tactics used by the military to remove or contain the leadership have been counterproductive.

During the later 1960s, establishment leaders such as school principals, mayors, and other former Jordanian officials attempted to contain demonstrations and other civil resistance, fearing that the situation would get out of hand. In 1969 the mayor of Nablus even assigned municipal constables to calm student unrest, and the Arab head of the Nablus Education Department called on school principals to obtain parental cooperation in ending student strikes. However, such attempts have nearly ended as strikers and demonstrators have increasingly disregarded the advice or admonitions of traditional establishment leaders. Rather, they have found new leaders outside of and beyond the establishment who have made the "traditionalists" all but irrelevant.

"GOOD WORKS" VERSUS ECONOMIC "INTEGRATION"

Israeli "good works" in the territories, a strategy that in the early 1980s was called "improvement of the quality of life," aimed at sustaining the Palestinian economy. Occupation authorities maintained that: "Since 1967 economic life in the area [West Bank] has been characterized by rapid growth and a very substantial increase in living standards, made possible by the interaction of economies of the areas with that of Israel."[7] There are sufficient indicators to demonstrate areas of economic improvement, such as the annual increase in the value of agricultural production, improved methods of cultivation, decreased infant mortality rates, decline of infectious diseases, larger percentage of girls attending schools, and total increase in school attendance—in sum, an overall rise in living standards. However, the value of such "good works" was vitiated in the eyes of the occupied Palestinians by the steady attrition of control and even influence over their own economic fate.

Most significant was the actual physical loss of territory through acquisition of land by Israeli authorities for Jewish settlement and usage. By the end of the first twenty years of occupation, Israeli authorities had requisitioned nearly half the total land area in the West Bank and a third in Gaza.[8] Concomitant with loss of the land itself was a sharp decline in the number of Palestinians employed in agriculture, which was the principal occupation until the late 1970s.[9] Most peasants displaced from agriculture found employment in a variety of mostly unskilled jobs at the bottom of the wage and social scales in Israel; several tens of thousands left the occupied territories to seek work in neighboring Arab countries.

There has been no substantial loss of agricultural land cultivated and irrigated by Palestinians in the West Bank, but in Gaza there was a decrease that forced many out of farming. Since 1967 little effort has been made by Israeli authorities to encourage further agricultural development through basic structural changes such as investment in infrastructure, extension of irrigation systems, or land reform. According to Meron Benvenisti, Israeli strategy sought to

> improve conditions as far as possible within the framework of existing resources, without any essential changes. . . . Palestinian agriculture was allowed to develop only insofar as it would not affect Israeli agriculture, and on condition that its development would not involve a fiscal or economic drain on the Israeli economy or government. West Bank agriculture has been made to fit into the Israeli system and adjust itself to the demands of the "common market" created after the occupation. Naturally, the stronger and more developed economy gained the advantage over the weak and undeveloped one.[10]

Attempts by Palestinian farmers to market their produce in Europe free of Israeli control entailed a long struggle. Until 1987 all agricultural exports to Europe had to be channeled through the Agricultural Export Company (AGREXCO), Israeli's export marketing organization owned by its farming establishment. This produce was sold under the Israeli brand name "Carel." Though forced to market through AGREXCO, Palestinian farmers did not receive the same rights as Israelis. The latter could sell their produce in the occupied territories without permits, but Palestinians had to receive government permission to market within Israel; moreover, Palestinians did not receive extension assistance from the agricultural ministry in developing new crops.[11] Only since 1987, at the insistence of the European Economic Community (EEC), have Arab farmers in the occupied territories been permitted to make direct sales to European markets.

A major constraint against expansion of Palestinian agriculture in the occupied territories has been the limited water supply. This vital resource was removed from the control of the indigenous population and integrated into the Israeli-imposed "common market." Israeli experts perceive Palestine's hydrological resources to be an integrated whole that must remain under their control to maintain the country's agricultural and industrial development. They argue that without control of water-sources potential, the entire system would collapse. While plans exist for expanding water supplies for Jewish agriculture in the West Bank, the supplement planned for the Arab sector is for domestic use only. Currently, the water available to the West Bank Palestinian population is 23 percent of the total potential; plans call for an allocation of 137 million cubic meters (mcm) for the 1 million West Bank Palestinians and 100 mcm for the 100,000 Jewish settlers in the area.[12]

In Gaza the situation is potentially more disastrous. The low water table is already endangered by the inflow of sea water, resulting in increased salination and damage to the local citrus crop. As a consequence, the Israeli water authority has imposed severe restrictions on water use and banned the digging of new wells by local Arab farmers. These restrictions have not applied to new Israeli settlements within the Gaza region, which have sunk dozens of new wells in recent years. In 1984 Israelis consumed an average of 14,200–28,000 cubic meters (cm) of water, as compared to the Gazan average of 200 cm.[13] The separate water systems that existed before 1967 in Gaza and the West Bank have been taken over in recent years by Mekorot, the Israeli national water system.

An integral aspect of the "common market" has been the employment of tens of thousands of Palestinians from Gaza and the West Bank in Israel. About a third of the Palestinian labor force works in Israel, although this estimate does not reflect the large number of black market laborers employed "unofficially." The largest numbers work in agriculture, construction, and services, occupations in which Jewish workers have been increasingly difficult to find, even during times of unemployment. While the pay received by Arab workers is usually higher than that in the occupied territories, it is generally at the bottom of Israeli wage scales. Furthermore, fringe benefits—though pro-forma—are minimal and often difficult to obtain.

Cash payments received by Arab workers in Israel have contributed significantly to building construction and to increased acquisition of household and consumer items such as radios, television sets, and refrigerators. But they have contributed little either to expansion of agriculture and industry or to development of the local economies of Gaza and the West Bank.

Israel has benefited from the availability of this large pool of cheap labor, which

it can utilize or marginalize [i.e., use to supplement Israeli labor] without great risk to its own economy. In periods of economic prosperity, for example, the availability of large resources of labor has had a stabilizing effect on wages inside Israel and in periods of recession, has acted as a repository for surplus labor. . . . The resulting state of dependency of the Palestinian labor market on the economy of Israel, renders the former vulnerable to the political, social and economic exigencies of the latter.[14]

12

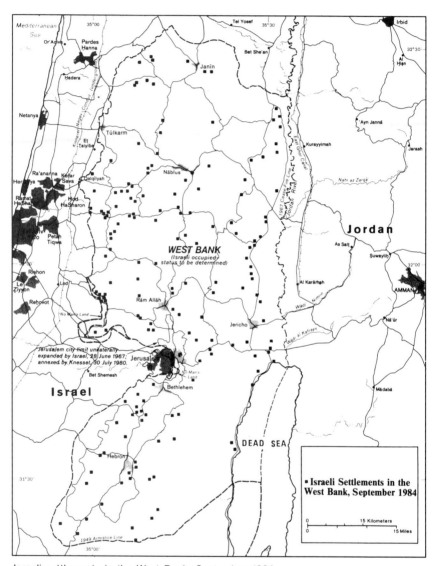

Israeli settlements in the West Bank, September 1984.

Industrial development in the territories since 1967 has been stagnant. The number of workers remains minimal: approximately 7,000 in Gaza and 15,000 in the West Bank. Most Palestinian goods sold in Israel have been subcontracted for Israel firms. Manufactured items sold in the territories must compete with Israeli products, which receive "massive protection as well as government subsidies and credit. . . . Moreover, lately the industry of the West Bank has had to compete with Israeli enterprises located in the territories and enjoying far-reaching benefits."[15]

Since the 1970s, the electricity supplies of the West Bank and Gaza have been gradually integrated into the Israeli national grid, despite attempts by the Palestinian population to maintain its own systems. The government waged a twenty-year legal battle against the East Jerusalem Electricity Company, which supplied power to Arab Jerusalem and several other places. Through a series of measures the Israeli Corporation extended its control such that, by the end of the 1980s, it dominated electricity supplies in all but a few towns and villages with their own grids or generators. Immediate plans for expansion call for providing Arab families with about half the kilowattage of Jewish families, which according to the Corporation reflects different living standards and levels of use.[16]

Israeli plans for economic integration of the West Bank and Gaza into its "common market" started in the late 1960s, when the Labor Alignment controlled the government. Despite Labor's assertions that it opposed annexation, Defense Minister Dayan, who had full power in the territories, proclaimed a policy of "new facts," emphasizing that Israel was in the territories by "right and not on sufferance, to visit, live and to settle."[17] Under the "new facts" policy, limited Jewish settlement was authorized in the West Bank at strategic sites not heavily populated by Arabs. Israeli Jewish investment was encouraged through cheaper prices for raw materials, low interest rates on loans, and other economic incentives. Within ten years some 4,200 Jews had established 36 West Bank settlements. Within the next ten years (i.e., by 1987), a threefold increase in settlements had occurred, and the number of settlers had grown nearly twenty times. The massive increase in Jewish settlement after 1977 was accompanied by acceleration of the economic integration process (i.e., consolidation of the "common market") and by increased severity in dealing with Arab opposition to the skein of measures initiated by the Likud government that replaced Labor in 1977.

Labor's policies in the West Bank had been more ambiguous than those of Likud, largely because of divisiveness within its ranks about the future of the territories, and because public opinion was also divided on the issue of annexation. Likud, by contrast, was a bloc of nationalist factions held together by the vision of territorial unification in the "whole

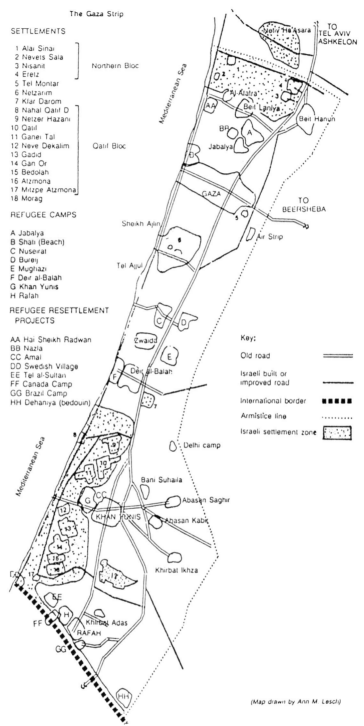

The Gaza Strip

SETTLEMENTS

1 Alai Sinai ⎫
2 Nevets Sala ⎪
3 Nisanit ⎬ Northern Bloc
4 Eretz ⎪
5 Tel Montar ⎭
6 Netzarim
7 Kfar Darom
8 Nahal Qatif D ⎫
9 Netzer Hazani ⎪
10 Qatif ⎪
11 Ganei Tal ⎪
12 Neve Dekalim ⎬ Qatif Bloc
13 Gadid ⎪
14 Gan Or ⎪
15 Bedolah ⎪
16 Atzmona ⎪
17 Mitzpe Atzmona ⎭
18 Morag

REFUGEE CAMPS

A Jabalya
B Shati (Beach)
C Nuseirat
D Burelj
E Mughazi
F Deir al-Balah
G Khan Yunis
H Rafah

REFUGEE RESETTLEMENT
 PROJECTS

AA Hai Sheikh Radwan
BB Nazla
CC Amal
DD Swedish Village
EE Tel al-Sultan
FF Canada Camp
GG Brazil Camp
HH Dehaniya (bedouin)

TO
TEL AVIV
ASHKELON

TO
BEERSHEBA

Key:

Old road

Israeli built or
improved road

International border

Armistice line

Israeli settlement zone

(Map drawn by Ann M. Lesch)

Jewish settlements, Palestinian refugee camps, and resettlement projects in the Gaza Strip. *Source: Journal of Palestine Studies,* No. 57, Autumn 1985, p. 50.

land of Israel." Among the campaign promises that brought it to power were removal of restraints and restrictions on Jewish settlement in the territories, tougher policies toward Arab dissidents, and eventual incorporation of the West Bank and Gaza under Israeli hegemony.

THE RISE OF RESISTANCE
TO "INTEGRATION"

As we have seen, Arab opposition to "integration" schemes began as early as July 1967 and has continued ever since. It was emphasized yet again in the West Bank municipal elections of April 1976, before the Likud hard-line policies were introduced. In the election for mayors of twenty-four towns and nearly two hundred municipal council representatives, "notables" representing established families and "moderates" known for their willingness to cooperate with Israeli authorities were defeated. Many of the new elected officials were militant opponents of the occupation and clearly supporters of the PLO as their "sole legitimate representative." The election results were in part a reaction to the 1975 proposals of then Defense Minister Shimon Peres to establish a "civil administration" authorizing Palestinian local "self-rule" under Israeli control. In several areas, nationalist blocs formed during the 1976 election campaign under the slogan "NO to [Peres's] civil administration; YES to [Palestinian] National Front!" As Danny Rubinstein, the Israeli West Bank correspondent for *Davar*, observed: "The Arab public regard this [Peres's] plan as eyewash, since the Israeli government will maintain its control and the autonomy will be false."[18]

Within six months of assuming office, Likud's Prime Minister Menachem Begin was confronted with Egyptian President Anwar Sadat's peace initiative. Begin responded in December 1977 with a new version of civil administration. His plan was to become the basis of the 1978 Camp David proposals for autonomy in the West Bank and Gaza. The new autonomy scheme aroused no more enthusiasm than had the previous Peres proposals for civil administration. Begin's plan only provoked increased tensions between the population of the territories and the Israeli military authorities.

In the early 1980s, the Likud government decided to proceed unilaterally with implementation of Begin's scheme through military order 947, which established another "civilian administration" in the West Bank to deal with "the civilian affairs of the inhabitants." Gradually, civil administration was assumed by local Palestinians who took on certain tasks of the military government. The new administration was to be not "an administration operated by civilians, but an administration dealing with the affairs of civilians."[19] A major objective in establishing the new procedures was to undermine PLO influence in the territories—an influence held accountable for resistance to the occupation and to Begin's autonomy plan. To counteract the PLO, which was most influential in the larger Arab towns and cities, a system of Village Leagues was organized whose members were traditionally at odds with their more sophisticated urban compatriots. Palestinians who cooperated with the "rules of the game" were rewarded with financial patronage and priority in employment and housing, and a special fund was made accessible to the Village Leagues. Those unwilling to "play the game" were subjected to harsh penalties and cut off from outside financial assistance. Within a few months of adopting the new policy, the pro-PLO mayors of the larger West Bank cities were dismissed, and the number of deportations, curfews, house demolitions, seizures of property, and imprisonments without trial increased.

Measures taken to implement order 947 during November 1981 sparked a new wave of popular opposition to military government, the largest since 1967. To many it seemed that the West Bank was about to erupt into full-scale insurrection. Many Palestinians and Israelis, as well, regarded the new "reforms" as a decisive move toward annexation. Opposition to civil administration was led by students at the four West Bank universities (Bethlehem, Hebron, an-Najah, and Bir Zeit), resulting in their shutdown by the military for weeks or months. When municipal councils refused to cooperate with the new Israeli "civil authorities," Palestinian officials were replaced by Israeli army officers and curfews were imposed. Nine mayors were dismissed, their authority turned over to Israeli officials by the end of 1982. The National Guidance Council (NGC), established in 1978 to coordinate protest activities, was disbanded in March 1982. The twenty-eight-member Council included mayors of the six largest West Bank cities and towns, as well as representatives of professional organizations in the West Bank and Gaza. Israeli authorities described the NGC as an "arm of the PLO," responsible for "subversive activity," "political and ideological violence," and deterioration of the security situation. On several occasions the military had debated outlawing the NGC: At the time, observers believed that the decision to act would favor the Village Leagues by silencing their strongest opponents.

Opposition intensified in response to the crackdown, beginning with a general strike called by the Association of Engineers and Lawyers in November 1981. The army ordered an end to the strike and detained several NGC members who had organized it. Israeli officials blamed the continuing unrest and civil disturbances on the PLO, pointing to broadcasts from abroad that called on the population to resist the new Civil Administration.

When the first West Bank mayor, Ibrahim Tawil of al-Bireh, was dismissed in March 1982, he denounced the Israeli order, insisting that he still maintained office as the legal representative of his town. Other mayors were divided on how to cope with this unprecedented situation. The moderate mayor of Bethlehem, Elias Freij, believed that it would better serve the interests of his population if he remained in office. Most mayors, however, followed the lead of Nablus's Bassam Shak'a, who preferred to wait for word from the PLO headquarters in Beirut. The majority finally concluded that the Israeli military would welcome their resignations; therefore, they decided to remain in office "to fight the Civil Administration with all their strength."[20]

By March rioting had again intensified, spreading through most of the West Bank and Gaza. Bloody clashes with the authorities were frequent, and civil unrest was greater than in any period since the occupation had begun. Demonstrators put up roadblocks, stoned Israeli vehicles, and often clashed with Israeli troops. Protesters chanted slogans such as "Palestine is Arab!" and "Get out of Palestine!" Stores closed by Palestinian proprietors during the strike were welded shut by the Israeli army. Against the advice by the Israeli civil administrator, who was an army colonel, Chief-of-Staff General Raphael Eitan increased personal and collective punishments and gave Jewish settlers greater freedom to participate in combating the unrest. Most settlers were members of Gush Emunim (Bloc of the Faithful), which for a long time has demanded more severe measures to repress Arab civil resistance.

Participation by Jewish settlers in dispersing demonstrations led to several incidents in which they killed or wounded Palestinians. The settlers asserted that they fired in self-defense only, although one settler was arrested for manslaughter. In "retaliatory actions" against Arab towns and villages, the settlers smashed car windows, broke into houses, and beat up youths for rioting or throwing rocks.

Following dismissal of Arab mayors, the army imposed a new series of restrictions. The Civil Administration began to reject requests for licenses and permits required to operate municipal services. When municipal employees struck, they were ordered to report for work or be dismissed. Censorship was tightened on the Arabic press in East Jerusalem, and when the pro-PLO dailies al-Faj'r and al-Sha'b rejected the new regulations, they were banned in the territories. They continued to be sold in Jerusalem, which was under Israeli law and not subject to military authorities. New restrictions were also imposed on trade unions; their members were harassed by repeated military interrogations, and several union leaders were arrested.

The cohesiveness of Palestinian sentiment was demonstrated in a joint statement issued by the twenty-five West Bank municipalities on

May 1. The statement threatened to shut down all services unless the Civil Administration was abolished and the Arab mayors reinstated. It also reaffirmed allegiance to the PLO. Differences between radical and moderate leaders concerned the extent of the strike: The radicals called for a total strike without a termination date, whereas moderates such as the mayors of Bethlehem and Gaza supported a boycott of contacts with the Civil Administration but continuation of basic services such as water and electricity. Communal solidarity was also evidenced by the refusal of any local Arabs to replace the deposed mayors. The failure of the Israeli authorities to break through the wall of civil resistance and to recruit replacements for striking Palestinians was attributed by the Israelis to PLO threats against Arabs who collaborated with the authorities.

For the first time since the occupation began, there was widespread public criticism within Israel of the tactics used by the military to deal with Palestinian resistance. Prior to 1982 many fringe groups were critical, and "dovish" elements from Labor expressed doubts within the party about such tactics. Now, even former army commanders were questioning the new methods. One former West Bank commander, Brigadier Benjamin Ben-Eliezer, argued that attempts to impose the Civil Administration caused a power struggle between indigenous Palestinian leaders and Israeli authorities—a struggle that could "only lead to increased terrorist activity, and therefore tied down stronger IDF [Israeli Defense Force] forces."[21] Another former West Bank commander, Major General Raphael Vardi, believed it pointless to try and foster "an unnatural and synthetic" leadership. Vardi argued that "it is better to have a long and hard dialogue with the recognized leadership than with an unpopular and powerless one."[22] Many observers saw parallels with unsuccessful French policies in Algeria and British rule during the Mandate, when attempts were made to counter radical urban leadership with compliant rural notables. As the *Jerusalem Post* observed, "It is hard to believe that anybody in his right mind expects the army's punitive measures to cause the Palestinians to warm up to the idea of autonomy." *Ha-Aretz*, a leading independent Hebrew daily, in comparing the army's civil administrator to an Indian reservation governor, accused him of blowing up houses, arresting labor leaders, appropriating land, and banning distribution of hundreds of books.[23]

The killing of thirteen Palestinian civilians by the military between March and May aroused a storm of Israeli criticism. Many accused the army of overreacting, of having inadequate training and equipment for riot control, and of placing troops in "dangerous, dehumanizing situations." Overt criticism of army tactics came from many reserve officers who charged that failure to provide means of riot control with anything other than firearms inevitably led to uncontrolled shooting and casualties. The Histadrut newspaper, *Davar,* observed that "moral harm inflicted on Israel itself by the killing of rioters was worse even than the political damage." Despite the outcry against these tactics, public opinion supported government policy according to a poll commissioned by the *Jerusalem Post.*[24]

THE LEBANESE WAR
AND THE OCCUPATION

The outbreak of civil resistance in the territories only reinforced the determination of the Begin government to weed out manifestations of Palestinian nationalism and to uproot PLO influences that were blamed for the unrest. Many in the government, especially Defense Minister Ariel Sharon, believed that if the PLO were eliminated, the government could, with far less resistance, implement its plans for the occupied territories, including the autonomy and Civil Administration schemes. As long as the PLO had its autonomous political and military base in Beirut and south Lebanon, no alternative leadership could be fostered in the West Bank and Gaza.[25] Among the numerous additional motives for the June 1982 invasion of Lebanon, pacification of the occupied territories was the most significant. Even prior to the invasion, Sharon told the U.S. ambassador to Israel that the operation would help "solve the problem of the West Bank and Gaza."[26]

Defeat of the PLO in Lebanon and forced evacuation from its Beirut headquarters by September failed to have the results in occupied Palestine desired by Sharon. Removal of the PLO leadership from proximity to Israel neither diminished civil resistance nor made the population more compliant. Rather, it led Palestinians in the territories to conclude that only the PLO held hope for future salvation. The impact of Israeli attacks on Palestinian bases in Lebanon, where many West Bank and Gaza residents had relatives, was perceived as an attempt to liquidate the whole Palestinian community. Especially intense was the reaction to the massacre of Palestinians in the Beirut Sabra and Shatila refugee camps by Maronite militiamen allied with Israel, leading to renewed strikes, demonstrations, and clashes with the Israeli army. The failure by the Arab states to intervene in Lebanon or take other actions that might deter Israel, the "Arab conspiracy of silence," was regarded as treacherous; it was even compared to the Palestinian defeat in 1948 and to the Jordanian repressions of 1970–1971. Palestinians were seen as isolated and lonely, as distinct from other Arabs; many were thus led to feel "shame for being an Arab, but pride in being Palestinian."[27]

The failure of Sharon's plans in Lebanon was reflected in the attempts to revamp Israeli policies in the occupied territories after 1982. The Village Leagues were no longer the focal point in efforts by the military authorities to wean local leadership away from PLO. In November 1982 a new military coordinator of activities in the territories clamped down on finances and limited the privileges of the Leagues. Upon entering office, the new civil coordinator described the atmosphere awaiting him as a "scorched earth situation," declaring that he would attempt to reestablish contacts with all factions regardless of political orientation so as to keep open options for the future.[28]

His successor in July 1983 also adopted a somewhat more low-keyed rhetoric. He emphasized the need for dialogue, but specifically with pro-Hashemites who he hoped would emerge to take over the municipalities and replace the Israeli officers running them. Rather than forcing a precipitous break with the PLO, he announced that he would encourage the population to "disengage slowly," hoping to persuade them about the benefits of autonomy. While dismissing the Village Leagues as "unrepresentative and corrupt," he took a determined stance against reinstating the pro-PLO mayors who had been dismissed or deported. This "carrot-and-stick" approach was reinforced by orders from Chief-of-Staff Eitan to clamp down firmly on "instigators," with measures including curfews and collective economic sanctions imposed on "troublesome" areas. The access to supplies such as fuel and cement was cut off. Parents were to be punished for misconduct of children, an order that a military court later declared illegal. The court did, however, sanction the use of "reasonable force" in curbing violent riots—a necessity, it stated, to protect soldiers' lives. Arab residents, the court declared, should be aware of the risk they were taking in resorting to violence. At the trial in December 1982 of several soldiers charged with beating and harassing Arab residents, the soldiers defended their actions as being part of the army's hard line authorized by instructions from above. However, the court decided that such authorization was not included in any order from the chief-of-staff. During the first three months of 1983, more than 300 Palestinians received jail terms of up to nine months, and many were heavily fined. To prevent rock throwing from refugee camps, several such camps were encircled by high walls and subjected to lengthy curfews, for punitive as well as preventative purposes.[29]

Violent conflict between Jewish West Bank settlers and Palestinians escalated in 1983 as a result of the increased stoning of Israeli vehicles. Rock throwing, mostly aimed at Jewish settlers, was beginning to replace direct confrontations between the army and the demonstrators. The settlers blamed the deterioration of security on the failure by the military to take strong enough deterrent measures, and they threatened to organize their own "security committees" if the stoning continued. In May 1983 an underground Jewish organization, "the Fist of Defence," whose members were believed to be militant settlers, claimed credit for several vigilante acts. These included placing explosives in a Hebron mosque and sabotaging scores of Arab-owned vehicles—in retaliation, they said, for attacks on Jewish traffic.

In reaction to public criticism of the government for failure to control vigilantism, the Ministry of Justice established a commission to investigate the failure by the authorities to deal with Arab complaints against Jews. The commission's report blamed Jewish settlers for failing to cooperate with the police and for threatening Arabs who refused to sell land or who lodged complaints against the settlers. When the government neglected to act on its findings, the commissions's head, Deputy Attorney General Yehudit Karp, resigned in protest.

Clashes between settlers and the Arab population of Hebron erupted during July 1983 after a Yeshiva student was killed in the city. Jewish residents of the nearby town of Kiryat Arba retaliated by destroying and setting fire to Hebron's Arab market, and they blamed Defense Minister Moshe Arens for the murder because of his "soft" policy toward the Arabs. Settlers were among the prime suspects in an attack by three masked men at the Hebron Islamic University, also in July; after breaking into the university, they fired weapons and threw grenades, killing three students and wounding thirty-two. The army immediately imposed a curfew on the city and tear-gassed the protesting crowd that surrounded the hospital where the wounded had been taken.

Another point of tension between militant Jewish nationalists and Palestinians was the Haram al-Sharif in Jerusalem containing the Dome of the Rock and the al-Aqsa mosques, two of Islam's most sacred places. In Jewish tradition, the same area is believed to be the site of the twice-destroyed ancient Holy Temple. Although most Orthodox Jews refrain from entering the area enclosing the mosque lest they tread on ground that once contained the Holy of Holies, militant nationalists insist that Jewish control be reestablished so that the Holy Temple may be rebuilt there. After Israel's conquest of Jerusalem in 1967, Jewish militants, many of them West Bank settlers, demanded that the government remove all restrictions on Jewish prayer at the Temple Mount; and on several occasions they tried to force entry in order to stage demonstrations and prayer vigils within the Muslim area. In January 1984, their attempt to place explosives at the two mosques failed. The incident further inflamed an already tense situation, for Arab nationalists have long accused Israel of secret plans to evict them, destroy the mosques, and rebuild the Jewish Temple. When word of the sabotage attempt spread, it provoked riots throughout the West Bank and became a focus for anti-Israel demonstrations, especially by pious Muslims.

Security measures used by the army and outbursts of settler vigilantism helped undermine the "carrot" aspects of Israeli policy. Efforts to wean the population from loyalty to the PLO by cultivating pro-Jordanian moderates and "pragmatists" such as the mayors of Gaza and Bethlehem were subverted by political developments beyond the territories. These included the sixteenth session of the Palestine National Council convened during February in Algeria; the rift within Fatah, the largest faction of the PLO, that broke out in Lebanon during May; and deterioration of relations between PLO Chairman Yassir Arafat and Jordan's King Hussein. Such events, even when they appeared to threaten Arafat's leadership, galvanized public opinion in the territories behind him. Even the pro-Hashemites issued statements supporting Arafat. While divisiveness within PLO ranks outside Palestine seemed to threaten prospects for a united front against Israel, it did not appear to undermine the strong support for the organization or its leader among Palestinians within the territories. A poll conducted in June 1983 by the weekly magazine *al-Bayander Assiyasi* showed that more than 90 percent of West Bank Palestinians supported continuation of Arafat's leadership.[30]

"IMPROVING THE QUALITY OF LIFE"

Following the 1984 elections for Israel's eleventh Knesset and establishment of a National Unity Government (NUG), with Labor's Shimon Peres as prime minister and Likud's Itzhak Shamir as deputy prime minister, innovations were introduced in the "carrot" approach. These "good will gestures" were urged on Israel by U.S. Secretary of State George Shultz during 1982 as ways to "improve the quality of life" in the territories, as "confidence building measures" that might diminish tensions and entice local Palestinians into political compromise. The Likud government had failed to respond to Shultz's suggestions, but Peres perceived them as an opportunity to improve Israel's image, even if the Palestinian leadership reacted negatively.

The series of measures taken by the NUG's new Defense Minister Itzhak Rabin, also a leader of the Labor party, included reopening an-Najah University in Nablus, which had been closed by the army; relaxing press censorship; developing West Bank industrial infrastructure; and establishing an Arab Bank in Nablus. By 1984–1985 Palestinian reaction against the 1982 introduction of the Civil Administration had become less militant, and the army stated that the boycott of Israeli authorities by Arab municipalities had ended. Consequently, the NUG decided to appoint new Arab mayors, not those removed during 1982–1983. Still, it was not yet time for new West Bank elections, the army declared. Appointees to replace the Israeli officers who had been running the municipalities would be selected by Israel. The most notable appointment was that of Zafir al-Masri as mayor of Nablus. From a notable family, he was the nephew of a former mayor and chairman of the Nablus Chamber of Commerce. Steps to the "improved quality of life" and reappointment of Arab mayors were regarded with skepticism by the population at large. They were seen as measures to implement the infamous autonomy scheme (part of the 1978 Camp David agreements) rather than as indications of real change in Israeli policies. Traditionalists and pro-Hashemites were willing to give Israel the benefit of their doubts, but young nationalists and those affiliated with PLO factions denounced the whole effort as a scheme to permit minimal Arab local government under continued Israeli control. In Nablus, opinion was divided between the notables who backed al-Masri, on the one hand, and those in the left wing of the trade union movement and the local Communists who accused him of giving in to the Israelis, on the other. The new measures, they charged, were an anti-PLO plot, in collusion with the "combined forces of Zionism, imperialism, and Arab reaction."[31]

In response, al-Masri argued that his appointment came not from Israel's initiative but from the residents of Nablus, that an Arab mayor was better than an Israeli officer; his purpose, he insisted, was to make life less unbearable. Two and a half months after taking office in December 1985, Zafir al-Masri was assassinated at the entrance of the Nablus Town Hall. Palestinian rejectionists claimed credit for the murder; it was a death sentence, they said, for his involvement in the "Zionist, Jordanian plan aimed at liquidating the Palestinian cause."[32]

As Arab resistance to the occupation became more militant, with increasing instances of violence, one Israeli observer perceived that it reflected "socio-political change, i.e., the rise of a new, more militant generation of West Bank Palestinians who had grown up under Israeli occupation and had gradually developed a deep hatred for the Israelis as 'Jews and people.'"[33]

A New Leadership Emerges

The emergence of a new generation of political activists meant new political influences among the Palestinians in the occupied territories. The traditionalists, many of them notables from established families such as the Shawwas in Gaza, the al-Masris in Nablus, the Jabris in Hebron, the Nusseibis and others in Jerusalem, were generally pro-Hashemite and thus inclined to favor turning the territories over to King Hussein and affiliation with Jordan. They were the least militant in resistance to the occupation and most receptive to the "Jordan option" as a solution, the one favored by the Israel Labor party and the United States. However, even they supported Arafat and hasty termination of the occupation.

PLO activists were divided among mainstream supporters of Arafat (probably the largest of all trends), fringe groups supporting the anti-Arafat faction of Fatah, and Marxist PLO groups including the Popular Front for the Liberation of Palestine (PFLP) and Democratic Front for the Liberation of Palestine (DFLP), often called "rejectionists" because of their opposition to Arafat's proposals for a solution and their hostility to King Hussein. To the left of the PLO "rejectionists" was the Palestine Communist party in the West Bank and Gaza Strip, a descendant of the movement in mandatory Palestine. While the Communists often identified with the "rejectionists" and opposed Arafat's leadership, they accepted coexistence between Israel and a Palestine state. A growing trend on the right was Islamic fundamentalism, especially in Gaza, where there were frequent fights between secularists and fundamentalists. Clashes between diverse PLO factions, and between secularists and Islamicists, were becoming more frequent on West Bank and Gaza university campuses.

Many differences between these groups are reflected within the Palestine trade union movement. Control over some two dozen unions was divided among the Communists, Fatah, and the rejectionist front. Similar divisions existed among the various professional organizations, women's groups, and other Palestinian institutions in the territories. The Arabic press, with publication offices in East Jerusalem to circumvent strict military government censorship, also reflected these differences. The three dailies, five weeklies, and several other journals represented the spectrum of Palestinian orientations, from pro-Hashemite to PLO and Communist.

Palestinian Refugees

Still another center of intense political activism and opposition to occupation was the Palestinian Arab refugee camp community. According to the United Nations Relief and Works Agency (UNRWA), by 1988 there were more than 385,000 West Bank and 459,000 Gaza registered refugees—that is, former inhabitants of Arab towns and villages or their offspring now within the pre-1967 borders of Israel. They left Israel during the first Arab-Israeli war in 1947–1949. In the West Bank, more than 100,000 people lived in twenty refugee camps; in Gaza, 250,000 lived in eight camps. Most of the camps were established in 1948 to accommodate Arabs who had fled the Israel-held territories. Originally intended as temporary refuge, these camps developed into more or less

Refugee homes surrounding "town square" in beach camp for Palestinian refugees. UNRWA photo by George Nehmeh.

permanent adjuncts of the urban districts. (A few are located in rural areas.) Homes and service buildings such as schools and clinics have become permanent fixtures during the past four decades, but the camps are usually situated in the least desirable locations. They have the appearance today of permanent slums rather than temporary shelters. Their sanitary facilities, such as water supply, sewage, and toilets, are minimal—barely adequate to prevent massive epidemics but hardly conducive to comfortable family life. A major problem facing camp inhabitants was little if any room for further household expansion, yet refugee families had one of the world's highest fertility rates; families with twelve children were not uncommon. In the two generations since 1948, the camps became among the most crowded living areas in the Middle East, bursting at the seams, with all the physical and psychological problems caused by such overcrowding. The pressure was somewhat relieved by departure of many males who went abroad to find employment. This was especially true in the 1970s, during the era of economic expansion in the Arab oil-producing states. Since the oil recession of the 1980s, not only has there been little opportunity for employment abroad, but many men who left families behind in the camps have had to return, thus exacerbating the crowded conditions to an unprecedented degree. The refugee camps have become breeding grounds for discontent and unrest, as well as for the political radicalism accompanying such situations. While the first generation of camp dwellers may have been docile from the shock of displacement, a new generation of street-wise youth has arisen, no longer willing to passively accept the fate of their parents and grandparents. A large part of the cadres in the most militant Palestinian resistance factions comes from the refugee ranks—born, raised, and educated in the camps.

The UNRWA school system run by Palestinian administrators and teachers was, unlike the government schools, relatively free from interference by Israeli authorities. As textbooks and curricula were less controlled by the Israeli Ministry of Education, UNRWA schools were freer to instill Palestinian national consciousness and patriotism. However, this did not exempt their teachers and older students from repeated interrogation by Israeli security and intelligence agents, or from arrest and imprisonment.

While many Palestinians from the nonrefugee community were socialized and radicalized in Israel's jails, refugees constituted a larger percentage of the prison population. The first generation of prisoners were the teachers; the second and third were made up of students who in turn taught younger children lessons in Palestinian nationalism.

By 1988 several thousand young Palestinians had served terms in Israeli prisons for security or political offenses, many of them multiple sentences. The conditions in Israeli prisons, even for Jewish prisoners, are far below those of model American or British institutions. Inmates live in crowded cells, there is frequent abuse by guards, and the violations of prisoners' basic rights are such that numerous international and human rights organizations have raised the issue. There have been frequent charges of torture during interrogations used by the General Security Services (Shin Bet) to extract confessions of guilt from detainees, both men and women. *The West Bank Handbook,* edited by Meron Benvenisti, points out that in addition to physical torture, arrest of relatives is not an uncommon means of putting pressure on suspects; masked interrogators are often used so that prisoners cannot identify them, and confessions are written in Hebrew, which the accused often do not understand. Conditions are such that new young detainees quickly join the ranks of Palestinian activism to become the vanguard in the civil resistance movement. As Benvenisti observes, "'Graduates' of Israeli prisons are accorded honored status by their peers and gain easier terms for West Bank university admission and for university examinations."[34] At the same time, they are already clearly marked as "troublemakers" and remain on blacklists, the first to be apprehended when security forces make their periodic sweeps during times of unrest.

TWENTY YEARS OF OCCUPATION

When Itzhak Shamir returned to the prime minister's office at the end of 1986 according to the terms of the rotation agreement with the Labor Alignment, he proclaimed that his government would proceed to consolidate "the Jewish presence in all parts of the Land: Jerusalem, Judea, Samaria, and Gaza, the Galilee and the Sharon."[35] A massive drive was prepared to establish forty-eight new Jewish settlements in the West Bank and Gaza, twenty-one of them laid out (but not yet populated) in a scheme by the previous Likud government. To encourage settlers, plans called for huge expenditures at a much higher rate than within the Green Line, which separates Israel from the occupied territories. A survey by a specialist of the Settlement Study Center in Rehovot revealed that per capita funding in West Bank Jewish towns was 143 percent higher than in comparable towns within Israel. Spending on resources in West Bank regional councils was 61 percent higher than in similar councils within the Green Line.[36]

Stepped-up Jewish settlement was to be supported by a tougher line against Palestinian opponents of government policies. The new "iron fist" was in reality a continuation of policy introduced by Defense Minister Rabin when the NUG was formed in 1984 and imposed on inhabitants of South Lebanon during Israel's withdrawal from that country. Rabin's "tough line" had led to permanent closure of three Arabic newspapers and one press service, as well as to the house arrest or administrative detention of several Palestinian journalists. The new Shamir-Rabin emphasis led to expulsion of Akram Haniye, editor-in-chief of the east Jerusalem daily *Asha'ab*. The expulsion order described him as "a leading Fatah functionary,"[37] but without even alleging that he had been involved in "anything like terrorist activity." This new policy was castigated by the *Jerusalem Post*, which commented: "If yesterday's expulsion order . . . means that Israel is now embarking on a policy on the West Bank which will alienate even further the bulk of the population . . . , it has chosen a precarious course guided by an overdose of wishful thinking."[38]

After twenty years of occupation, many observers asserted that for all practical purposes the West Bank with its 60,000 Jewish settlers and its 800,000 indigenous Arabs had been annexed. Benvenisti, a former deputy-major of Jerusalem and Israel's most prominent authority on the occupied territories, has argued that a gradual process of consolidation had taken place since Israel captured the territories, and that with termination of the Six-Day War in June 1967 the "Second Israeli Republic" was established in the Land of Israel. This second republic now ruled all mandatory Palestine "and has the monopoly on governmental coercive power in the entire area under its dominion. The distinction between Israel's sovereign territory and the area in which it rules by military government has long since lost its meaning, as it acts as sovereign, for all intents and purposes, in the whole of the area west of the Jordan river, changing the law as it wishes, and creating permanent facts."[39]

Benvenisti believed that "all Israeli objectives have been attained in the territories and Jewish interests have been assured. The process of economic integration has long since been accomplished." Palestinians in the territories were citizens of a foreign state—Jordanian in the West Bank, stateless in Gaza, and deprived of all political rights. The Second Israeli Republic had become a binational entity with "a rigid, hierarchical social structure based on ethnicity"; it was a "Herrenvolk Democracy." Because each community, Palestinian and Israeli, denied the other's legitimacy as a collective, "perpetual conflict" would prevail. "This delegitimization is vital for both sides, for it enables both to believe in the exclusivity of their claim and in the absolute justice of their position." Despite internal divisions within the Palestinian Arab and Israeli Jewish communities, each "outwardly present[s] a monolithic facade." The vast majority of Israelis were determined "to preserve the Jewish character of the Second Republic, i.e. its superior status, even at the cost of domestic values," whereas the Palestinians were united in their "desire to destroy Jewish hegemony." This struggle was accompanied, said Benvenisti, "by the development of stereotypes, a lowering of the threshold of moral sensitivity, the loss of humanistic values, and despair leading ultimately to psychological withdrawal, to anarchy or fundamentalism."

Benvenisti scorned the "carrot-and-stick" policies of the Israeli government, although it was the inevitable means of control in the absence of any long-term political approach. But it "only exacerbates the conflict." As in other, similar situations, a rise in living standards and exposure to the open society only hastened "the modernization process of the minority and the sophistication of its political struggle." Nevertheless, the rising level of Palestinian expectations and the consequent political militancy did not threaten the Israel-imposed system, for the balance of power decisively favored the Jews. Their superior services, "and the sophistication of [their] system of enforcement, ensure that any attempt to threaten the system will be crushed." There was little threat to the system of control from Jewish feelings of guilt because

> the ethnic stratification of superiors and inferiors serves as a barrier against unresolvable ideological and cognitive contradictions. . . . The status quo is perceived as tolerable, because an unflinching analysis of its implications would only raise unanswerable questions and spell danger for national

consensus. . . . Self-delusion, therefore, plays a vital role in maintaining sanity and a sense of tribal affiliation.

Benvenisti feared that when the character of the Second Israeli Republic became clear to Israelis and "when the outside world manages to overcome its reticence about preaching morals to the Jews, when feelings of shame overcome the defence mechanism of 'a nation apart,'" it would be too late. Self-delusion will then have deteriorated "to the point of loss of all contact with reality, and the Second Israeli Republic, which, from its birth, manifested worrisome signs of emotional instability, will then become a 'crazy state.'"

Many Israeli critics of government policies disagreed with Benvenisti. They argued that it was still not too late to reverse the steps toward integrating the occupied territories and to prevent outright annexation with all its dire consequences. But among Arabs in the territories, the Benvenisti jeremiad seemed to carry more weight and provoked greater apprehensions about the future. In the year prior to the Intifada, numerous measures and incidents intensified Arab anxieties about the intentions of the Israeli government.

For instance, great concern was aroused with a scheme announced by the Israel Water Commission and the state-owned Mekorot Water Company to utilize several million cubic meters of West Bank water in Jerusalem and the surrounding Jewish settlements. Arab mayors in the Bethlehem area were outraged because the project would deplete Arab wells and provide only a small quantity of pumped water to their villages and towns. Bethlehem mayor Elias Freij, whose city suffered an acute water shortage, insisted that: "This plan threatens our very existence. . . . [It is] a matter of 'to be or not to be' for us." The scheme contradicted Israeli statements about peaceful coexistence, he asserted. The plan was dropped in October 1987 as a result of divisions over its implementation within the cabinet and opposition from Egypt, Jordan, the United Nations, the European Community, and the United States. Some attributed the resignation of Efraim Sneh from the post of West Bank civil administrator to these objections. Nevertheless, the harm had been done, and Arab anxiety about Israeli policies was raised several notches, even among West Bank moderates.[40]

Controversy between Jewish militants and the Islamic clergy was reignited in 1986–1987 when a Jewish faction, the Faithful of the Temple Mount, brought a suit against Israeli government authorities charging them with permitting the Muslims to undertake illegal construction. The Grand Mufti of Jerusalem and head of the Wakaf was enraged by the suit. He insisted that the Muslim Wakaf establishment had exclusive sovereignty over the Temple Mount and that the real intent of the Jewish organization's court application was to drive Muslims from their mosques in the Temple area.[41]

Arab fears of increasing control by military government authorities were sparked by the introduction of a computerized data bank in the West Bank during 1987. The $8.5 million project became operational in August, providing the army with a "black list" to be consulted when issuing permits, licenses, and travel documents. The new system would supply extensive information about property, family ties, and Palestinian political attitudes, thereby facilitating control and immediate checks by security agents. This system, warned a study from Benvenisti's West Bank Data Base Project, "might develop into a sinister 'Big Brother' control apparatus in the hands of the administration that already possesses absolute power and is free of any checks and balances."[42]

During the months before the Intifada, settler vigilantism erupted again with increased violence against Arab towns and refugee camps. Tensions also increased between the vigilantes and the army. Military commanders threatened to stop the vigilantes and to treat them like common criminals unless they got "a hold of themselves." Their activism nearly created a rift within Gush Emunim when several members criticized the movement's leader, Daniella Weiss, for conducting a rampage through the West Bank town of Kalkiliya in retaliation against a petrol bomb attack on Jews near the town. Weiss's critics charged that many vigilante actions were stirring up hysteria, denigrating the army, and creating an image problem for Gush Emunim. The *Jerusalem Post* asserted that "last week's vigilante orgy of bottle smashing and garbage bin overturning in Kalkiliya, and rioting in Nablus and Hebron presided over by Gush Emunim's Secretary-General Daniella Weiss, was on the face of it a cry of outrage over insufficient safety for Jewish settlers across the Green Line. . . . Its purpose was to coerce the military authorities . . . into putting the screws on the local Arab population so painfully that they would either meekly subject themselves to Israel's rule forever—or get out."[43]

Public opinion in Israel seemed to be gathering momentum against Arab unrest during 1987. A poll conducted during July by *Modi'in Ezrahi* for the newspaper *Ma'ariv* suggested that two-thirds of the Jewish population "would not part for any price with any portion of Judea and Samaria." The majority supported "outright annexation," and of these "only a few would award the annexed Arabs the rights of Israeli citizenship." Half those favoring annexation "are in fact looking forward to the West Bank Arabs being kicked out." On the eve of the Intifada in November, a poll by Dahaf indicated that more than 40 percent of Israeli teen-agers surveyed (612 between the ages of fifteen and eighteen) wanted to reduce the rights of Israeli Arab citizens. These trends so alarmed Education Minister Itzhak Navon that he promised to put additional funds into the school system for courses on democracy and racial tolerance.[44]

The attitudes of Israeli youth seemed to reflect the growing sense of xenophobia, particularly toward Arabs. This trend intensified on the eve of the Intifada as discussion of "transfer" again became legitimate in right-wing Israeli political circles. The proposal to "transfer" all Arabs out of territory under Israeli control had been the more or less exclusive property of Meir Kahana and his Kach party until 1987. But with a new Israeli election approaching in 1988, the subject was no longer confined to such discredited political figures. It sprang up within the Likud and National Religious parties, and several times aroused a storm of debate on the Knesset floor. Within the Herut party, the backbone of the Likud movement, a group of Knesset members led by Deputy Defense Minister Michael Dekel openly came out for "transfer" of Arabs, beginning with inhabitants of refugee camps from the West Bank, across the Jordan River. Another cabinet minister, Yosef Shapira of the National Religious party, made a similar proposal, including a $20,000 incentive for any Palestinian who emigrated from Israel. Both schemes were sharply attacked within the respective parties and on the Knesset floor. Labor's Shimon Peres blasted the "transfer" idea as a "twisted, perverted" notion that would undermine Israel's good name. Despite opposition from "respectable" politicians, "transfer" later became the raison d'être for establishment of a new political party, Moledet (Motherland), led by a former army general, Rehovam Ze'evi, who is currently director of Tel Aviv's Haaretz Museum. Moledet offered a haven to "transfer" advocates who found Meir Kahana's approach to the "Arab problem" too crude or embarrassing.[45]

These militant trends provoked counterreactions within the Jewish community. An increasing but still small number of youths who were approaching military service openly voiced opposition to government policies in the territories. Public attention to their dissent was aroused by the letter of sixteen high school students to Defense Minister Rabin in September asking to be exempted from service in the territories. The youths protested that the occupation had turned the IDF from a defense force into an army of occupation. Several vowed that they would go to jail rather than serve in the territories. Some teachers reported that this was not an isolated incident, that the phenomenon was becoming widespread. "I've never faced problems like this with my pupils in all the years and all the schools that I've taught," stated one high school civics teacher.[46]

At a higher, more official level, lack of unanimity within army circles was underscored during September by the resignation of West Bank

Civil Administrator Brigadier General Efraim Sneh. Considered a "liberal," Administrator Sneh had been at odds with his superiors for a long time. The disagreement leading to his resignation was caused by the plan to divert West Bank water sources to Israel. Sneh had maintained contacts with all Palestinian factions including moderate PLO supporters. His resignation worried many such supporters, who feared that it was a harbinger of change for the worse in government policy. Whereas Arabs commended him for improving services and increasing expenditures on health facilities (Sneh, forty-four years old, was a physician), Jewish settlers rejoiced at his departure, accusing him of "soft" policies that encouraged Arab terrorism. Two months later, upon leaving the army altogether, Sneh declared that there could be no such thing as "an enlightened occupation." The idea is *kishkush* (nonsense), he insisted. Israelis, he complained, "fail to realize that an educated, intelligent, Western-oriented elite has emerged among the Palestinians over the past twenty years."[47]

Two decades of close contact had led to changing Palestinian perceptions of Israel and of Israelis. New generations who had lived all their lives under occupation adapted to various aspects of Israel's material culture and were influenced in their thinking and world views by attitudes from across the Green Line. Israeli products such as soap, clothing, canned goods, and bottled beer were sold in shops throughout the occupied territories. Many Jewish companies became dependent for a substantial share of their sales on markets in the West Bank and Gaza. Many advertised extensively in the Palestinian press and pitched their sales campaigns to the Arab market. Throughout the West Bank, Palestinians could be seen wearing Israeli-made jeans, shirts, and sandals. *Jerusalem Post* correspondent Joel Greenberg wrote of visiting a billiard hall in Jenin, where he found young Palestinians dressed like Israeli "greasers" sporting similar haircuts and listening to Israeli pop music. He observed that one area in which cooperation existed was the underworld; Israeli and Arab criminals even looked and dressed alike. "The short haircut, jeans, and sneakers make them virtually indistinguishable." The Arab press kept its Palestinian readers informed about details of Israeli politics, scandals, and criminal life.[48]

Greenberg's conversations with Palestinians revealed ambivalent feelings about their encounter with Israeli society and culture, and its impact on their lives. They were no longer "overwhelmed" by "Israel's power, technological superiority and modern culture. . . . [Now] they can see through the dazzling facade into Israel's weaknesses, faults and divisions." One Palestinian journalist remarked to Greenberg that "Israel is no longer virgin. . . . Now there are jokes about Israelis, about the stupidity of the occupation, and its corruption. Israel isn't the perfect model anymore. Palestinians now feel superior to the Israelis."

Daily employment within Israel of tens of thousands of Palestinian youths, both men and women, not only exposed them to "modern" ways but frequently also disrupted traditional family patterns and sex roles, as these workers became financially independent, adopted modern dress and behavior patterns, and were exposed to Western mass entertainment and media.

While many Palestinians admired the relative political and social democracy and freedom of press across the Green Line, they felt a "total absence of physical security" in their own environment because Israeli standards were not applicable in the territories. Nevertheless, young Palestinians were no longer cowed by the Israeli presence. Youths were beginning to rebel, not only against their parents and teachers but against Israel's authority as well. Palestinians could see the Israelis arguing with their own leaders, so why shouldn't they stand up to Israeli officers? West Bank lawyer Jonathan Kuttab pointed out to Greenberg that "rejection of Israeli occupation has paradoxically given a new social legitimacy to rebellion against authority. Boys who throw stones at soldiers, disrupt classes to organize demonstrations, and go to jail, gain the status of heroes, and are no longer considered troublemakers who should be disciplined."

In the end Greenberg concluded, "Palestinian perceptions of Israeli society cannot be separated from the pervasive political and military reality of occupation. Palestinians say it poisons the atmosphere, filling it with mistrust, severely limiting opportunities for natural contact between cultures very different from each other."

By 1987 the struggle against occupation was characterized by what political scientist Emil Nakhleh called the "new *sumud*." *Sumud*, or steadfastness against the occupation, was acquiring new meaning as "a more indigenous Palestinian struggle to stay on the land." He maintained that the new *sumud* was concerned with the urgent and immediate questions of daily survival. These problems included the rapid increase of Jewish settlement and loss of Arab land, and danger to debt-ridden institutions "ranging from Bir-Zeit University to charitable societies. . . . It is a populist concept based on the long-term demographic struggle." Nakhleh believed that Palestinians in the territories had become more active as leaders and independent of PLO chieftains abroad. A debate had begun about possible political options; Palestinians were feeling increasingly isolated from Arab factions in the outside world and were beginning to make their own decisions about the present crisis and future possibilities.[49]

An indication of this independent initiative was the series of meetings between several West Bank leaders and members of Herut to discuss the possibilities of a peace settlement. The contacts began during the spring of 1987 between a member of the Herut Central Committee, Moshe Amirav, and Faisal Husseini, head of the East Jerusalem Arab Studies Society. Husseini, son of a Palestinian hero in the 1947–1948 war, was considered by the Israeli security forces to be a leading PLO activist responsible for organizing much of the opposition to the occupation. The two men developed a "peace plan" that was later denounced by Likud leaders. Amirav was expelled from the party for his efforts; Husseini was arrested in September and imprisoned, one of several incarcerations he experienced during 1987–1988.

Another example of independent initiative was the unprecedented announcement by Hanna Siniora, editor of the East Jerusalem daily al-Fajr, that he intended to head a Palestinian list during the next elections for the Jerusalem municipality. Siniora's intent was to confront Israelis with a strong opposition bloc that would take an active role in defending Arab rights in Jerusalem. This plan meshed with Bir-Zeit Professor Sari Nusseibeh's call on Israel to annex the territories, whereupon occupied Arabs would receive the vote and thus become powerful enough to influence the government and determine their own future. The suggestions of both Siniora and Nusseibeh were rejected by other Palestinian leaders, including Feisal Husseini. Siniora withdrew his plan to run for mayor, and Nusseibeh was severely beaten at his university by an unknown group of Arabs. The beating was perceived as a threat to others against going public with schemes so far removed from mainstream political thinking.[50]

At the far right of the political spectrum there was increased activity among Muslim fundamentalist groups who were becoming more militant. By September 1987, several Islamic Jihad cells had been uncovered in the Gaza Strip, and many fundamentalists had been arrested and imprisoned, charged with violent actions against Israelis and against fellow Palestinians with whom the Muslim zealots disagreed. Israeli intelligence operatives feared that the zealots would influence other Palestinian groups, such as Fatah, to join in spectacular suicide attacks, car bombings, and assassinations.[51]

Increased Palestinian militancy in the territories and feelings of isolation from the Arab world were reinforced by the outcome of an emergency Arab League summit conference that convened in Amman, Jordan, during November, a month before the Intifada. Although the summit reiterated its pro-forma support for the Palestinians and called for an international Middle East peace conference, Palestinian issues were overshadowed by debates about the Iraq-Iran War. Many in the occupied territories felt slighted, even betrayed, by the summit's off-handed way of dealing with their problems. Palestinians were further alienated from the Arab world by what appeared to be a lack of concern for and failure to halt the massacre of their kinsmen by Shiite Amal militiamen at refugee camps in Lebanon. Fighting between Amal and Palestinians had continued since 1985, causing the deaths of several thousand refugees, many of them with close relatives in the territories. Efforts to mediate the conflict or to suspend military activity had been futile; Palestinians in the West Bank and Gaza believed that their kinsmen in Lebanon were being sacrificed because of unconcern by Arab world leaders.

During October 1987 tensions within the territories were palpable. In Jerusalem, according to correspondent Hirsh Goodman,

> you can feel the tension. Worshippers—Jew and Moslem alike—scurry rather than walk. Tourists cluster together and are protected by armed soldiers. Shopkeepers keep one hand on their shutters in anticipation of the next riot.
>
> In Gaza, you drive a car with Israeli plates at peril. . . . The marketplaces are empty of Israeli shoppers and thousands of Gazans have stayed away from jobs in Israel—some in protest, others out of fear. . . . The atmosphere . . . is reflected throughout Judea and Samaria and even in some parts of Galilee.
>
> Suspicion has become endemic in our lives. A car crash in which two officers were killed by an Arab truck driver is immediately attributed to terrorism, as is almost every murder. . . .
>
> Fear, suspicion and growing hatred have replaced any hope of dialogue between Israelis and Palestinians. Moshe Amirav . . . was humiliated and threatened with expulsion from the party for having dared to explain to West Bank Palestinians his view of how the territories could be "annexed humanely." . . . Voices of reason have been drowned out by the rallying cries of the extremists and solutions that once seemed possible now appear unattainable. Yesterday's moderates have become either immoderate or silent, and the thin line that separated "terrorist" from "nationalist" has become blurred. Continued political inaction will guarantee that the vacuum will be filled by more terror, more protest, more reaction and more innocent casualties.[52]

Israel's army commanders were much more sanguine about the situation than many journalists. Less than two months before the eruption of Intifada, General Amram Mitzna, in charge of the country's Central Command, told a press conference that "fewer than one in a thousand" West Bank Palestinians had been involved in anti-Israel violence. "The limited extent of public participation, and the varying styles of attack

Israeli soldiers in Dheisheh, a Palestinian refugee camp. UNRWA photo by George Nehmeh.

over the years indicate that there is no clear-cut trend towards spontaneous popular resistance," he asserted. According to the optimistic general, casualties on both sides were few during 1987—only three Israelis killed and twenty-eight wounded in disturbances, and five Arabs killed and seventy-six wounded in clashes with the IDF. The number of incidents—involving petrol bombs, grenade attacks, stabbings, shootings, stone throwing, tire burnings, and erection of barricades—had declined during the previous three months. Most of these attacks, stated Mitzna, were not directed from abroad but had local origins; however, they did "not reflect a long-term trend towards a popular uprising."[53]

On November 25, an incident occurred that cast some doubt on the capacity of Israeli military intelligence to forecast danger signals. A brigade headquarters near the Lebanese frontier was attacked by Palestinians who flew two motorized hangliders from the Biqa region in Lebanon. One glider landed within Israel's self-declared "security zone" on the Lebanese side of the frontier; the other landed next to the military base. One Palestinian entered the base, killing six Israeli soldiers and wounding seven before he was shot and killed. The incident led to reprimand of a brigadier general and disciplinary actions against other officers. The army's investigation committee was critical of IDF intelligence for failing either to ward off the attack or to foretell renewed activity by the attackers—namely, the Popular Front for the Liberation of Palestine/General Command, led by Ahmad Jibril.

In the territories the attack caused "widespread satisfaction." It was seen as "a heroic operation . . . which destroyed the myth of Israeli defenses. . . . For once the Palestinians made it hurt." With banner headlines, *al-Fajr* termed the attack "courageous" and displayed a picture of the Israeli chief-of-staff describing it as "a painful and powerful blow."[54]

Early in December, a UN official in Gaza predicted that within a week, the twenty years of occupation, Palestinian frustration, disillusionment, and feelings of abandonment would reach the boiling point.

NOTES

1. Ann Mosely Lesch, *Israel's Occupation of the West Bank: The First Two Years* (Santa Monica: Rand Corporation, 1979), p. 6.

2. Sara Roy, *The Gaza Strip Survey* (Jerusalem: West Bank Data Base Project, 1986), p. 123; Meron Benvenisti, *The West Bank Handbook: A Political Lexicon* (Jerusalem: Jerusalem Post, 1986), pp. 143–145.

3. Lesch, *Israel's Occupation*, pp. 94–95.

4. Benvenisti, *The West Bank Handbook*, p. 85.

5. Lesch, *Israel's Occupation*, pp. 89–90.

6. *Ibid.*, p. 104.

7. Israeli Ministry of Defense, *A Fourteen-Year Survey (1967–1981)*, p. 3; cited in Don Peretz, *The West Bank: History, Politics, Society, and Economy* (Boulder, Colo.: Westview Press, 1986), p. 109.

8. Benvenisti, *The West Bank Handbook*, p. 104; Roy, *The Gaza Strip Survey*, p. 38.

9. Benvenisti, *The West Bank Handbook*, p. 1.

10. *Ibid.*, p. 2.

11. Benvenisti, *1987 Report: Demographic, Economic, Legal, Social and Political Developments in the West Bank* (Jerusalem: West Bank Data Base Project, 1987), p. 21.

12. Benvenisti, *The West Bank Handbook*, pp. 223–225.

13. Roy, *The Gaza Strip Survey*, p. 51.

14. *Ibid.*, pp. 36–37.

15. Benvenisti, *The West Bank Handbook*, p. 113.

16. *Ibid.*, pp. 75–77.

17. *Jerusalem Post Weekly* (hereafter JPW), no. 470, 10/27/69.

18. Lesch, *Political Perceptions of the Palestinians on the West Bank and The Gaza Strip* (Washington, D.C.: Middle East Institute, 1980), p. 66.

19. Peretz, *The West Bank*, p. 87.

20. Colin Legum, Haim Shaked, and Daniel Dishon (eds.), *Middle East Contemporary Survey* (hereafter MECS), Vol. VI: 1981–1982 (New York and London: Holmes & Meier, 1984), pp. 81–82, 367–368.

21. *Ibid.*, p. 367.

22. *Ibid.*

23. Peretz, *The West Bank*, pp. 85–86.

24. MECS, Vol. VI, p. 168.

25. *Ibid.*, p. 110.

26. *New York Times*, 5/28/85.

27. MECS, Vol. VI, p. 376.

28. MECS, Vol. VII: 1982–1983, p. 332.

29. *Ibid.*, p. 335.

30. Peretz, *The West Bank*, pp. 102–103.

31. MECS, Vol. IX: 1984–1985, pp. 241–242.

32. *Ibid.*, p. 242.

33. *Ibid.*, p. 235.

34. Benvenisti, *The West Bank Handbook*, pp. 58–60, 176.

35. *Jerusalem Post International Edition* (hereafter JPI), no. 1,355, 10/25/86.

36. JPI, no. 1,371, 2/14/87.

37. JPI, no. 1,358, 11/15/86.

38. *Ibid.*

39. Meron Benvenisti, "The Second Republic," JPI, no. 1,367, 1/17/87.

40. JPI, no. 1,391, 7/4/87; no. 1,392, 7/11/87; no. 1,393, 7/18/87; no. 1,396, 8/8/87; no. 1,400, 9/5/87; no. 1,408, 10/31/87.

41. JPI, no. 1,394, 7/25/87.

42. JPI, no. 1,402, 9/19/87.

43. JPI, no. 1,385, 5/23/87; no. 1,389, 6/20/87.

44. JPI, no. 1,394, 7/25/87; no. 1,409, 11/7/87; no. 1,410, 11/14/87.

45. JPI, no. 1,404, 10/3/87; no. 1,409, 11/7/87; no. 1,393, 7/18/87; no. 1,411, 11/21/87; no. 1,396, 8/8/87.

46. JPI, no. 1,405, 10/10/87.

47. JPI, no. 1,403, 9/26/87; no. 1,410, 11/14/87.

48. Joel Greenberg, "A Flawed Model?" JPI, no. 1,405, 10/10/87.

49. JPI, no. 1,400, 9/5/87.

50. JPI, no. 1,388, 6/13/87; no. 1,389, 6/20/87.

51. JPI, no. 1,400, 9/5/87; no. 1,411, 11/21/87; no. 1,387, 6/6/87.

52. Hirsh Goodman, "When Extremism Eclipses Reason," JPI, no. 1,407, 10/24/87.

53. *Ibid.*

54. JPI, no. 1,413, 12/5/87; no. 1,414, 12/12/87.

2

Israeli Policies—
Coping with the Uprising

The boiling point came, as predicted by the UN officer in Gaza, on December 8, 1987. The incident that sparked the Intifada was relatively minor—a road accident that failed to attract attention in most of the local media and was overlooked by the foreign press. Attention still focused on the hang-glider incident and the IDF investigation of army intelligence for failure to prevent the Palestinian guerrilla incursion.

The road accident occurred in Gaza; four Arab workers were instantly killed and seven seriously injured when an IDF tank-transport crashed into a truck bringing the workers back into the occupied territory from jobs in Israel. The driver of the army transport was supposedly the brother of another Israeli who had been killed earlier by Gaza Arabs. Rumors quickly spread that the accident was deliberate, a vengeance taken by the Israeli for the death of his brother.

Three of the four dead Palestinians were from the large Jabalya refugee camp adjoining Gaza; their funeral on December 8 and 9 became the occasion for another massive demonstration against the occupation and its policies. As on previous occasions, the Israeli army entered Jabalya to quell the funeral-protest demonstrations and, also as before, the soldiers were met by a hail of stones and iron bars thrown by hundreds of demonstrators. This time, however, the grief and anger of the demonstrators, most of them teenage youths, seemed more determined and fierce. The soldiers, as usual, fired tear gas and live ammunition into the crowds, injuring many and killing a 20-year-old youth who became the first "martyr" of the Intifada. His death only inflamed the anger, and the demonstrators in Jabalya were joined within the next day or two by protesters throughout Gaza and the West Bank. Now, however, they refused to disperse; the demonstrations, instead of ending after an initial outburst, increased in number and spread like a bush-fire. The IDF was unable to contain the unrest. The Intifada had started.

A NEW SITUATION?

In Israel it was soon evident that this was a new situation. The press reported that the "unrest" was the worst since 1981, when protests had erupted against imposition of the Civil Administration. Some placed the beginning of the new "unrest" during the week before, when a 45-year-old Israeli salesman was fatally knifed on a Gaza street. A high-ranking IDF officer blamed the spreading unrest on celebration of the anniversary commemorating formation of the Popular Front for the Liberation of Palestine. The "celebration" was in the Balata refugee camp near Nablus on the West Bank. The army reported that, after Friday prayer services, hundreds of worshipers leaving mosques, including women and children, attacked two Border Police patrols with stones, hatchets, and other objects. Unable to disperse the crowd with tear gas and rubber bullets, the policemen fired live ammunition, killing three people and wounding seven. Attacks on the troops continued even after a curfew was clamped on Balata.

Army spokesmen asserted that these "incidents," or "troubles," would pass "in due course." The IDF would remove its gloves, revealing an iron fist; some refugee camps would be put under curfew; some high schools would be closed for a few weeks; some PLO activists would be placed in administrative detention, perhaps a few expelled; and the demonstrators would cool off. True, dozens of young Palestinians had dared to attack the IDF patrols with stones, bottles, Molotov cocktails, and iron bars, knowing that the soldiers would shoot back. Now they seemed more daring than in the past, many encouraged by the hang-glider attack. Legends already abounded in refugee camps, universities, and high schools about "the lone Palestinian hero who won the battle against the whole Israeli army."[1]

The *Jerusalem Post's* Yehuda Litani observed that "since the politically paralyzed government cannot provide an answer, the army and civil administration authorities will once again have to act. But their answer will provide a short-range solution, if anything at all."[2] Even IDF officers, Litani commented, admitted that their "remedies" were short-term, and that continued "disturbances" could be expected, probably the next on Fatah day (January 1), commemorating the founding of the largest Palestinian guerrilla organization, led by Yassir Arafat. "As long as the government does not provide the Palestinians with some answer, we are just dispensing aspirin, instead of serious treatment," Litani went on to say.

The troubles in Gaza set off a new round of bickering within the National Unity Government. Foreign Minister Peres, who had long considered Gaza more a burden than an asset, suggested to the Knesset

Beach camp for Palestinian refugees (population 42,000) in the Gaza Strip, during the February 1988 unrest. UNRWA photo by George Nehmeh.

Foreign Affairs and Defense Committee in mid-December that the Gaza Strip should be demilitarized but remain under Israeli supervision, and that the thirteen Jewish settlements there should be dismantled. This would be part of eventual peace negotiations, not an immediate or unilateral move. Shamir attacked Peres for the suggestion, calling him a "defeatist with a scalpel who wants to put Israel on the operating table so he can give away Gaza today, Judea and Samaria tomorrow, and the Golan Heights after that." Does Peres "simply mean handing Gaza over to terrorist rule?" Shamir asked. Peres' surrender, Shamir told his Likud colleagues, called for starting the 1988 election campaign "forthwith!"[3] Throughout the first month of the Intifada, Shamir repeatedly blamed the uprising on Peres and the Labor party, accusing them of encouraging the Arabs into "violent agitation."

The *Jerusalem Post* supported Peres, commenting that "only the blind, it seems, could see in the Gaza Strip anything but a hell-hole made to order for terrorism."[4] Unfortunately, however, any suggestion that Gaza was not really essential for the country's security "promptly met with a torrent of abuse from the country's 'patriotic' Rightist Corner." In 1980 even ex-Prime Minister Begin had proposed to diminish Israel's responsibilities in the Strip by granting "full autonomy" to the Palestinians there before granting it to inhabitants of the West Bank, but nothing came of the suggestion. The establishment of thirteen settlements with some 3,000 Jewish inhabitants failed to prevent "terrorism" in Gaza. Rather, "the settlers, symbols of Israeli claims to unshared rule over the entire Land, help solidify the bond between the terrorists and Gazans in general—and compel the army to divert scarce resources to their protection. And all this to ensure that the fast-growing demographic monster represented by the Gaza Strip is *not* lifted from Israel's shoulders. What sense does all that make? None, said Foreign Minister Shimon Peres. . . ."

The *Jerusalem Post* asserted that even within Shamir's Herut party there are those who realize that Gaza "is an awesome burden rather than an asset for Israel, and that the area can never be brought to heel except by the most brutal and un-Israeli methods, possibly by mass expulsion." Many Herut members were prepared to "dump" the Strip but dared not speak their minds for fear of being disavowed by their party. "Moderately clear-eyed though they are, they allowed their blind-folded colleagues to blandly lead the country to a point of no return."[5]

By the end of December 1987, after three weeks of Intifada, more than a dozen Palestinians had been killed and scores wounded. Now observers were calling the unrest the worst, not since 1981 but since the occupation began in 1967. The rioting spread to the capital, Jerusalem, with no indications of dampening Palestinian spirits. Security authorities feared that it would spill over into Israel proper and cause unrest among the country's own Arab citizens (see Chapter 4).

SPONTANEOUS REBELLION OR PLO-DIRECTED REVOLT?

Israelis began to debate whether this was a spontaneous rebellion caused by "genuine despair" or "merely another outburst inspired by the Palestinian Liberation Organization and enforced by a minority of agitators acting on outside orders."[6] The cabinet, relying on its military and civilian security "experts," perceived that these disturbances, though reaching a peak, were not the uprising that some of the media believed them to be. The army said it saw not "even the beginning" of a rebellion but, rather, "a rash of events centered on various locations and instigated by a minority. The population of the territories was not taking to the streets though this eventuality is a source of concern." Jerusalem's mayor, Teddy Kollek, said that although the disturbances were a "difficult blow," their importance should not be exaggerated. The rioting in the capital was merely caused by "a small group of inciters and [was] not a sign of civil revolt."[7]

One of Israel's leading academic authorities on the Palestinians, Yehoshua Porat, thought otherwise. He saw differences between the current disturbances and those in the past. The recent events, he stated, were the "first signs of an uprising by the population." The December actions were carried out in public; they were not secret terrorist operations. Women and children were now participating in attacks on soldiers. This mass participation "divides Israeli society while terrorist activity unites Israeli society," he noted.[8]

In Gaza the masses were galvanized by the pervasive influence of Islamic institutions and leaders who were in the forefront of the Intifada. In recent years Israeli security authorities treated many of the Muslim leaders with less severity than other agitators, believing that they would become an effective counterweight to the PLO. But this theory backfired, for the fundamentalists were now among the leaders in opposition to the occupation. The dozens of mosques amplified calls to the faithful to rise against the occupation, and they became centers of information or rumor about the Intifada.

In the midst of the December turbulence, Industry and Trade Minister Ariel Sharon, long an advocate of a tough approach to Arab dissidence, moved into a house he had purchased in the Muslim section of Jerusalem's walled Old City. To ensure that his presence became known to all, Jews and Arabs alike, Sharon erected a large menorah on the roof of the building. On the first night of Hanukkah in mid-December, he invited the cream of Israel's social elite to a candle-lighting ceremony. As some 300 policemen patrolled neighboring alleys and rooftops, women clad in furs and men in dinner jackets assembled to celebrate Sharon's Hanukkah victory. Not only Arabs but many Jews considered the action provocative, especially in light of the spreading unrest throughout the country. The Mufti of Jerusalem denounced this act by "the butcher of Lebanon, the blood-thirsty Sharon" as "dangerous and infuriating." A group of protesting Palestinian women and youths who marched toward the Sharon house from the al-Aqsa mosque was dispersed with tear gas. Jewish protesters from Peace Now also demonstrated. Moshe Amirav of the Herut Central Committee stood in front of the Sharon building and stated that although he did not object to Jews living in the Muslim quarter, he did not "think that a minister should come here in a provocative way at the worst possible time." Another cabinet member, Absorption Minister Yaakov Tsur, labeled the Sharon move as "hooliganism under government auspices."

Sharon insisted that his move would improve security in the Muslim quarter and lead to more Jewish settlement there. Prime Minister Shamir supported him and failed to see any provocation. "Jews have lived here, and Jews will always live here," he insisted. To ensure Sharon's tranquillity, the government would have to spend an estimated $500,000 a year in police salaries alone.[9] Some forty men were designated to watch the Sharon residence around the clock. Sharon's Arab neighbors and their guests were now required to undergo lengthy security searches before entering their homes. One Arab reported that he was forced to remove his shoes and coat and stand outside in the cold before being permitted to enter.[10]

By the end of the year, Israeli officials had begun to worry about the country's image abroad. The foreign press and media were saturated with news stories, press photos, and television coverage of the unrest showing Israeli soldiers firing into crowds of stone-throwing Arab youths, many not yet in their teens. The Foreign Ministry was flooded with reports from consulates and embassies in Europe and North America about Israel's battered image. An emergency team was organized to cope with the situation, the most difficult since Israel had bombed Beirut in 1982. Major energies were now poured into saving the country's good name, a task that to many in the government seemed as important as suppressing the Intifada. Prime Minister Shamir, however, felt that there was no need to apologize for Israel's actions. After all, what was going on in Gaza, Judea, and Samaria was "right and just" and should not be difficult to explain to the world. Were it not for the IDF, Shamir warned, the PLO would take over. "It is basic and simple. Our neighbors must come to terms with our presence in the country." Israel's ambassador to the United Nations, Benyamin Netanyahu, explained that the riots were "incited" by the PLO; and, in any event, "look at the demonstrations you had in France a year ago. Students were killed." He compared the casualties in the occupied territories with those in India, Saudi Arabia, and Syria, where according to his account hundreds were killed in a single day.[11]

It took about a month for an Israeli consensus to emerge, a consensus that the "disturbances" were not a flash in a pan, a passing series of incidents that could be suppressed in routine fashion by the normal complement of occupation forces. The consensus was that this was a spontaneous uprising, politically inspired—an uprising whose origins were within the territories, not abroad. Army commanders agreed with Defense Minister Rabin that a political rather than military solution would have to be found. Still, they insisted, tough new measures would be necessary to maintain law and order and to keep the situation in hand, and larger doses of force would be required. This would necessitate more arrests, more expulsions, destruction of more homes belonging to "rioters," extended curfews, and rougher physical treatment of demonstrators. Unless the IDF could assert "complete control" of the territories, it would not be possible to find a political solution, stated the IDF

Chief-of-Staff Dan Shomron.[12] By early January the army had nearly doubled its forces in the West Bank and tripled them in Gaza. Gaza looked like a war-zone, with armored vehicles and tanks rolling over the barricades of stones and burning tires placed every few yards along the main highway. Shomron acknowledged that there were more troops in Gaza alone than had been used to occupy all the territories in 1967. His officers began to worry that if the troop diversion continued for long, their best front-line units would be kept from training schedules and border duties "to play policeman to the population of the territories."[13]

IRON FIST MEASURES REQUIRED

This was an unprecedented situation in which the IDF, trained and psychologically honed to deal with external threats, had to face the enemy within. Most officers argued that the army had far more important tasks than police duty. Some suggested turning the job over to the Border Police, an assignment for which they were better trained and equipped. During 1986 the government increased the number of Border Police in the territories to a ratio of one policeman for every two or three soldiers. Now the IDF asked for a ratio of one to one. Other senior officers, however, believed that the Border Police would have to be closely supervised; though better trained, they were much less restrained than military units and, according to some, may have triggered rioting in Balata because of their uncontrolled beatings and furniture smashing. "We are caught between the hammer and the anvil," stated one military source. "On the one hand, we are responsible for the territories. On the other, we have serious reservations about involving our soldiers in the necessary evils of occupation." Recalling the traumatic experience of the IDF with the civilian population of Lebanon in 1982, another officer observed: "We are just beginning to get Lebanon out of the army and I don't want to think about having to do it again."

The tough new measures recalled previous army tactics for dealing with unrest in the territories, especially during the protest demonstrations of 1976 and 1981–1982. Rabin was quite candid about baring the IDF's iron fist and in January openly proclaimed a new policy of using "might, power, and beatings" to quell the unrest. This, he argued, would save lives; it was preferable to using live ammunition.

Memoranda and protests about the harsh new tactics began to pour out of the territories from human rights and social welfare organizations. International civil rights organizations, including Amnesty International and the International Commission of Jurists, were alarmed at the growing ferociousness of the occupation forces. Within Israel daily press accounts and eyewitness reports from occupation troops led to a cascade of protests about government policy in the territories from opposition factions in the Knesset such as Shinui, Mapam, and the Citizens Rights Movement. The number of Israeli Jewish protest groups seemed to grow daily, ranging from Peace Now, which considered itself part of the loyal opposition, to Yesh Gvul (There Is a Limit/Border), whose members refused military service in the occupied areas (see Chapter 4).

Representative of the protests was the January open letter from thirty Palestinian medical and health care organizations, including the Gaza Arab Medical Society, Union of Palestinian Medical Relief Committees, Union of West Bank Pharmacists, Palestine Red Crescent Society, Hebron Union of Dentists, Nablus Union of Physicians, and several health facilities. They charged that during the previous month, under the guise of security,

> a large number of Palestinian health and medical institutions were subjected to invasion and harassment by the Israeli military. Physicians and nurses were harassed and even stopped from performing their duty of providing the necessary medical and first aid care to the wounded. Some health professionals were even subjected to beating and other forms of physical violence. Wounded civilians were also attacked by the Israeli army.

The letter cited several instances in which Israeli soldiers threw tear gas into hospitals, stopped ambulances from transporting wounded, prevented blood donors from reaching clinics, used live ammunition against civilians, and arrested wounded or injured Palestinians.[14]

In a statement to the forty-fourth session of the UN Commission on Human Rights in New York on February 5, 1988, Amnesty International reported that "human rights violations on an extensive scale have become a feature of the Israeli occupation in the West Bank and Gaza in recent months." It charged that Israeli troops "repeatedly resorted to the use of lethal force and have inflicted severe—often indiscriminate—beatings on demonstrators and others in the occupied territories opposed to continued Israeli administration." Palestinians were injured, not only by gun fire, "but also often soldiers have deliberately carried out beatings." Commenting on Rabin's "might, power, and beatings" policy, Amnesty observed that the armed forces appeared to be given "license to beat indiscriminately"; that not only demonstrators but also "bystanders, including women and children, were beaten by soldiers with clubs and rifles butts. Many have been hospitalized with broken limbs, fractures, head wounds, and extensive bruising. Some were reportedly beaten after soldiers had taken them into custody and after being injured by gun fire." Soldiers were reportedly seen dragging wounded Palestinians from hospitals and beating them.

Additional charges included arbitrary arrests in the absence of warrants and without telling those seized why they were detained. Tactics described in the Amnesty statement included sweeps into areas at night during which the army staged mass arrests of all teenagers present in the homes visited. Many of those arrested were held incommunicado and denied access to lawyers or to their families for up to two weeks. Often 14 and 15 year olds were tried and convicted without legal representation. Palestinian lawyers in the territories decided to boycott the trials because they were not given enough time to prepare, were denied details of charges, were not informed of trial dates, and were refused access to their clients before trial.

There were numerous reports of ill treatment and torture of detainees "to extract information or confessions or to harass and intimidate." The forms of torture mentioned in the statement included beating and kicking of prisoners all over the body, including the head and genitals; falaqa (beating soles of the feet); hanging by rope from the ceiling and being swung from wall to wall; prolonged exposure to cold; use of electric shocks; long periods of solitary confinement and sleep deprivation; and verbal abuse and threats.

Amnesty noted that for many years it had been concerned about administrative detention or restriction to towns and villages of Palestinian activists, including journalists, students, trade unionists, and members of women's and human rights organizations. Often they were not informed as to why they had been detained. Routinely withheld were full or precise details about detention orders and evidence upon which such orders were based, making it impossible to challenge such detentions effectively.[15]

Most of the charges in the Amnesty International statement, the letter from the health and medical personnel, and other similar reports were again catalogued by the U.S. Department of State in its 1988 report to Congress on worldwide human rights violations.

IMPACT OF IDF METHODS
ON ISRAELI TROOPS

The use of "might, power, and beatings" soon began to have negative impact on the Israeli troops administering the new policy. Some officers were concerned "that eventually our soldiers will become callous about other people's suffering and about human values and they will use force even when it's not necessary."[16] A debate ensued within the high command about the effect of the Intifada on the average recruit. Arab resistance since December had been of an entirely new magnitude, and the reactions

Israeli soldiers at the entrance of Aida Refugee Camp, Bethlehem, during the unrest in February 1988. UNRWA photo by George Nehmeh.

among both Palestinians and occupation troops were totally unexpected. As the resistance intensified and the number of troops required to deal with it increased, several officers believed that they could expect more callousness and blind use of force. History proves it, they asserted.

"Take two civilian teenagers—would one ever dream of harassing the other? Of course not. But put them in uniform, make one the NCO and the other a new recruit, and see what you see. Why? Because one has power, and the other hasn't."

Now the Israeli soldier had power to rule over every aspect of the Palestinian's life. He could order the Palestinian to clear roadblocks and remove burning tires; he could seize identity cards, close shops, impose curfews, shoot people in the legs, and fire tear gas at them.

Some officers were alarmed at warnings from psychologists that their late-teenage soldiers might get so accustomed to using force in the territories that they would use it in Israel, possibly against their own families. If they get used to a certain kind of behavior, many think that they are supposed to act that way all the time. "A society which stresses the use of force will find force used in all places," an officer confided. There was apprehension that accepted standards would become impossible to sustain. The deterioration "won't occur in a few months, but it's certainly not a matter of years. You can't tell when we'll reach that point. We'll only know when we're there, and then it will be too late. The situation will be irreversible," the high-ranking officer feared.[17]

In an attempt to prevent such a situation, the IDF's chief education officer called up from the reserves extra lecturers to instruct recruits that "Palestinians are not sub-humans, that overreaction will breed more violence, and that restraint should be exercised, because we have to live in peace with them." Since most troops had not been born when the occupation began, for many there was no big difference between Nazareth and Nablus; both were Arab cities under Israel's jurisdiction, and many young soldiers could not understand why inhabitants of one and not the other were creating disturbances. "Don't make the Arabs monsters; don't lose your humanity" was to be the message from the IDF high command.

Despite the education program planned by the army, its message seemed never to have reached a large number of the troops; or perhaps the pressure of daily excursions into the hostile territories inured most soldiers to the high-flown lessons about human relations. Within the government itself there were often conflicting statements, some disavowing the use of brutal measures, others justifying them. Most confusing were the signals from Defense Minister Rabin himself.

In response to charges from a fact-finding team of U.S. physicians who had discovered evidence of "an uncontrolled epidemic of violence by army and police" in the territories, Rabin asserted that action had been taken against soldiers using extreme force. The delegation sent by the Boston-based Physicians for Human Rights had researched medical aspects of abuses in twenty countries. It included psychiatrists, an expert on trauma and emergency medical services, and several Harvard Medical School professors. They visited the occupied territories in February, two months after the Intifada began, and reported that "the sheer numbers [of wounded] that we have estimated, indicates that the rate and scope of beating and other forms of violence cannot be considered deviations or aberrations, and they come closer to being the norm." The team found that hospitals in the territories were "overwhelmed" by the flood of casualties and that their condition is "worse than the TV series 'MASH.'" One delegation member noted: "If this were a war, many of the actions whose results we have seen would be declared atrocities." Apparently the IDF's declared policy on the use of force was not "being fulfilled in the field." The delegation acknowledged that the army was going against its norms and that 10 to 15 percent of the soldiers were emotionally "torn apart" by the tasks assigned them. Some soldiers refused to participate. Characteristic was the plea of one interviewed: "The more I break other people's bones, the more I am broken myself."[18]

The issue of beatings and of other uses of force was to plague Israel again and again in the months ahead. It seemed that not only thousands of Palestinians had become victims but also that the reputation of the army was at stake, as was the good name of Israel itself. Were these measures an inevitable consequence of the occupation? Were the Palestinians to blame? Had Israelis been deceiving themselves about the "humanity" of their youths? Questions such as these began to divide the country. They insinuated themselves into political debate and became central in the forthcoming election campaign (all of which will be discussed in Chapter 4).

Defense Minister Rabin never seemed able to devise a coherent or consistent policy on the use of force. While taking umbrage at criticism of his troops in the field, he continued to issue statements about the necessity for using the methods criticized. The Arabs had to be deprived of the "sense of power" they had acquired as a result of their protests during the first fortnight of the uprising. "They felt they were getting the upper hand over the IDF . . . [and that] they were making their mark politically." Rabin and the high command decided that "residents of the territories must not be allowed to make political gains as a result of violence." The army therefore "decided to stamp out violence entirely."

In answer to questions about beginning the beatings policy, Rabin stated that it was introduced on January 4 or 5 but was not announced publicly for several days because reporters had not asked about it. To prevent confusion in the country, he decided to reveal the facts "so as not to create a situation in which one set of directives is transmitted within the army, while another picture is presented to the public. The soldiers must feel that they have the backing of the political echelon and the senior command." Tear gas, rubber bullets, beatings, all had to be used, he insisted, to put down the disturbances. According to Rabin, the use of beatings—though authorized—was circumscribed by the use of restrictions: Beating was to stop when a detainee was caught, should not be used when entering a home to make an arrest unless there was resistance, and should not be used to force merchants to open shops or as punishment for keeping them closed. "No blows for the sake of blows," he said. The world complained when Israel fired live ammunition at rioters; now it was protesting the use of nonlethal weapons (beatings). "They will always complain unless Israel speaks to the demonstrators nicely, over a cup of coffee," he protested.[19]

The general responsible for the West Bank, Amram Mitzna, Officer Commanding (OC) Central Command, acknowledged the inconsistencies of the situation. "We, the Israelis, as Jews, have a very sensitive conscience, because brutality is against our way of thinking and behaving," he declared. Mitzna pointed out that a number of soldiers had been court-martialed or dismissed as punishment for excessive beatings. His soldiers, trained to fight a clearly defined enemy, were now carrying out a "confusing" mission, forced to police "a mostly innocent civilian population." But no soldier had refused to beat Palestinians, he asserted.[20]

Army Chief-of-Staff General Dan Shomron opined after the first few weeks of the Intifada, and following the initial outbursts of international criticism, that his troops had neither the training nor equipment for police duties. The army was making do with what it had at hand. At the beginning of the year, he promised that the occupation forces would be given more riot training and control equipment. While no special IDF riot squads would be formed, special clubs would be manufactured for the disturbances, whose scope and intensity had taken the army by surprise. Instead of sending in young soldiers with rifles and combat gear against the stone-throwing Arab youths, troops would be assigned who had riot-control training and were equipped with special helmets, shields, tear-gas grenades, rubber bullets, and clubs. The army was so unprepared for the situation that it had to borrow a water cannon from the Jerusalem police to use in the Gaza Strip, Rabin told a press conference.[21]

To the Israeli public and the international community, the uprising was characterized by the daily confrontations between stone-throwing Palestinian youths and Israeli occupation forces. Although foreign television displayed hundreds of such altercations, one incident in particular seemed to capture the disproportion between the antagonists, between Israeli ruthlessness and Palestinian oppression. Early in March a CBS television crew in Nablus filmed from a distance, without being seen, a sequence in which four Israeli soldiers beat two Arab youths who were sitting on the ground with their hands tied behind their backs. The soldiers kicked the Arabs in the head and chest, and then beat them on the arms and legs with heavy rocks. According to the CBS Israel bureau chief, the beating lasted about forty minutes. Within a day the television clip was being shown throughout Europe and the United States. The incident aroused a storm of protest, and Israeli embassies in Washington, London, Paris, and Amsterdam were flooded with angry calls. In some countries the incident sparked anti-Israel demonstrations; even supporters of Israel were shocked or chagrined.

General Mitzna still insisted that such incidents were "aberrations" but acknowledged that this one so shocked him that he and fellow officers "couldn't say a word after we saw this film." He canceled all appointments to personally investigate the incident and freed the two Arab youths even though they had thrown stones. "They feel O.K.," and their arms were not broken, he claimed.[22]

This incident and the hundreds of other clips showing violence so dramatized the physical confrontation that other, perhaps more significant, aspects of the Intifada were either overlooked or relegated to insignificance. By January, the street fights between soldiers and demonstrators had become only outward manifestations of the uprising. It began to take a political shape: Leaders were beginning to emerge; tangible goals were being discussed; economic and social changes were evolving; and a community-wide cohesiveness was forming within the Palestinian population of the occupied territories.

NONVIOLENT CIVIL RESISTANCE

An initial sign of political resistance was the call in January by Hanna Siniora, editor of the East Jerusalem Arabic daily *Al-Fajr*, for civil disobedience. His plan envisaged a Palestinian boycott of Israeli-made cigarettes, the first attack on the economic front. Civil disobedience would be escalated in subsequent stages with a boycott of Israeli soft drinks, refusal to pay taxes, and a strike against Israeli employers.

Israeli authorities were at first nonplussed by this new dimension of the uprising. Was Siniora's plan unlawful, and could he be punished for contravening military government regulations? One complication was that *Al-Fajr* was published in Jerusalem and Siniora was a resident of the city. Since Israel had annexed Arab East Jerusalem, it was considered part of Israel proper and was not subject to the military administration or to the law applied in Gaza and the West Bank. The attorney-general ordered a probe of the editor's public statements to see if he could be charged with incitement or some other technical violation of the law. After being summoned to the Jerusalem police station at the notorious Russian Compound, Siniora was grilled for about two and a half hours and released, but ordered not to leave the country without police permission.

About the same time, leaflets appeared throughout the West Bank and Gaza spread by an anonymous "popular committee" with a seventeen-point program expanding the scope of civil resistance. The committee called on Palestinians to sever all connections with the occupiers by refusing to work for Israelis and by boycotting Israeli goods and those sold by Arabs who dealt with Israelis. A form of nonviolent activism was proposed in which all village residents would present themselves at police stations for arrest when security forces tried to seize a fellow villager. When the military imposed a curfew in towns and refugee camps, all residents were urged to leave their homes simultaneously (in order to break the curfew at a given time) and to raise Palestinian and UN flags.

This list of civil disobedience actions closely resembled those advocated by a Palestinian Jerusalem resident, Mubarak Awad, in an article published by the *Journal of Palestinian Studies* during 1984. Awad, a Jerusalemite who lived in the United States for some fifteen years and who studied at a Mennonite College, had become a U.S. citizen. He returned to his native city in 1985 with his Quaker wife, who was principal of the Friends school for girls in Ramallah. Following his return, he established in Jerusalem the Palestinian Center for the Study of Non-Violence, an institution that Awad hoped would become instrumental in teaching Palestinians under occupation how to cope with their plight without using armed force. Some in the Israeli government believed Awad to be a principal leader of the uprising and sought to have him deported.

Though supposedly influenced by Gandhi and Martin Luther King, Awad's approach—according to his explanations—was based more on practical than on moral considerations. The use of nonviolence, he argued, was "the most effective strategy" for Palestinians in the West Bank and Gaza. It "does not determine the methods open to Palestinians on the outside; nor does it constitute a rejection of the concept of armed struggle . . . [or] the possibility that the struggle on the inside may turn into an armed struggle at a later stage." For the present (1984), however, nonviolence appeared to be the most effective method "to obstruct" Israeli objectives. Among the arguments presented for this strategy were that it could use "the largest possible amount of the potential and resources of Palestinians" under occupation and would offer "all sectors of the Palestinian society an opportunity to engage actively in the struggle, instead of observing it passively." It could "neutralize to a large degree the destructive power of the Israeli war machine, and enlist in our service, or at least neutralize, important sectors of Israeli society." By removing "the irrational fear of 'Arab violence,' which presently cements Israeli society together, . . . it contributes to the disintegration of hostile Israeli . . . [elements] and helps to isolate Israel politically and morally." Furthermore, nonviolence would increase "any beneficial public international attention to our cause by revealing the racist and expansionist features of the Zionist movement and denying it the jus-tification built on its purported 'security.'"[23]

The use of nonviolence, however, should not assume reciprocal non-violence by "the enemy." Great sacrifices would be demanded by the use of this strategy. "Martyrs and wounded will fall, and Palestinians will suffer personal losses in terms of their interests, jobs, and possessions. Non-violent struggle is a real war, not an easy alternative," Awad cautioned. Lest Palestinians mistakenly perceive that nonviolence is negative or passive, he warned, on the contrary, that it is a form of "mobile warfare" requiring "special training and a high degree of organization and discipline."

The crux of Palestinian nonviolence was to be based on the assumption that "the Israeli soldier is a human being, not a beast devoid of conscience and feeling. He has an understanding of right and wrong. . . . He constantly needs a reasonable justification for his activities. On the other hand, he has the potential for evil and oppression like any other person. He is often an intolerant racist and shares most of his government's evil assumptions." Public opinion, both Israeli and international, were significant cards in this strategy. Israel is in constant need of international support and is dependent on public opinion at home; therefore, it could not ignore the effect of its actions on these constituencies.

The "suffering and pain" resulting from subjecting themselves voluntarily to the consequences of nonviolent methods would forge unity among the Palestinians, Awad believed. They would achieve "moral superiority" over "the enemy," and "set in motion historical factors which insure the survival of the Palestinian people and their eventual victory." There could be no guarantee of victory through either armed struggle or nonviolence. The latter could achieve "its goals, and affect the hearts and minds of the Israeli soldiers." This would be evidenced by their "loss of fighting spirit," by protests against the government, by growing Israeli emigration, and by an increase in the moral and political isolation of Israel abroad.

Implementation of a nonviolent strategy would require "points of contact" between Palestinians and Israeli occupation authorities—contact that some Israeli leaders had sought to circumvent. For example, when he was defense minister, Moshe Dayan attempted to reduce the number of confrontations between Arabs and Israeli troops by minimizing the military presence in the occupied territories, especially the urban areas. However, it would be useful to draw the army into direct confrontation with demonstrators, to set in motion the use of nonviolent confrontation strategy.

Mubarak Awad borrowed a number of tactics for his proposed strategy from the book by Gene Sharp, *The Politics of Non-Violence* (Boston: Sargent, 1973). These included demonstrations, obstruction of plans from the authorities, refusal to cooperate with the occupation government, harassment of occupiers, boycotts of Israeli goods, strikes, establishment of alternative institutions to replace those of the authorities, and civil disobedience.

Demonstrations, already a frequent occurrence since the occupation began, could be devised to educate not only Palestinians but Israelis and international public opinion as well. Demonstrations would manifest solidarity within the community. They might include not only street marches but also fasting, protest prayer vigils, guerrilla theater, flying the Palestinian flag, and other public expressions of solidarity. As the Intifada progressed, all of these tactics were used. One that particularly annoyed Israeli troops was the collective blowing of whistles, which created confusion and angered soldiers who chased the whistle blowers with the same vigor that they pursued stone throwers.

Placing obstructions, such as boulders, burning tires, and other large objects, in roads used by the military was a tactic that had also been employed for twenty years before the Intifada. Awad proposed more extensive obstruction, to be achieved by interfering with communications and cutting electricity, telephone, and water lines. He even recommended that Palestinians throw their bodies in front of Israeli bulldozers to prevent them from clearing land for new Jewish settlements or military outposts. If obstruction tactics were violent (such as stone throwing), the Israeli reaction would inevitably be violent. Soldiers could then claim that their response, probably shooting, was in self-defense. The use of nonviolent obstruction tactics might also elicit a violent response, but it would send a clear message that Palestinians were willing to martyr themselves for their land. Nonviolence would prove false the myths about Palestinian "terrorism," that the disturbances were incited by a handful of cowardly trouble-makers and provocateurs. However, organization of a mass passive resistance movement using many of these tactics was to prove extremely difficult because the tactics required far more discipline than the Intifada could command in its initial phases.

More successful were organized efforts at noncooperation. As the uprising gathered momentum, increasing numbers of Palestinians refused to make the daily trek to Israeli construction sites, orange groves, street cleaning details, and factory assembly lines. However, economic pressures precluded a total boycott by Arab labor: Most Palestinians continued to work across the Green Line because they needed the income to sustain their families. Still, Jewish employment of Arab labor became much more uncertain. Employers often were unable to determine who would report for work, or when. Had another strike occurred? Were laborers prevented by fellow Palestinians or by Israeli troops from appearing? (The impact caused by disruption of Arab labor in Israel and Israeli plants in the territories will be discussed in Chapter 4.)

Awad's plan of noncooperation with authorities involved total severance of all official contact. He proposed that the occupied Palestinians refuse either to use Israeli identity cards or to fill out government forms required for permits or information, fail to appear when summoned by the authorities, reject payments of any Israeli taxes or fines, boycott work as employees of the occupation authorities, and avoid social contact with Israelis. Although the leaders of the Intifada advocated many of these measures, compliance was far from total. Merchants and shopkeepers required permits to stay in business; those with automobiles needed licenses to keep them on the road; travelers abroad had to obtain Israeli exit and reentry permits, and nearly anyone who left home would need the required Israeli identity card or risk immediate arrest and imprisonment. Thus it was not easy to break the Israeli bureaucratic throttlehold on the territories. For the average person involved in noncooperation with the government, the economic and political risks were far too high.

As the Intifada progressed, boycotts of Israeli goods became widespread; starting with cigarettes, they broadened to include the host of manufactured items that had captured consumer markets in the West Bank and Gaza. Soft drinks, soap, household cleaning items, beer, clothing, canned foods—item after item was added to the list, until the boycott began to have a telling effect on both the local Arab and Israeli economies (a matter that will be discussed in Chapters 3 and 4).

Local strikes by shopkeepers, merchants, and nearly all other businesses, from travel agencies to law offices, soon began to acquire a pattern. (Pharmacies were exempted from closing.) At first, the strikes were sporadic, declared for a day or as long as a week. The military government attempted to break the pattern by sending troops to forcibly open shops. Soldiers would swoop down on a street of closed stores, catch an owner, and order him to open; or they would cut the lock on shuttered windows and doors, forcing the establishment to open. When leaders of the Intifada later permitted shops to open at certain hours, the army ordered them shut; and when they were shut, the military forced them open. As it became apparent that the uprising would continue indefinitely, shopkeepers and businesses faced the prospect of financial ruin and women found it increasingly difficult to sustain their household. A pattern emerged throughout the territories of the daily strike such that transactions were permitted between the hours of 9 A.M. and noon. Evidence of the new "short business day" existed in all large towns and cities. Visitors to the Old City of Jerusalem could observe that the Arab sectors suddenly came to life at 9 A.M. as the streets were crowded with shoppers who thronged the stores during the daily three hours allotted for business. Shortly after noon, nearly every Arab establishment closed, and the Arab Old City once again seemed deserted.

An important aspect of Mubarak Awad's strategy was the establishment of alternative institutions to provide services and community infrastructure replacing those imposed by the military government's Civil Administration. The foundations and framework for Palestinian institutions already existed long before the occupation began. Since 1967, however, such institutions—women's organizations, schools and universities, technical training facilities, hospitals and clinics, welfare associations, professional groups including lawyers, physicians, and engineers—had developed at a more rapid pace. (These developments will be discussed in Chapter 3, which deals with the social and political impact of the Intifada.)

There were many Israelis and Palestinians who regarded Mubarak Awad and his ideas as peripheral, almost irrelevant, to the Arab-Israeli conflict. Palestinian militants scoffed at the idea of nonviolence; many perceived it as an imported fad that had no chance of success in the "serious" war of rocks, knives, and Molotov cocktails. Many Israelis also belittled the nonviolent "fad" as something of which Arabs were incapable: They could never effectively organize, and if they did, they would not be able to sustain the discipline required for such a strategy.

Yet Awad became enough of a threat to Israeli authorities that they decided to deport him early in 1988; after three years, as unrest began to escalate in Gaza and the West Bank, they suddenly took notice. Some now argued that he was as much if not more of a threat than the Palestinian terrorists who killed innocent women and children.[24]

Behind the scenes, a struggle ensued between the Israeli Foreign Ministry, then controlled by the Labor party and considered moderate, and the officials affiliated with the militantly nationalist Likud over the fate of Awad. Strong pressure was exerted on Israel by the U.S. State Department and Ambassador Thomas Pickering to renew Awad's request for an identity card, which was required for his continued stay in Jerusalem. Since Awad was a U.S. citizen, the legal course taken by the government was to deny renewal of either the necessary identity card or his visa. (U.S. Jews generally had little difficulty in renewing visas for a prolonged stay in the country.)

Many Israelis resented the U.S. pressure. The Shin Bet (domestic intelligence service) argued that Awad threatened the country's security and challenged its sovereignty. Charging that he had instigated civil disobedience, it noted that he and his organization had removed the surveyors' markings that had been prepared for a new Jewish settlement in the West Bank, and that his followers had broken open houses sealed by the army, planted trees on disputed lands, and urged Palestinians to refuse tax payments to Israel. An official in the Ministry of Interior, responsible for issuing identity cards and residence permits, accused Awad of "the most flagrant breaches of the law." After months of internal discussion over the Awad case and sharp exchanges with the State Department, Awad was placed under police guard and shipped off on a TWA jet to New York in June 1988. The U.S. government "strongly objected" to the deportation. "We think that it is unjustifiable to deny Mr. Awad the right to stay and live in Jerusalem where he was born,"

White House spokesman Marlin Fitzwater stated.[25] Foreign Minister Peres asserted that Awad's appeal to Israel's High Court of Justice, albeit unsuccessful, proved that the "rule of law prevails."

Many recognized that Awad's deportation was a blow to Israel's image abroad. When he arrived in the United States, Awad launched a media campaign and stated that he wanted to return to Jerusalem, his birthplace, and organize a Palestinian peace movement. The *Jerusalem Post* observed that the government had handled the situation "in typical club-footed fashion," almost assuring Awad wide publicity and creating one of the worst instances of bad relations with the United States in forty years. Although Awad was no friend of Israel, "and his non-violent persona is in large measure bogus, . . . Mr. Shamir may yet come to realize that he would have been less trouble for Israel here, than there."[26]

THE IDF AND DEPORTATIONS

When it became apparent to the IDF high command that the uprising could not be crushed by force, at least not through measures that would be acceptable to the Israeli public or tolerated by Israel's friends abroad, especially the United States, a decision was taken to undermine the leadership of the Intifada. If the leaders could be uncovered and deported, that would be "a proven short-term deterrent to further disturbances," a former head of the West Bank Civil Administration told the media. Although expulsion of "troublemakers" was not a new procedure employed by the military, it was not used lightly. Deporting Palestinians from their homeland for political or security reasons stirred up opposition from Israeli civil rights groups and was another cause for censure by the United States. Many Israelis argued that it was a violation of international law. Nevertheless, since the occupation had begun, Palestinians and civil rights groups in Israel had claimed that more than 2,000 Arabs had been deported by the IDF. They included mayors, teachers (among them the president of Bir Zeit University), journalists, and editors of Arabic newspapers. Israel official sources claimed that only 60 bona fide West Bank residents had been expelled on security grounds. The others, they said, were found to be in the country illegally.[27]

When Mubarak Awad brought his case to the Israeli Supreme Court, he argued that deportation violated the 1949 Geneva Convention; the Court, however, argued that the Convention was not applicable in the West Bank and Gaza; its purpose, the Court stated, was to prevent mass deportations of civilian populations in occupied territories. A major purpose of the Convention was to prevent atrocities like those committed by the Nazis, who deported millions to labor camps and gas chambers; it was not intended to undermine the occupation power's capacity to maintain law and order. Nevertheless, the Court warned, deportations should not be used arbitrarily but only in accord with the 1945 Defence (Emergency) Regulations used by the British during the mandate and retained by the government of Israel. The military could issue deportation orders "whenever necessary or desirable to preserve public security, defend the area, secure public order, or to put down sedition, revolt, or riots."

Recipients of deportation orders could appeal to an advisory committee for redress, although local military authorities were not bound to accept the committee's recommendation. As in Mubarak Awad's case, appeals could be made to the High Court of Justice; but few such appeals were ever made, and only a handful of deportation orders had been rescinded.

After less than a month of the tough "iron fist" policy, the IDF selected nine Palestinians for deportation, a mix of individuals from diverse backgrounds. They included the deputy editor of a woman's magazine, the vice-chairman of the Gaza engineers union, a Ramallah lawyer, three religious fundamentalists, two refugee camp residents, and a man jailed for "terrorist attacks" in 1979 but released in the 1985 prisoner exchange when Israel freed several hundred jailed Palestinians in exchange for three Israeli soldiers captured by a guerrilla faction in Lebanon. They ranged from 26 to 45 years of age, and from university students to graduates. Most of them had served previous jail sentences for subversive activities. According to the IDF, they were leading operatives of Palestinian nationalist (in IDF terms, "terrorist") factions including Fatah, the Popular Front for the Liberation of Palestine, and Islamic fundamentalist groups. It appeared that the IDF was attempting to send a message to a wide range of factions, from Marxist to radical Islamic.

Since no neighboring country would accept the deportees, they were taken to the 15-kilometer-wide "security" strip of southern Lebanon, still controlled by Israel after its evacuation in 1985. As expected, the United States and the United Nations protested the expulsion; Washington supported a Security Council resolution calling on Israel not to carry out the deportations. The Israel Association for Civil Rights condemned the measure as a violation of international law. The usually pro-Labor *Jerusalem Post* asked what useful purpose could be served "by even limited resort to a sordid . . . mandatory ordinance which directly clashes with Israel's paper commitment to the humanitarian provisions of the Fourth Geneva Convention, and which makes something of a mockery of Israel's claim to be running a benign occupation. Deportations will create more problems than they solve, helping to rekindle rather than put out the fires of resistance in the territories." If the banished Palestinians really did turn out to be "big fish," their places would soon be taken by "small fry."[28]

Neither international nor internal criticism of the deportation procedure prevented the army from using it frequently during the first year of the Intifada. The number of expulsions did not reach the peak of the late 1960s and early 1970s when hundreds were deported, sometimes in a single year. But the more than fifty deportation orders during 1988 were double the number during the previous two and a half years. That number might have been even larger had it not been for the reprimands by the U.S. government, which opposed Israel's use of the measure. Washington's strictures reached their highest intensity in August, when Deputy Secretary of State John Whitehead warned that Israel's failure to reconsider its latest deportation order could "damage our bilateral relations."[29]

International pressures and those of Israeli civil rights groups were more than counterbalanced by Israeli militants such as those in Gush Emunim and in right-wing political parties who continued to demand that outspoken leaders of the Palestinian community be banished. The use of deportations as a device to undermine the uprising acquired particular significance during 1988, an election year in which discussion of the "transfer" of Palestinians from the territories became an issue in the campaign. A new political group, the Motherland party, was formed with "transfer" as the centerpiece of its platform (see Chapter 4).

Deportation orders were served on leaders who seemed to be specially chosen or randomly selected, as in the case of the Beita incident. A large number of those targeted were journalists, lawyers, student activists, and trade unionists (six unionists were ordered to be deported in 1988) charged with membership in popular committees that had been labeled "terrorist organizations" by the IDF. Among the more obvious individuals not served with deportation orders were outspoken nationalists in Jerusalem such as Hanna Siniora and Faisal Husseini. Because Jerusalem was considered by Israel to be part of the Jewish state, they were not subject to provisions of the Defence (Emergency) Regulations, which could be enforced only in the occupied territories.[30]

POLITICAL ASSASSINATION

Unable to end the uprising by eliminating the Gaza and West Bank leadership, the IDF attempted another tactic in April. Although it acknowledged that the Intifada had begun spontaneously within the territories, by April all concerned recognized that direct contacts had been established between the local leadership and PLO headquarters in Tunis. Perhaps a blow could be struck directly at the highest echelon outside the country, demonstrating again Israel's long punitive arm and, at the same time, striking a blow at morale within the territories. In April, Khalil al-Wazir (also know as Abu Jihad), PLO Chairman Arafat's closest aide, was assassinated at his home in Tunis along with his chauffeur and two body guards. They were gunned down by an unidentified group of men, generally suspected of affiliation with Israeli intelligence. When queried about the shooting, Israeli officials had no comment. The *Washington Post* reported that the operation was in retaliation for an attack during March by the PLO on an Israeli bus in the Negev. According to the report, which was republished in the *Jerusalem Post*, the assassination plan was given a "yellow light" by the ten-man Israeli inner cabinet. At the time, Foreign Minister Peres and two other ministers opposed the operation. It was presented again to the inner cabinet in April according to the *New York Times*, during a time of "increasing desperation" over the uprising. Army intelligence now believed that Abu Jihad was a key leader, directing the Intifada from abroad. Ze'ev Schiff, a leading Israeli military commentator, asserted that until the Intifada a presumption had prevailed that PLO chiefs would not be attacked personally. "There was a sort of unwritten asylum for chieftains." But since December 1987 the rules were changed across the board, including those concerning administrative detention, when to open fire on demonstrators, and attacks on PLO leaders. The only cabinet member who publicly criticized the assassination was Ezer Weizman, who believed that it would increase hostility between Palestinians and Israelis and harm peace efforts.[31]

The attack in Tunis was a windfall for Israeli hardliners. It not only weakened peace prospects then being explored by U.S. Secretary of State George Shultz but also helped to undermine moderates in the Labor party such as Peres, Weizman, and Education Minister Itzhak Navon, who were pressing for an international peace conference.

As predicted by Israelis who were close to the situation in the territories, Abu Jihad's assassination poured fuel on the fires of unrest. A new wave of violence erupted after what had been a short period of fewer demonstrations and diminishing confrontation. In Jerusalem the Supreme Muslim Council declared three days of mourning and a general strike, during which hundreds of black flags were flown. In Gaza, where Abu Jihad had been raised, there was a new wave of Molotov cocktail attacks on occupation troops. As the PLO chief was being buried in Damascus, mock funerals were held in several towns in the territories. Orders came from the Intifada United Leadership designating the Saturday after Abu Jihad's death as a "day of rage" on which protests and demonstrations were to be escalated. (The "day of rage" was repeated the following year.)

The Tunis operation again underscored the differences within the Israeli government and public over the appropriate measures for dealing with the uprising. While nearly all Likud supporters were enthusiastic about the operation, there was division within the Labor party. The Likud attitude was epitomized by the comments of its Knesset member Benny Shalita, who congratulated "whoever performed the 'mitzva' [religious obligation] of killing Wazir." Labor Minister of Knesset (MK) Benjamin Ben-Eliezer, former IDF general in the Civil Administration, asserted that the killing would not quell the unrest; after the assassination Weizman called it "folly," whereas Rabin, Labor's second highest leader, gave it his backing.[32]

Rabin's support for operations like the Abu Jihad assassination underscored the inconsistency of his policy. Although he favored undermining the Intifada leadership, he also argued against the idea that there was an organized movement in the territories. In July 1988 Rabin told the Knesset that it was "nonsense" to talk of civil disobedience "because violent elements . . . were intent on undermining their local ruling bodies." He insisted that there was "no organized command or logistic structure" for the Intifada. "They act on the spur of the moment and make use of whatever comes to hand," he said of the leadership.[33]

Although the government was noncommittal about the use of assassination abroad, it adamantly denied that it organized "death squads" in the territories, a charge raised by Palestinian human rights organizations. The Ramallah-based al-Haq (Law in the Service of Man) maintained that there was a deliberate and calculated policy to physically incapacitate or eliminate Palestinian leaders. It cited a *Jerusalem Post* report of December 11, 1987, that Rabin had announced deployment of snipers in all army units who would aim "at the legs only" of demonstration ring leaders. Rabin accused masked organizers of forcing Palestinian pupils, "often against their will, to riot." In July 1988 another *Jerusalem Post* story cited by al-Haq told of an undercover military unit code-named "Shimshon" (Samson). Operating in Gaza, its members were disguised as foreign press representatives who kidnapped or liquidated ring leaders and troublemakers. A similar unit, code-named "Cherry," allegedly operated in the West Bank; its orders were to shoot to kill Palestinians "with blood on their hands." The IDF official spokesman indignantly disassociated the military from such activities, and several foreign journalists had their press credentials temporarily suspended for reporting the alleged incidents. Since those carrying out the work of "death squads" usually operated in civilian clothes and from civilian automobiles, sometimes using fraudulent press identification, some Israelis maintained that this was the work of civilian settlers. Al-Haq speculated that such squads "would presumably consist of units attached to the intelligence services (Shin Bet) rather than the armed forces, although the possibility of coordination between them and the army should not be excluded."[34] To prevent members of Israeli intelligence from using the journalist disguise to penetrate the territories, leaders of the Intifada began to issue their own foreign press cards through the "Palestine Press Office" in Jerusalem, a tactic that aroused the ire of right-wing Knesset members. They demanded that any correspondents who used the Intifada-issued credentials be thrown out of the country.

ADMINISTRATIVE DETENTION AND MASS ARRESTS

Unable to remove the top leadership of the Intifada, the IDF made attempts to strike at lower echelons through mass arrests and administrative detention. If the head could not be severed, then the arms and legs—the cadres that carried out the orders of the United National Leadership—would be crippled. This meant that thousands of activists, not merely stone throwers and those who distributed leaflets, in the scores of towns and hundreds of villages would have to be stopped. The result was the most extensive use of arrests, imprisonment, and administrative detention since the occupation began.

Under the Defence (Emergency) Regulations, any soldier or police authority could make an arrest in the occupied territories without a warrant. Suspects could be detained up to four days by any soldier or policeman and could be held for another four days. Detainees could be kept up to eighteen days before being brought to a military court, which could extend detention up to six months without a trial. The time of detention exceeded by far that permitted by authorities within Israel. Administrative detention, also called preventative detention or internment, authorized the government, acting through the armed services, to hold individuals without either charge or trial for up to six months, an arrest that could be repeated indefinitely. This procedure was used between 1967 and 1980 but gradually diminished until 1985, when it was resumed again. Between 1985 (the period of "iron fist") and December 1987, an estimated 316 Palestinians were held in administrative detention.[35]

While under detention those arrested were usually interrogated by the Shin Bet, which used a wide variety of methods to elicit information and to undermine the self-confidence of detainees. There has been extensive condemnation of such treatment, which included torture, by reputable human rights organizations within Israel and abroad. Their reports have been published by Amnesty International and by the U.S. State Department in its report to Congress on human rights violations.

Once a week, the families of Palestinian detainees are allowed to visit their relatives held in Ansar II detention camp (seen in background), Gaza town. UNRWA photo by George Nehmeh.

Israeli authorities acknowledged that some 18,000 Palestinians were arrested during the first year of the Intifada, many times the number in any similar period since the occupation began. Al-Haq estimated that between 9,000 and 10,000 were held at any given time during 1988. Of these, between 3,000 and 4,000 were in administrative detention, subjected to interrogation by the Shin Bet and denied access to legal council or to a court hearing for extended periods of time. Those arrested included women and children as young as 14 or 15 years old, the latter accused of stone throwing and other "terrorist" acts.[36]

After the Intifada began, military legislation was amended to permit more flexible use of administrative detention orders. As the rules of evidence were relaxed, those held in administrative detention were in effect considered guilty until proven innocent and prisoners were denied access to facts about their detention. The number of officers permitted to issue detention orders was increased when the authority to do so was granted to any military commander rather than being restricted to the commanders of the West Bank and Gaza. Palestinian lawyers in the territories believed that these new provisions so limited their capacity to deal with clients that they decided to boycott the military courts.

Since December 1987 extensive use was made of mass arrests either as a form of collective punishment or as a way to discourage participation in civil disobedience. During 1988 there were several instances of roundups in which hundreds were arrested, many of them during curfews or army raids when the whole male population from age 14 to 50 or 60 in a village or camp would be detained for questioning. A familiar pattern after an Israeli soldier or settler was attacked was to collect all males over 14–16 years of age in the village square or school for interrogation. In one case, the male population of Beita was detained at the village school for five days. While the use of mass arrests probably intimidated many individuals and deterred them from active participation in the uprising, there is no doubt that it undermined what little respect they may have had for the Israeli system of justice, and on many occasions it politically activated youths who before their detention were merely observers.

A "profile" based on 330 cases of those held in administrative detention was presented in a report to the Israel Bar Association and heads of law faculties by Knesset member Dedi Zucker of the Citizens Rights Movement (CRM). Fifteen percent were between 16 and 21 years old, 58 percent between 21 and 30, and the rest over 30. A quarter were enrolled in high schools; 4 percent had less than six years of school, 53 percent between seven and eleven years of school, and 6 percent twelve years; and 10 percent had university degrees. These figures showed that most leaders of the uprising were under 30 and fairly well educated. Zucker believed "that the political echelon has clearly lost control over the situation," and that failure by the Israeli legal community to take a firm stand on the issue was "tantamount to complicity and support for the system."[37]

Within weeks after the Intifada began, existing jail and prison facilities were swamped, and the IDF found that it had to open new and often makeshift detention centers in schools and in hastily improvised prison camps where detainees were kept for lengthy periods. Among the more notorious were Ansar II in Gaza and Ketsiyot Military Detention Center (Prison Seven), called Ansar III, which was established in the Negev Desert to take the overflow from the Intifada. Ansar II and III were named after the detention center improvised during the Lebanon War, when thousands of Palestinian and Lebanese prisoners were kept in tent encampments.

Conditions in these makeshift prisons were so abysmal that they sparked protest within Israel, leading to an investigation during the summer by a judicial committee. Three Israeli Supreme Court justices decided to visit Ketsiyot after an appeal from seventeen detainees about "inhuman" conditions, a charge denied by the camp commander. During the justices' visit in September, inmates told of insufficient food, water shortages, prisoners having to share food trays and limited to one shower a week, lack of exercise, physical mistreatment, and boredom. Earlier reports from Ansar II described how fifty detainees were packed into old army barracks approximately 9 by 5 meters in size. According to regulations, prisoners were locked in the barracks during the day, with only a ten- to fifteen-minute exercise period at midnight or dawn. They were allowed to use toilet facilities once every twenty-four hours, provided they ran there and back. Soldiers demanded that detainees answer them "Na'am Ya'effendi" (Yes, sir—in Arabic). Prisoners who refused or were caught walking to daily latrine visits could be locked in the *zin zin*, a 1-meter square booth where they had to stand with their hands tied behind their back. Often new arrivals were isolated for between two and eighteen days for initial interrogation. Thereafter they were sent to a barracks containing thirty to sixty inmates. Many detainees were 12- or 13-year-old children for whom this was an initial "life experience" away from their families. A *Jerusalem Post* correspondent, Bradley Burston, reported that six IDF soldiers were court-martialed for physical and verbal humiliation, including "the use of a 12-year-old detainee as a 'football' in a pick-up 'soccer game.'"[38]

Ansar II, a "holding pen for suspected rock throwers," was about to become "perhaps the single most efficient operational institution for the indoctrination of Gaza youth," Burston believed.

> Minutes from the heart of Gaza City, a new military force is taking shape, with scores of draftees arriving every night. For the moment the outfit lacks a formal name, but odds are that what is being formed here—right under the noses of the Shin Bet and the IDF Southern Command—is nothing less than the future army of Palestine. It is the site of detailed and intensive courses in such subjects as introductory Palestinian nationalism and making explosives in one's own home. In fact, the "campus" is an Israeli military installation: the Coastal Detention Facility, better known as Ansar 2.[39]

CURFEWS

A major difference between previous uprisings and the new Intifada has been the latter's pervasiveness and persistence and the ability of new leaders to rally participation on the part of the total or nearly total populations in towns and villages. Mass participation led to a decision by the IDF to impose mass curfews on towns and villages as another form of collective punishment. However, it was limited in its capacity to impose authority, especially in the West Bank where there are more than 500 villages, many of them in remote or isolated hill country. Without a substantial increase in manpower and equipment, the IDF was unable to establish a presence throughout all the occupied territories at once. Since the resources of the military (both personnel and equipment) were already overstrained, with reserve duty for many increased from forty-five to sixty days a year, selective mass pacification had to be used. It was believed that more frequent curfews, a tactic used often since 1967, would be effective. Villages, towns, refugee camps, even cities could be isolated, and collective punishments could be used to wear down resistance to the occupation, area by area.

During the first year of the Intifada, al-Haq determined that a minimum of 1,600 curfews was imposed throughout the occupied territories. An estimated 400 were prolonged, lasting from three to forty days around the clock. According to this estimate, nearly every Palestinian resident of the territories was subjected to enforced home confinement during the year at least one time; most endured long curfews, some repeatedly. On almost any given day, at least 25,000 Palestinians were under curfew, frequently hundreds of thousands at a time. On several occasions all Arabs in the West Bank and Gaza were curfewed—notably, on Land Day commemorating the confiscation of Arab lands by Israel, and when the PLO proclaimed Palestinian independence during November 1988. And for the first time since the early days of occupation in 1967, a curfew was imposed in the Arab sections of Jerusalem.

During curfews no one was permitted to leave home for any reason; inhabitants were ordered to stay away from windows and balconies; curfew violators were often shot; even being seen at a window by patrolling soldiers could result in being shot at or intruded upon by troops. Soldiers often used curfews to search homes for weapons, Molotov cocktail materials, and young men or boys who might have participated in demonstrations or stone throwing. There were many cases documented by al-Haq of people in areas under curfew being beaten, shot, rounded up, and taken away for questioning; of furniture, windows, and food being destroyed; of tear-gas grenades being thrown into homes and other enclosed structures, contrary to instructions for their use.

An alternative measure to isolate a town or village was to declare it a "closed area," thus placing it under siege by the army. Although inhabitants were permitted to leave their homes in "closed areas," the military could exclude outsiders and prevent food and other items from entering. During "closure," water, electricity, and telephone services were often disconnected. Even cities like Nablus were periodically "closed"; the army surrounded the city by setting up checkpoints at entrances and confiscated all food to prevent it from reaching the inhabitants. Even tourist buses were searched and sandwiches confiscated.

One of the longest "sieges" during 1988 was imposed on the West Bank village of Kabatiya as punishment for the lynching of a local resident suspected by the inhabitants of being an IDF informer. When the mob besieged his home, he opened fire, killing a 4-year-old boy and wounding several others. The mob then burned his house, killed him, and hanged the body from an electricity pylon. In retaliation, the IDF "closed" the village from February 24 to April 3; telephone, water supplies, and electricity were cut off. Kabatiya's leading export, stone from its quarries sent to Jordan for construction, was not permitted to leave. As a result, many villagers were left without work. The houses of four villagers suspected of involvement in the lynching were bulldozed or blown up by the army, and the families left in tents supplied by the Red Cross. In all, some 400 of the 7,000 villagers were arrested. Periodically the army would reenter to conduct searches, during which they beat residents, vandalized property, and destroyed food supplies. At times, the full curfew was reimposed.[40]

The villagers attempted to cope with or circumvent army restrictions by smuggling contraband from neighbors through hillside trails and footpaths not accessible to IDF vehicles or not yet blocked off with boulders or earth. When caught, the smugglers were tried and heavily fined. The military kept watch for violators with helicopters circling above the village.

After a few weeks of isolation, Kabatiya's residents began to devise ways of going back to premodern self-sufficiency. Resorting to devices of an earlier era, they replaced idle tractors with donkeys and used branches pruned from trees instead of kerosene for cooking fuel. Many started to plant small vegetable patches to supplement meager food supplies; fruit from local orchards was dried and stored along with supplies of sugar, flour, beans, lentils, and olives. New wells were dug or old ones reopened in place of the severed water pipeline. *Jerusalem Post* reporter Joel Greenberg, who visited Kabatiya during the siege, observed that "despite the hardships, the people in Kabatiya seemed to have adjusted grimly to their new conditions of life, which they say are a return to the way the village lived only a generation ago." Some of the villagers he interviewed commented as follows:

> We're making do with what we have. . . . Instead of milk, we give the kids bread and tea. We'll hold out. . . . The situation has brought people together, strengthened their solidarity, and people are helping others who don't have enough food. . . . It's of secondary importance to the people here whether they eat olives or fresh vegetables. There is a far more important issue which matters much more to them. . . . We can hold out for months, even years.[41]

CONFLICT WITH SETTLERS

The deteriorating relations between the military and the Arab inhabitants of the West Bank were often exacerbated by the free-lance activities of Jewish settlers. Long used to having their own way in the territories, the settlers traveled freely through Arab villages; they were armed, whereas the villagers were forbidden to own guns. The settlers lived under Israeli law, not the Civil Administration of the IDF. After the settler movement had begun during the Labor government and gathered momentum under Likud after 1977, only a handful of Jews were apprehended for misusing their privileged position, most notably those arrested for participation in an underground Jewish "terrorist" organization that had planted explosives among Palestinians during the late 1970s and early 1980s. The settlers perceived themselves as similar to the American frontiersmen living in "Indian country," but living there by right, not on sufferance. Most of them criticized the IDF for exercising too much restraint against the Intifada and insisted on more forceful action. Some claimed for themselves the authority to shoot stone throwers in the legs and demanded that the army destroy and clear away houses along the roads that might offer cover for ambushes. If the stone throwers could not be apprehended, perhaps their families should be deported. On several occasions, settlers stormed into Arab villages, broke into homes, and beat the inhabitants in retaliation for stoning their vehicles. It mattered little whether the Palestinians attacked were actual perpetrators; the important thing was to teach the villagers a lesson. Although the military authorities occasionally attempted to restrain settlers, the latter were generally free to harass and intimidate Arab inhabitants in a pattern that appeared to be consistent with the IDF's pacification schemes.[42]

The Beita incident of April 1988 was typical of the serious complications that resulted from settler attitudes and actions. The incident was caused when two settlers led a group of teenage hikers from the Jewish settlement, Elon Moreh, to the outskirts of Beita. When the villagers started to throw stones at the group, one of their guides shot and killed a Palestinian. Hundreds of villagers then surrounded the hikers and, after a discussion between the two groups, the settlers agreed to pass through Beita to reach the main road, understanding that they would be given safe passage. Upon entering the village, the sister of the Palestinian who was shot hurled a rock at the armed Israeli who had killed her brother. This started a melee in which a crowd attacked the hikers with stones, sticks, and other objects. During the altercation, the villagers grabbed the settlers' guns; one of the guides was wounded and a girl hiker shot dead. The group was finally permitted to leave the village, and the guns were later returned.

Initially the villagers were blamed for shooting the two Jewish hikers, thus provoking a hue and cry of demands for vengeance. Several thousand people attended the funeral of Tirza Porat, the girl who was shot, turning it into a massive anti-Palestinian demonstration. Knesset member Haim Druckman of the NRP thundered at the funeral: "The village of Beita must be wiped off the face of the earth!" His supposedly more moderate NRP colleague Zevulon Hammar, the minister of religious affairs, agreed, stating that "there's no room on the map of the country for Beita!" He called on the government to immediately approve establishment of a new West Bank settlement named Tirza Porat. Prime Minister Shamir, the first of the funeral orators, opined that the settlers were motivated by "love of the land," whereas the Arab attackers were guided by blind hate. "There's no question that every Jew, young or old, man or woman, instinctively awakens their thirst for blood and their thirst for murder," but "every murder strengthens Israel, unites Israel, and deepens our roots in this land."

Not all Israelis were swept up in this paroxysm of emotion. Several Knesset members called for an investigation to determine just what happened at the village and who was responsible for the confused reports about the incident. Even before the investigation, the IDF had detained hundreds of villagers for questioning for up to five days at the village school and had arrested sixty. The army took reprisals by blowing up the homes of fourteen villagers and deporting six of them to Lebanon. The village was sealed off between April 6 and April 30, scores of olive and almond trees were uprooted, and the sister of the man who had been killed was prosecuted, convicted, and sentenced to prison for throwing a rock and injuring the Israeli guide. Finally, when the army report was made public, it stated that the girl was shot not by Arabs but inadvertently by her Israeli guide who reacted instinctively, when he was hit on the head with a rock, by shooting several bullets. Nor was any proof found that other weapons were used by the Beita villagers. Still, the report placed major blame on them, because they had initiated the altercation with stone throwing. "The motivation and aggression of local Arabs and the readiness to harm a group of Jewish hikers are the main causes for the development of the incident and its tragic end." However, the report went on to say that "the incident and its tragic results would have been prevented had the hike been planned and cleared according to standard procedures." Army Chief-of-Staff Dan Shomron angered many of those demanding vengeance when he remarked that most villagers had no intention of harming the hikers. All but one of the hikers got out alive—"not because they were rescued by the army, but because the villagers themselves didn't let the inciters hurt them, and it was they who called the ambulances. . . . I sincerely believe . . . they didn't want to kill them."

The incident demonstrated several things. It underscored the inequitable relations between Palestinian villagers and Jewish settlers. Although no settlers were killed by Arabs, the village of Beita was subjected to the harshest punitive measures for an incident that resulted from poor judgment by settlers leading a group of teenagers so close to an Arab village in a region where there was great tension. The leaders of the children from Elon Moreh used them to make a point: that Jews were free to move at will in the West Bank, any time, tension or no tension. The incident at Beita, observed Joel Greenberg, "seems to be a microcosm of the psychological workings of the Palestinian-Israeli conflict. The hikers and villagers played out roles dictated by the nightmares and prejudices that have locked Jews and Arabs into a seemingly endless struggle."[43]

PUNITIVE ECONOMIC MEASURES

By the middle of 1988 it had become clear to Israeli policymakers that the Intifada could not be suppressed by military force alone. Still, they believed that continued use of forceful measures was necessary to keep things from getting totally out of hand, to demonstrate Israel's capacity to remain in the territories, and to maintain control. If the uprising could not be broken by force, then other measures were necessary—tightening the economic screws and undermining communal institutions. True, Israel suffered because of Palestinian strikes against Jewish employers and boycotts of Israeli products, but the Arab economy was much more vulnerable, especially since it was an adjunct of the much larger Israeli economic system (see Chapter 3).

By mid-1988 Palestinian unemployment had increased and a major economic recession was threatening the West Bank and Gaza. Many policymakers believed that what the IDF had failed to do, deteriorating economic conditions would accomplish. Customs regulations were tightened at the Jordan river crossings between the Hashemite Kingdom and the West Bank. More extensive use was made of government authority to issue permits and licenses for trade and commerce, and tax collection was tightened by closing loopholes and clamping down on tax evasion. In March, as winter approached, fuel supplies to the West Bank were halted, telephone links to the territories were frequently cut, and troops increasingly forced open shops during strike hours or welded them shut when merchants disobeyed orders to open. Periodically the army prevented Arab workers in the territories from crossing the Green Line to their jobs in Israel. Although many workers either refused to continue employment for Israelis or worked erratically, most needed the pay to sustain their families.

Major attempts were made to undermine the economy by exerting pressures against Palestinian farmers. In October 1988 the marketing and export to Jordan of olive oil, a mainstay of the West Bank economy, was blocked. In "noncooperative" villages, the harvesting and processing of olives were prevented. General Mitzna openly warned that recalcitrant villagers would suffer economic sanctions. In many instances, the army ordered olive presses to shut down, uprooted olive and other fruit trees, and destroyed food supplies and farm equipment as punitive measures for rioting, refusal to surrender suspects, or nonpayment of taxes. Imposition of curfews or sieges on agricultural towns or villages often prevented farmers from reaching their fields or orchards to spray, irrigate, or harvest, resulting in crop losses. In June Defense Minister Rabin threatened to demonstrate that civil disobedience and the boycott of Israeli military government institutions were "an unattainable dream," given the IDF's capacity to undermine the Palestinian economy. "We try to limit [punitive] administrative and economic measures to definable centers of civil disobedience, but it is not always possible to localize the effect of such measures."[44]

Limiting the circulation of funds in the territories was still another measure taken to exert economic pressure. As early as February 1988, restrictions were placed on the amount of cash that travelers from Jordan could bring into the country. By mid-March the amount was limited to 400 Jordan dinars (at that time equivalent to between US$650 and $700). Official money changers were prevented from crossing to Jordan, where they obtained the dinars used as common currency in the West Bank. These restrictions greatly circumscribed daily business and commercial operations. Transactions with the Jordanian banks in which many Palestinians kept their funds were undercut, and the remittances that many received from abroad for sustenance were greatly diminished. Israeli authorities explained that these new, more severe restrictions were necessary to cut the flow of PLO funds into the territories. Indeed, PLO funds were significant in supporting many institutions and individuals, including stipends for hundreds of students attending universities in the West Bank and Gaza.

By 1988 the refusal to pay Israeli taxes, especially the Value Added Tax (VAT), had begun to have a telling effect on the military government, and measures were initiated to break this form of resistance. In June any Palestinian in the territories applying for a driver's license, a permit to travel abroad, a construction permit, or an import-export permit had to present certification from several Israeli offices showing that all due taxes were paid. Often receipts were demanded to prove payment of income tax, municipal taxes, customs duties, and auto registration fees, each from a different office, each requiring a visit of several hours or days. Teams of tax collectors accompanied by soldiers raided shops and homes of merchants for an accounting. Roadblocks manned by the IDF stopped Arab vehicles, impounding those whose drivers did not have the required tax receipts. Army raids swept into villages, especially those known for recalcitrance, to check on and enforce tax payments. In some villages, homes built without the required building permits were razed.

Lest any Arab inhabitant escape the bureaucratic dragnet, valid credentials were sometimes canceled and new ones required. Thus in December 1988 and January 1989, all West Bank drivers had to replace their license plates with new ones. To obtain the new plates, each owner had to present the necessary lists of taxes and fees paid. Each receipt required hours of waiting. In Gaza, the same procedure was imposed on the whole population, thus requiring every Palestinian there to obtain a new identity card. Without the necessary receipts a new ID was unobtainable, and without the ID it was all but impossible to move out of or within the district.[45]

The major objectives of this bureaucratic war were to undermine economic life and morale, and to demonstrate that the IDF remained in control and that the local population was dependent on the Israeli administration in every aspect of its daily life. By January 1989 the IDF high command believed that it had won a victory, that the leadership of the Intifada had failed to create institutions alternative to those of the Civil Administration, and that the Palestinian population had demonstrated by waiting hours in long queues that it recognized Israel's authority. The army pointed out that although many Palestinians had resigned in protest from offices of the Civil Administration, they were replaced by other Arabs; many of the protesters were now appealing to be rehired.[46]

A notable example of civil resistance in the bureaucratic war was the village of Beit Sahur near Bethlehem, considered a "tough nut" by the IDF. In July, its 9,000 residents, nearly all Christian, were placed under curfew because they had returned their Israel-issued identity cards as a protest against a government tax raid. The raid was a response to the villagers' rejection of notices to pay the VAT and Israeli income taxes. After serving residents with notices to pay, the government placed a lien on the automobiles of those with outstanding debts. Some 300 villagers, encouraged by the local "people's committee," responded by returning their ID cards to the municipality. Within hours, leaders of the local committee were arrested and placed under six-month administrative detention.

After the IDF closed off the village and imposed curfews lasting several weeks, local committee leaders, following the pattern of nonviolent resistance already initiated by the Intifada, began to organize a variety of passive resistance efforts. These included cultivating home-grown vegetable gardens to replace Israeli products and organizing an informal "civil" guard to replace the policemen who resigned in protest against Israeli authority.

Lessons in planting "victory gardens" were given by a Bethlehem University biology professor, Dr. Jad Issac, who opened a small garden shop to provide materials and tools. As a result, Dr. Issac was subjected to IDF harassment and later was placed in administrative detention. Before his arrest, his telephone service was cut off, he was daily summoned to the local military governor's office for interrogation, soldiers were stationed near his home to question visitors, and at night the military shined bright lights into his home to awaken him. The IDF accused Dr. Issac of inciting the population in a violent demonstration following the return of ID cards. He and other villagers countered that he had urged the demonstrators to go home and that some had attacked him when he tried to calm the crowd. Later, the army broke up the same demonstration with tear gas and clubs.[47]

The IDF Civil Administration claimed that the authorities had broken civil resistance in Beit Sahur and that the inhabitants later took back their ID cards. Nevertheless, the town was placed under curfew for several weeks "to restore calm."[48]

BREAKING COMMUNAL STRUCTURES

Long before the Intifada began, IDF pacification measures in the West Bank and Gaza included forays against Palestinian communal structures and organizations such as schools and universities; professional organizations of lawyers and engineers; trade unions; and charitable, medical, and research groups. After December 1987 these attacks were intensified, for the army high command perceived them as centers of civil resistance and breeding grounds for the Intifada's new leadership that were competitive with government institutions. It was feared that those affiliated with such organizations were among leaders of the uprising and would provide cadres for a future Palestinian entity. Therefore, policymakers for the territories believed it prudent to undermine or weaken these communal organizations before they acquired the strength to challenge Israel's supremacy. The rationale provided by security authorities for the campaign was that such organizations either harbored or were the breeding grounds for "terrorism"—that they were "centers of unrest" and of "violent protest."

Schools and universities and eventually the whole educational system were among the first to be hit. They were obvious targets because they provided "foot-soldiers" of the Intifada, youths who staged the mass demonstrations and threw stones at Israeli soldiers and settlers. Palestinian schools had long been "infused with a political intensity alien to the American academy." Israeli authorities perceived Palestinian universities "not so much [as] universities as 'institutions of political activity,' part of the infrastructure of the Palestine Liberation Organization." Some IDF officers charged that the educational system was the backbone of the "anti-Israel campaign orchestrated by PLO terrorists." Even before the Intifada, some Israelis called for closure of Palestinian universities. In 1986 Tehiya Knesset member Yuval Ne'eman, a former president of Tel Aviv University, demanded that the government close all higher education institutions in the occupied territories.[49]

While permitting universities to function, military government authorities had for years imposed on them a regime of severe restrictions and frequently raided campuses. During upsurges of civil resistance before December 1987, schools and universities had been closed by the military for lengthy periods. After December these measures were intensified; hundreds of students were arrested, many were held in administrative detention, and several were deported. As the Intifada progressed, closures increased in frequency and lasted for several months. Although schools were reopened for the 1988–1989 academic year, universities remained closed for most of 1988 and later were ordered not to reopen until further notice.

School and university closings seemed to have little effect on the level of student participation in anti-Israel demonstrations. If anything, thousands of youths were freed from daily discipline and orderly schedules; their boredom increased and many more participated in the very activities that school closures were intended to prevent. The closings exacerbated economic pressures because many school employees and teachers lost their pay for most of 1988. The interruption of education also stymied the entrance of thousands of students into the economy. The research of more than 17,000 university students and 2,500 faculty and researchers was halted. Libraries and laboratories were off-limits, and many experiments had to be abandoned precipitously.

Local committees attempted to organize alternative classes for school children, and to acquire professors for their students, at off-campus locations in homes or community centers. The Israeli authorities declared those classes illegal and periodically raided them, arresting both students and teachers. In October 1988 the military informed schools that distribution of workbooks to school children would not be tolerated.[50]

The informally organized *shabiba* (youth) movement in the territories, an obvious target for the military, was outlawed in March 1988, accused of being a front for Fatah. It consisted of a loose network throughout the West Bank, Gaza, and East Jerusalem whose members, while not formally affiliated, were certainly sympathetic to Arafat and the PLO. While shabiba activities did include communal self-help projects and aid to the elderly, there is little doubt that the organization provided middle and lower cadres of the Intifada who relayed messages from the leadership, distributed leaflets, organized demonstrations, and the like. At the next level were "popular committees" organized on an extensive scale. The members constituted a cross-section of the Palestinian community and represented a principal bulwark of the uprising (see Chapter 3). These committees, too, were banned along with the other communal organizations listed above.

Among the prominent charitable organizations banned was In'ash al-Usra of al-Bireh, a women's group established in 1965 that offered a wide range of services and vocational training. These included sewing, knitting, and embroidery workshops; a bakery and food-processing projects; financial aid and scholarships for children whose parents were killed or imprisoned; and medical assistance for the needy. The director of In'ash al-Usra, Samiha Khalil, called Umm Khalil, was an outspoken nationalist and leader of opposition to the occupation; as such, she aroused the ire of the military. In retaliation for her activism, the army raided the offices of the organization in June 1988 during a curfew of al-Bireh. The searchers claimed to have found letters, videotapes, and other materials that were anti-Israel and supported the uprising; as a result, the organization was closed and its director apprehended.[51]

Faisal Husseini's Arab Studies Society in East Jerusalem, the largest research organization and resource center in the territories, was also closed for a year in July 1988 for "security" reasons. It was labeled an Arafat-financed front, Fatah's "tool to promote its aims and attain the objective of the uprising."[52]

Throughout 1988, when conventional tactics and strategies tried during the two previous decades of occupation failed to suppress the uprising, the army experimented with refined techniques; these included aerial photos that divided each Palestinian community into sections. Every structure in each section was numbered on the photo-map and assigned to an IDF patrol. Observation posts were scattered throughout troublesome areas, and patrols were linked with them through radio contact. The observation posts were equipped with powerful binoculars and night-vision devices, some with television cameras, to spot trouble and call in a patrol for the exact location of the disturbance. New anti-riot devices were installed on army vehicles to deal with rioters. A stone-hurling machine was invented to counterattack youthful rock throwers; another type of vehicle was equipped to fire canisters of hard-rubber balls and small explosive propellants into crowds.[53]

However, neither conventional tactics nor new technology changed the overall situation. Mass demonstrations continued, sometimes at longer intervals but still with the potential to flare up unexpectedly, leading to still another serious altercation with the army. Passive and civil resistance persisted; at times it, too, would diminish as Palestinians reluctantly paid their taxes or returned to work for the Israelis; but then some new manifestation of nonviolent hostility would appear. Despite the rise and fall of morale, determination to end the occupation and the struggle for self-determination persisted. Morale was given a significant boost in November 1988, when the Palestine National Council in Tunis proclaimed the independent state of Palestine (see Chapters 3 and 5). IDF attempts to subvert any celebrations of the anticipated declaration had begun on November 11, four days earlier, when a curfew was imposed on Gaza's 650,000 inhabitants and the West Bank was sealed off. Phone lines in the territories as well as the electricity supplies in several cities were cut off, lest the population listen to broadcasts of the National Council proceedings. Although the Israel government announced that the declaration was "irrelevant and unimportant," apprehension about its impact in the territories seemed great among Israeli officials.

By the end of the first year of Intifada, the number of Palestinians killed, wounded, arrested, imprisoned, deported, and whose homes were blown up exceeded by several times the number in any previous uprising or in any other year since 1967. There had not been an uprising on such a large scale since the Arab revolt of 1936–1939 against the British mandate. Figures varied between those of the Palestine human rights organizations and those of the army, but, on average, a Palestinian a day had been killed, some 20,000 wounded, and 20,000 imprisoned in 1988. More than 150 Palestinian homes were blown up, and more than 50 were sealed by the army. Forty-five suspected Intifada leaders were deported. Three times the number of soldiers were used to suppress the uprising as had been used to conquer the territories in 1967. The cost in 1988 of occupation and of the suppression of Intifada was estimated to be $2–3 billion; this figure included additional military expenditures and the impact on Israel's economy (see Chapter 4).[54]

After a long period of ambivalence, the high command openly acknowledged that "there is no military solution to what we are facing. . . . It is mainly a political problem." It also acknowledged that the uprising had broad popular support. Some senior officers recognized that the Intifada "might continue indefinitely," requiring the "necessary

Gaza during the Palestinian uprising in the Israeli-occupied West Bank and Gaza Strip.
UNRWA photo by George Nehmeh.

adjustments." The army admitted that "there is no return to the pre-December-1987 status-quo."[55]

Many officers now agreed with Yehoshua Porat, Israel's leading scholar on the Palestinians, that "this is the first time that there has been a popular action, covering all social strata and groups. . . . The whole population is rebelling, and this is creating a common national experience." City, town, and village were participating in the uprising in an exceptional demonstration of national cohesion. Porat contrasted the current Intifada with the 1936–1939 rebellion, which, according to him, was not a popular uprising. In the 1948 war, only a small proportion of Palestinians had participated, primarily those near Jewish centers or close to the front lines. According to Porat's evaluation, the Intifada accomplished more in its first few months than decades of PLO terrorism had achieved outside the country. It greatly increased the political weight of the territories as compared to the PLO.[56]

Some army officers were now also beginning to agree with professor Shlomo Avineri of the Labor party that the "West Bank and Gaza under Israeli rule are a threat against which the whole might of Israeli army may not suffice. . . . An army can beat an army, but an army cannot beat a people. . . . Israel is learning that power has limits. Iron can smash iron, it cannot smash an unarmed fist." By January even President Haim Herzog, apprehensive about the violence in Jerusalem, had warned Christian leaders that the city could become another Belfast or Beirut.[57]

Many Israelis worried that the methods considered necessary by the army commanders were corrupting the IDF and Israel itself. The *Jerusalem Post* expressed concern about the growing frequency with which soldiers lost control. When troops had occupied a school in Nablus during May, not only did they vandalize the building but, when they left, they failed to erase the "DEATH TO THE ARABS!" graffiti on the walls. Although graffiti, unlike the Palestinian fire bombs, does not kill or maim, "it is hard to believe that the host of recently reported exceptions to Israeli norms of military conduct will not have a long-term impact." The paramount issue, however, was not the methods employed to suppress the uprising but what goals were being pursued. Without more clarity about future goals, "suppression of the *Intifada*, even if successful, will most likely sow the seeds of another, more violent uprising that could destroy any hope of Jewish-Arab accommodation. That is the writing, oddly invisible to some Israeli eyes, on the wall."[58]

After several months of confrontation between the military and the residents of the territories, when the high command became convinced that the uprising was not an aimless eruption of violence for its own sake, attempts were made to initiate a dialogue with the local Palestinian leadership. Both sides were faced with a serious dilemma. The army's policy had been to eliminate or remove those it considered Palestinian nationalist leaders; yet in June 1988 Defense Minister Rabin began to talk about dialogue with those who, until now, he had been intent on removing from the scene. For the Palestinian leaders the question was, Would dialogue be a trap, leading—after initial talks—to their incarceration or deportation? The army's approach toward leaders had been ambivalent, and it continued to be so. There was little consistency in treatment of those who were Palestinian spokesmen or recognized leaders, such as Faisal Husseini, Hanna Siniora, Sari Nusseibeh, and others. Some were arrested and released, some were deported, and some were never imprisoned.

The first of Rabin's dialogues began in June 1988 as "an exchange of views about the current situation" with several Palestinians in the territories, including a physician, a former Nablus city councillor, a journalist, and a Baptist bishop. These parleys were continued periodically but began to acquire more significance following the Palestine declaration of independence in November. As the impossibility of weaning any credible or significant number away from the PLO became clear, and as the organization rapidly acquired support of an international consensus, even the IDF began to modify its appraisals of effective tactics for dealing with the PLO (see Chapter 4). In March 1989 an Israeli intelligence report was leaked, stating that the uprising could not be ended in the near future—that a political solution could be found only if the government entered dialogue with the PLO. The report also maintained that "there was no serious leadership in the occupied territories outside of the PLO and that the PLO had truly moved toward moderation."[59]

After a year and a half, what had the Intifada accomplished? Although the IDF had inflicted severe damage on the inhabitants and economy of the West Bank and Gaza, it failed either to end the uprising or to eliminate the grassroots Palestinian leadership. The political and social transformation of Palestinian society that began in recent decades was greatly accelerated with the emergence of a new leadership and the decline of the "traditionals." Palestinian society was more unified than it had been before. And this was a unity that cut across class and religious lines, shaping a common outlook among the diverse geographic regions and political factions in the West Bank and Gaza (see Chapter 3). Palestinian nationalist sentiment burned more intensely than before December 1987, and a clear-cut political program was formulated within the territories, forcing PLO leadership abroad and the surrounding Arab rulers to clarify their goals in the Arab-Israel dispute (see Chapters 3 and 5). Israeli government and society no longer took the occupation for granted as Israelis were now forced to seriously consider alternatives to the status quo. The Palestine question emerged in the 1987 election and in Israeli politics as an issue of primary significance. Israelis were now polarized over the Intifada and the strategies for dealing with it. Even hardliners like Prime Minister Shamir and Defense Minister Rabin were forced to make proposals for political change favoring the Palestinians. There was serious introspection in Israeli society about national values, about the role of the army, and about reaction of youths to the tasks imposed on them in 1988–1989. Much of this inner turmoil was reflected in the world of writers and artists (see Chapter 4). At the international level, the Palestine question again became critical, focusing attention on proposals for solutions, the "rights of the Palestinians," and Israeli-Arab relations. Americans, too, were forced to confront the Palestine issue again, and it became a major priority in U.S. foreign policy. The U.S. government was forced to reevaluate its relationship with the PLO, and American Jews were torn between their loyalty to Israel and what they were learning about the Palestinians (see Chapter 5).

NOTES

1. *Jerusalem Post International Edition* (hereafter JPI), Yehuda Litani, no. 1,415, 12/19/87.

2. *Ibid.*

3. JPI, no. 1,416, 12/26/87; no. 1,415, 12/19/87.

4. *Ibid.*

5. *Ibid.*

6. JPI, no. 1,416, 12/26/87.

7. *Ibid.*

8. *Ibid.*

9. *Ibid.*

10. JPI, no. 1,419, 1/16/88; no. 1,421, 1/30/88.

11. JPI, no. 1,416, 12/26/87.

12. JPI, no. 1,417, 1/2/88; no. 1,418, 1/9/88; no. 1,419, 1/16/88.

13. JPI, no. 1,418, 1/9/88.

14. *Journal of Palestine Studies* (hereafter JPS), no. 67, Spring 1988, pp. 178–180.

15. JPS, pp. 169–172.

16. JPI, no. 1,421, 1/30/88.

17. *Ibid.*

18. JPI, no. 1,424, 2/20/88.

19. JPI, no. 1,422, 2/6/88.

20. *Ibid.*

21. *New York Times* (hereafter NYT), International Edition, 12/30/87.

22. JPI, no. 1,426, 3/5/88.

23. Mubarak Awad, "Non-Violent Resistance: A Strategy for the Occupied Territories," JPS, no. 52, Summer 1984, pp. 22–36.

24. JPI, no. 1,413, 12/3/87; no. 1,419, 1/16/88; no. 1,442, 6/25/88.

25. JPI, no. 1,422, 6/25/88.

26. *Jerusalem Post* (hereafter JP), 6/15/88.

27. JPI, no. 1,418, 1/9/88; no. 1,419, 1/16/88; Meron Benvenisti, *The West Bank Handbook: A Political Lexicon* (Jerusalem: Jerusalem Post, 1986), pp. 86–87.

28. JP, 12/28/87.

29. *Los Angeles Times*, 8/26/88.

30. *Punishing a Nation: Human Rights Violations During the Palestinian Uprising, December 1987–December 1988*, mimeograph edition (West Bank: al-Haq Law in the Service of Man, 1988), pp. 143–145.

31. JPI, no. 1,433, 4/23/88; no. 1,434, 4/30/88; NYT, 4/23/88.

32. JPI, no. 1,434, 4/30/88.

33. JPI, no. 1,445, 7/16/88.

34. *Punishing a Nation*, pp. 34–40.

35. *Ibid.*, p. 148; Benvenisti, *The West Bank Handbook*, pp. 58–60.

36. *Punishing a Nation*, pp. 147, 151, 242.

37. *Ibid.*, p. 151.

38. JPI, no. 1,430, 4/3/88; no. 1,453, 9/10/88.

39. JPI, no. 1,430, 4/3/88.

40. JPI, no. 1,431, 4/9/88; Joel Greenberg, "'Lynch Village' Shows No Remorse," *Punishing a Nation*, pp. 194–196.

41. JPI, no. 1,431, 4/9/88.

42. JPI, no. 1,455, 9/24/88 (Abraham Rabinovitch, "Settlers Leaving to Live in 'Indian Country'").

43. JPI, no. 1,432, 4/16/88; no. 1,434, 5/7/89; no. 1,433, 4/23/88 (Joel Greenberg, "The Killings at Beita—A Tragedy of Errors").

44. *Punishing a Nation*, p. 284.

45. JPI, no. 1,441, 6/18/88; no. 1,470, 1/7/89 (Joel Greenberg, "Bureaucrats Vs. the Intifada").

46. JPI, no. 1,470, 1/7/89.

47. JPI, no. 1,446, 7/23/88.

48. *Ibid.* (Joel Greenberg, "Intifada Without Stones and Bombs: The Quiet Front of the Uprising").

49. Anthony Thrall Sullivan, *Palestinian Universities Under Occupation* (Cairo: American University in Cairo Press, 1988), pp. 17, 2–3, passim.; Lynne R. Franks, *Israel and the Occupied Territories*, World Education Series (Washington, D.C.: American Association of Collegiate Registrars and Admissions Officers, 1987), passim.

50. *Punishing a Nation*, Chapter 8.

51. *Ibid.*

52. *Ibid.*

53. NYT, 3/30/89 (Bernard E. Trainor, "Israel Vs. Palestinians: Tactics Are Refined").

54. NYT, 2/2/89 (Anthony Lewis, "Israel Against Itself"); *Punishing a Nation*, p. 11.

55. NYT, 10/12/88 (Joel Brinkley, "Some Israelis Sense a Futility in Steps to Quell Arab Revolt"); 7/14/88 (Joel Brinkley, "For Israel, Uprising Is the Status Quo").

56. JPI, no. 1,427, 3/12/88.

57. JPI, no. 1,424, 2/20/88 (Shlomo Avineri, "The Limits of Power"); no. 1,470, 1/7/89 (Herzog).

58. JP, 5/25/88.

59. JPI, no. 1,440, 6/11/88; NYT, 3/21/89.

3

THE IMPACT OF THE UPRISING ON POLITICAL AND SOCIAL LIFE IN THE OCCUPIED TERRITORIES

From the early days of the Intifada, stones and those who threw them, "children of the stones," came to symbolize the spontaneity, pervasiveness, and wide popularity of the uprising. Yet, as we have seen, the Intifada was much more than an epidemic of sporadic, violent incidents against Israel's occupation of the West Bank and Gaza. Within days it developed into an organized movement; within weeks a coherent set of objectives was articulated; and within a few months the social and political impact on Palestinian society was evident.

The stone throwers, the foot soldiers, as it were, of the uprising, were described by Palestinian journalist Daoud Kuttab as children who had learned the language of resistance early in life. They were raised in an environment with all the symbolism and slogans of Palestinian nationalism permeating their daily lives from infancy, Kuttab writes. They "often learn the names of PLO leaders before they learn to read and write. They can explain the difference between Zionism and Judaism and are able to make a strong argument against any political solution involving Jordan's King Hussein." Those in refugee camps "drink their mothers' milk while their camp is under curfew; they wake up in the middle of the night to the sound of rubber bullets and rumors of a possible settler attack.[1]

Stone throwing was an old tradition among school boys, according to Kuttab.

To throw a stone is to be 'one of the guys'; to hit an Israeli car is to become a hero; and to be arrested and not confess to having done anything is to be a man.

Stone throwing is normally carried out as part of a large demonstration. Demonstrations may arise in response to a particular Israeli action: arrests, provocations, closing the entrance to a camp, injuring camp residents, and the like. They may also coincide with certain national days. Only on rare occasions is stone throwing an isolated incident. In some cases the stone throwing is carried out by small, well-trained teams. More often it is undertaken by a large group of people, including adults, both men and women, who are participating to protest actions taken by settlers against camp residents, for example.[2]

Children's participation in the uprising involved much more than stone throwing or provoking Israeli soldiers. Nationalist or popular committees affiliated with PLO or Islamic fundamentalist factions organized youth in a variety of educational and volunteer programs, from street or building construction in refugee camps to lessons in Palestinian history. Most social activities from weddings to sports encounters have taken on the coloration of the Intifada. Attempts to break up concentrated organization of anti-Israel manifestations by closing the schools only backfired, for youths became even more restive and less controlled by their elders when they wandered the streets and formed "patriotic" gangs between the frequent Israeli-imposed curfews.

Whereas parents used to be protective of school-age youths and apprehensive about their participation in political demonstrations and activity, many now support and even encourage their children to become involved. To be the parent of a young man or woman who has become a martyr in the struggle against the occupation, though tragic, is a source of pride, a badge of communal honor. Such parents, rather than traditional leaders, are often chosen to be members of the local committees that organize the Intifada at the grassroots level.

Kuttab observed that there was a consistent pattern in organizing youthful participation in demonstrations "from Gaza to Nablus." The youngest group was between ages 7 and 10, entrusted with the task of rolling tires into roads, pouring gasoline on them, and setting them afire. Those under 10 are usually not arrested if caught but, rather, are beaten and let go. The 11 to 14 year olds place large rocks in the roads to block traffic. Many in this group have become skilled at making and using homemade slingshots to fire stones at the occupiers. The 15 to 19 year olds are "the veteran stone throwers" who inflict the most damage on passing cars. Often masked with kufiyyahs (traditional headcloths), they are the most pursued by the IDF. But their familiarity with the alleyways and warrens of Arab towns and villages makes them difficult to catch. They are often given responsibility for obtaining food during curfews, and they assist in its distribution. Those over nineteen have key positions, leading the entire team.

Youth preparing for "battle" with Israeli troops in Jalazone Camp, West Bank (population 5,100). UNRWA photo by George Nehmeh.

They are in contact with observers on the hillsides and on high houses and they help determine which cars are to be attacked and which are to be let go. They stand at an elevated point and direct the stone throwers as to when and how far to retreat when the soldiers advance. They decide on the moment of a countercharge, which is carried out with loud screams and a shower of stones. The leaders know the range of the Israeli weapons and are able to differentiate between rubber bullets and real bullets. When rubber bullets are used, the leaders scream, "Don't worry. They are shooting *al fadi,*" which means roughly, "empty" or "blank." When the soldiers shoot real bullets, the leaders shout that the soldiers are firing *al malan,* meaning "full" or "the real thing." Even with real bullets, the leaders learn through experience the range of the various weapons being used. Leaders also seem to have the ability to determine whether soldiers plan to shoot in the air or at the demonstrators.[3]

The use of children to provoke the IDF was described by a Gaza leader in an interview with Israeli journalist Makram Khuri Makhul:

The order was that the youngsters should go in the front, facing the fire, and they don't hesitate to do so. They block the army's central route. It is the first time in history that this has happened. I go through the whole Strip and instruct them in the camps. It's not just school children. By now it includes everyone, aged from nought to a hundred. Here is a 55-year-old woman who took part in the events and was hit with a stick by the soldiers. The women are not afraid. Ninety percent of the people in Gaza belong to political groups. They don't need instructions from anybody. In any case, people who live under occupation and oppression do not need someone to incite them.

Once, in order to start a demonstration, we would send the children to organize a disturbance. Now, everyone is out in the streets at 3 in the morning. Not ten or twenty people, but hundreds. We don't have a timetable, but we already have a custom, waves of people going out, at 3 AM, in the morning, at midday, early evening. From the evening until 3 AM, we sleep and organize. Sometimes, if the situation demands it, we even go out at 10 PM, because during the night, the army doesn't effectively control the streets and doesn't know the local topography, so we are in control. For instance, yesterday in Jabalya refugee camp, there were demonstrations all night and there was not a single soldier, even though there was a curfew. The soldiers simply fled, because thousands of people formed a sort of human wall, and nothing will work against something like that, neither an iron fist nor bullets.[4]

Demonstrations and youth participation since December 1987, compared to those of the previous twenty years, have been marked by qualitative change—a change soon recognized by the IDF. Before 1987 the army was confident that it could easily suppress protests with the "iron fist" and scare tactics. Since the Intifada, however, "some top IDF officers admire the bravery shown by the Palestinian youth in the territories. These youngsters have demonstrated unusual courage. Their actions aren't terrorism—but rather the actions of a national movement," according to Brigadier General (Reserves) Giora Forman.[5]

LEADERSHIP OF THE INTIFADA

By early January 1988 it had become clear that an organized leadership had taken control of the uprising and was attempting to coordinate the series of spontaneous demonstrations and protests that erupted in December. The infrastructure for an organization to lead the resistance already existed in the scores of committees and self-help groups that had been established by Palestinians since the beginning of the occupation. They were organized both horizontally and vertically, along geographic lines at the village, town, and district levels and on a functional basis in groups of women, physicians, medical technicians, lawyers, students, teachers, and other professional or trade-union organizations. These groups also represented political and religious interests; some were affiliated with PLO factions such as Fatah, PFLP, and DFLP, whereas others were affiliated with the Palestine Communist party or the Islamic fundamentalists.

In contrast to the traditional leadership of the West Bank and Gaza, which had close links with Jordan and at times could accommodate its positions with those of Israel, the members of these groups were younger and much less identified with the notable families of Palestinian society. Many individuals in these groups represented Palestinians of the refugee camps and of the urban working class. However, as was traditional in Palestinian society, the rural sector was underrepresented.

The political orientation of these groups became much less rejectionist after 1974, when the Palestine National Council (PNC) at its twelfth session decided to include "political, popular, and democratic struggle" as well as armed struggle in its program to liberate Palestine. The PNC also took the first steps toward a two-state solution (a Palestinian state coexisting with Israel) by abandoning the goal of "democratic secular state" in all of Palestine. In 1976, after pro-PLO candidates had won municipal elections in most towns of the occupied West Bank, the PLO urged its supporters to establish grassroots organizations in the territories, following the example of the Palestine Communist party. One of the first PLO-affiliated groups was the Social Youth Movement (Shebab) formed in 1982. At first concerned with social, cultural, and sports activities, the Shebab soon became involved in communal and political action. During the 1970s and 1980s, dozens of other groups (such as

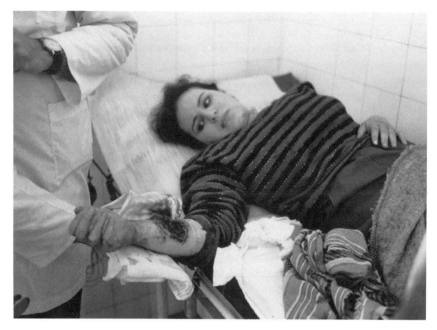

Palestinian woman shot in the arm during the disturbances in the Gaza Strip in January 1988. UNRWA photo by George Nehmeh.

those mentioned above) were organized to galvanize Palestinian society in an effort to maintain *sumud* (steadfastness) under occupation.[6]

The Palestine Relief Committees formed early in the 1980s by a group of physicians who volunteered to establish clinics in West Bank villages were representative of the origin and modus operandi of these groups. By 1983 "every section of the West Bank and Gaza was covered by one of eight such organizations," which formed the Union of Palestine Relief Committees. They provided the model for other committees, including agriculture, engineers, and women's groups, which also worked in villages and deprived urban neighborhoods.[7]

With the outbreak of the Intifada and the imposition of Israeli curfews, the committees served as models for coping with the hardships caused by the new situation. Food supplies had to be organized for besieged refugee camps and villages; a much more extensive medical emergency network was required for the mounting casualties; care was needed for families bereft of wage earners; and child care was necessary for younger children locked out of schools. Committees to deal with these needs were organized in camps, villages, and sectors of larger cities to meet the demands of the new emergencies. As the committees grew, their activities and objectives expanded. "Local neighborhood committees became responsible for alternative education, health needs, guard duties, and agriculture. They have become the backbone of the uprising, comprising as many as a hundred small committees in each of the major cities and up to ten in every refugee camp and village. The process of leadership developed from the base up."[8]

According to Daoud Kuttab, the Unified National Leadership of the Uprising (UNLU) emerged from these groups; it became responsible for making the major national decisions and for producing and distributing the periodic leaflets (bayanat) that direct the uprising. During the first few weeks, the uprising was led by individuals inside the territories without direction from or consultation with PLO chiefs abroad. The leadership in Tunis was taken by surprise at the events, and it was a while before they became orientated to the new situation. After a few weeks, lines of communication were set up between directors of the Intifada in the territories and PLO headquarters so that the two sets of leaders could coordinate their political statements and strategic planning. Contrary to the expectations of many outsiders, the PLO abroad did not take over management of the Intifada, nor did the leaders within the territories become mere agents subservient to the headquarters in Tunis. Rather, a partnership evolved in which the UNLU assumed a much more prominent role in the decisionmaking processes of the PLO. Since neither the PLO outside Palestine nor the UNLU within could veto the actions, statements, or plans of the other, the Palestinians in the territories were now a political weight at least equal to those in the diaspora and to the PLO leadership. According to many observers, their importance as frontline combatants in the struggle for a Palestinian state gave them far more importance than Palestinians abroad and made their leadership more significant than the combined leadership of diverse factions outside the country. Thus, when Israel attempted to lop off the head of the Intifada by assassinating Abu Jihad in April 1988, it failed to undercut the UNLU. Instead, the assassination, while an immediate blow to the PLO, only intensified the resentment and hostility of the Palestinian community at large and played into the hands of the most militant factions of the PLO and the UNLU.

Given the grassroots origins of the UNLU, it is not surprising that its decisions are the result of a democratic process, made unanimously after consultation with local committees and at times with the PLO abroad. Because the political orientation of the UNLU is so diverse, unanimity is almost a prerequisite to prevent internecine bickering and even violence of the kind that disrupted Palestinian university campuses during the late 1970s. According to some authoritative Palestinians, the UNLU was organized with fifteen rotating members, three each from Fatah, PFLP, DFLP, the Palestine Communist party, and the Islamic

Jihad.[9] The role of Islamic fundamentalists has been uncertain; at times they cooperate with the UNLU, and at times they oppose its positions. Israeli attempts to eliminate the leaders by means of arrests and deportations have been ineffectual; even if those apprehended were among the fifteen members of the UNLU, they were almost immediately replaced by new representatives from local committees of the organizations mentioned above.

In 1988 Israeli authorities hoped to eliminate upward-bound leaders by banning all popular committees, making membership a criminal offense. However, the network of local organizations had become so pervasive, having spread since December 1987 throughout the whole body of Palestinian society, that it was impossible to control. The network spread to sectors that before December were relatively immune to political activism. Many of the 500 Arab villages in the West Bank were isolated and remote from the mainstream of political activity and Palestinian nationalism. Since 1987, however, nearly every hamlet had become involved in the Intifada and had set up its own local committees. Many even issued their own bayanat to supplement those of the central leadership.

The "shock troops" of the uprising, which carry out the orders of the local and central committees, are organized into strike forces of Palestinian youth. In larger centers, such as Nablus, teenage activists are organized into strike forces of ten to fifteen members. Virtually every block in town is covered to see that orders issued in the bayanat are obeyed, that merchants honor strike hours, and that information in the leaflets is distributed throughout the community. Following the resignation of Palestinians from the Israeli-controlled police force, many of their functions were taken over by local strike forces or committees. They mediate disputes, patrol neighborhoods to prevent crime, and crack down on known criminals, drug dealers, and collaborators with the IDF.[10]

COMMUNITY ORGANIZATION

Before the Intifada, Israeli intelligence had established a wide network of Palestinian informers who operated in the West Bank and Gaza. Some collaborated for money, some out of fear, and some because they were blackmailed by means of unsavory information that the intelligence services had collected about them. In exchange for a family reunification permit, a driver's license, or other official favors, some Palestinians were willing to provide the authorities with regular intelligence about nearly all aspects of life in the territories. However, since 1987 the benefits of such collaboration have been greatly diminished. As the balance of power between Israelis and local Palestinian authority changed, the provision of such information came to be considered not a minor sin but treason against the Palestine people. Orders came from the UNLU to deal with collaborators, many of whom were armed by the Israelis. In several instances, such as Kabatiya (see Chapter 2), collaborators were lynched or assassinated. By the middle of 1989, more than forty had been killed—some by mobs, others by enforcers (i.e., members of shock teams designated to eliminate collaboration). Although the PLO abroad and the UNLU in the territories adopted a calculated policy of refraining from the use of arms against Israelis, this did not apply to collaborators.

In May 1989 members of a shock team were killed in an armed battle with the IDF when they inadvertently ran into an Israeli army patrol— a confrontation that was notable because it was the first armed clash in seventeen months between the military and armed Palestinians acting on orders from the UNLU.

Not all collaborators were executed or physically harmed; hundreds repented after being apprehended by local committees and brought to trial. Many confessed, turned in their weapons, and asked for forgiveness from the people over mosque loudspeakers. Some who refused to admit their collaboration had their houses burned. Despite the diminishing returns of collaboration for both Israeli intelligence and the collaborators themselves, the IDF continued to regard as one of its principal tasks the protection of Palestinian informers who were armed by and received financial subsidies from the IDF. In some cases, Arab collaborators from several villages banded together under the protection of Israeli army outposts.

Bayanat

Israeli attempts to eliminate the bayanat were also of no avail. Early in the uprising, bayanat became the chief source of information about daily events among the Palestinians and the main form of communication between the Intifada leadership and inhabitants of the territories. Other bayanat were issued locally, sometimes repeating information from the central leadership, sometimes giving orders or information of primary local interest. Islamic fundamentalist groups issued their own bayanat at times parallel to and at times conflicting with those of the UNLU. Early in 1988 Israeli intelligence published a few bayanat in an effort to confuse residents of the territories. But the populace quickly recognized that these were not authentic; they were detected because of fraudulent content and style. During the first year and a half of the Intifada, both UNLU and the fundamentalists issued some forty bayanat, each giving instructions to followers concerning strike days and when and how to demonstrate; asking for resignation of policemen, tax collectors, and others from Israeli service; encouraging boycott of Israeli goods; and issuing political exhortations and ideological exegeses.[11]

Examination of the first seventeen bayanat from the UNLU by the Center for the Study of Non-Violence in Jerusalem showed that the great majority of 163 actions called were specifically nonviolent in nature. Among twenty-seven methods of resistance to the occupation, twenty-six were nonviolent. During the first six months, general strikes were called thirty-two times, representing about a fifth of all protest activity. The strikes were called to commemorate an important national event and to protest Israeli orders or actions. Seventeen actions demonstrating solidarity accounted for more than 10 percent of resistance activity; these included calls to express support for and appreciation of contributions by individuals or groups, such as visiting families and graves of martyrs, giving financial support to Palestinian institutions, visiting prisoners, and undertaking agricultural or land reclamation labor. Some two dozen other nonviolent actions of the type described in Chapter 2 were enumerated in the Center's study.[12]

The bayanat issued by the UNLU were initially written by the leaders and printed on an underground press, but the source was soon discovered by the Israelis. The bulletins are still composed centrally, but their content is transmitted by telephone, facsimile machine, or radio to numerous points throughout the territories, printed or typed in many different places, and distributed by local committees or shock teams. Many reach neighboring countries and are broadcast from places such as Damascus or Baghdad. The clandestine al-Quds (Jerusalem) Palestine Arab Radio comes from Syria and the Voice of the PLO from Baghdad. Contact is maintained with PLO headquarters in Tunis through Cyprus by means of fax machines. Often the PLO suggests political themes and recommends changes in the bayanat but usually leaves strike days and other such actions to the local people's committees. The bayanat are written in a highly rhetorical style, using exhortations in the name of past Palestinian heroes or martyrs of the present. They deprecate Israel, Zionism, the United States, Western imperialism, fascism, and the occupation; but unlike the rhetoric of the past, the bayanat of the UNLU do not attack individuals as Jews or the Jewish people as the enemy.[13]

Since the second leaflet was issued in January 1988, the bayanat of the UNLU contained the name of the PLO as a co-equal in leadership. Periodically, the leaflets addressed those participating in the uprising as "grandchildren of al-Qassam" or "you new Qassamites," referring to Sheikh Izz al-Din al-Qassam, an Islamic religious figure who was killed by the British in a skirmish during 1935. The political themes emphasized are rejection of American and Israeli government peace proposals, "reactionary initiatives," and attacks on pro-Jordanian elements within the territories. The bayanat call for an international peace conference at which the Palestinians will be fully represented as an independent participant. The ultimate political objective discussed is establishment of a Palestine state, and the political themes generally follow the line set by PLO Chairman Arafat.

The bayanat issued by the fundamentalists, mostly by the Islamic Jihad, are often similar to those of the UNLU, but they have a far more militant political tone. They reject any compromise with Israel or a two-state solution, and they emphasize the religious character of the uprising for which they claim credit. They insist that "Islam is the solution" and often attack Jews as the enemy.

The Arabic Press

The Arabic language press, for the most part centered in Jerusalem, has been a principal pillar of Palestinian nationalist mobilization since the 1970s, a fact recognized by the occupation authorities. Therefore, they have imposed a far more restrictive censorship on the Arabic than on the Israeli Hebrew press, and have continually harassed Palestinian journalists. Although the total circulation of the principal daily and weekly Arabic publications does not exceed 30,000, the per capita distribution (22 daily newspaper copies per 1,000 population) compares favorably with distribution in other Arab countries. According to a study by the West Bank Data Base Project, the Arabic press "is a major area-wide instrument for Palestinian public official discourse."[14]

The language of the Palestinian media reflects "a militant style of mobilization and advocacy. . . . [It is] aggressive, combative, hyperbolic, quick to react to events and to paint black-and-white pictures," similar to the model of Third World journalism in other Arab countries.[15]

Indeed, so influential is the Palestinian press in the eyes of Israel security authorities that since December 1987 they imprisoned thirty Arab journalists, including five members of the nine-person board of the Arab Journalists Association. Censorship was intensified, and several West Bank newspapers were closed. In May 1989 seven Arab journalists were tried by military courts, charged with leading the Intifada under the guise of covering the news. According to a senior security official, the Palestinian journalists have "a network of informants all over the territories, and under the cover of reporting the news they can be in touch with everything. . . . These people are making the events, instead of writing about them."[16] Israeli officials accused the journalists of using their network of correspondents to collect information for PLO leadership abroad, as a transmission network for messages from the Intifada leadership, and to test ideas. All journalists accused of using their profession to further the uprising denied the charges and maintained that the Israeli officials were using them as an excuse for harassment.

SOCIAL CHANGE

The social and political changes in Palestinian society within the territories, hastened by the Intifada, began during the 1970s. One of the first manifestations was the 1976 municipal election, which turned out of office representatives of the traditional elites (see Chapter 1) and replaced them with a new generation of pro-PLO activists, many from the middle class, without ties to or subservient to notable families.

As we have seen, the pace of social change within the Palestinian community was greatly accelerated after December 1987. Intergenerational relations were altered as youths in their teens and early twenties played the vanguard role, providing not only foot soldiers but many leaders of the Intifada. Many of these youths were not from the professional elite but from the lower strata of society, the refugee camps and villages, often regarded with disdain by the urban bourgeoisie.

Villages that for generations had been isolated from the mainstream of politics were galvanized into action and became full-fledged supporters of the uprising, often leading the insurrection. With its limited manpower and facilities, the IDF was unable to occupy every one of the 500 villages simultaneously. Thus, scores were left to their own devices, becoming "little Palestines" or "liberated zones," while the larger cities and towns lay incapacitated by military occupation. These "little Palestines" set up their own local committees, issued their own bayanat, flew the Palestine flag, and plastered walls with slogans of the Intifada—all in spite of the military regime that outlawed such actions. Often their independence had tragic consequences when, to demonstrate that it still controlled the land, the Israel army would swoop down in a surprise attack to reassert its authority. Many casualties of the Intifada resulted from clashes between such villages and occupation forces; but each such attack, and each casualty it produced, only intensified the spirit of resistance and strengthened the growing solidarity between urban and rural sectors.

Traditional regional differences among the various districts, towns, and large cities of Arab Palestine greatly diminished. These differences—between the West Bank and Gaza, and between cities such as Nablus, Hebron, and Jerusalem—became less significant since the occupation began in 1967. The common plight and problems experienced after December 1987 were, however, a much more unifying factor than any suffered during the previous twenty years. Arab Jerusalem, which had

Children play atop the ruins of a demolished house in the West Bank camp of Jalazone.
UNRWA photo by George Nehmeh.

held a relatively privileged position because it was incorporated into
Israel, became a full participant in the uprising. When its residents found
that they could no longer stand aside during periods of repression in
the West Bank and Gaza, they too joined the demonstrations, boycotts,
resignations from government service, and other manifestations of *sumud*.

Jerusalem did contribute a larger percentage of personnel to the
political leadership, including journalists and individuals who were
spokesmen for the Palestine community, such as Hanna Siniora, Sari
Nusseibeh, and Faisal Husseini. Though spokesmen, they were not
necessarily grassroots leaders. But their location in Israel's capital gave
them high visibility, and they were often designated to participate in
parleys with foreign dignitaries such as Secretary of State George Shultz,
who came to Jerusalem for "on-the-spot," "first-hand" investigation of
the Arab-Israel conflict.

Although Muslim-Christian tensions were never as acute among the
Palestinians as in other Middle East societies, Christians—even if militant
nationalists—did not find it easy to overcome the stigma of their religious
background. Since the occupation and, especially, since the Intifada,
many of these interfaith tensions seemed to have dissipated. Christians,
among the prominent leaders of the Palestinian community at large,

have for years headed two of the most militant nationalist factions, the PFLP and DFLP. Many are also prominent in Fatah and the leadership cadres of the PLO. In Jerusalem, where the Christian clergy have usually refrained from political outspokenness since the occupation, most now openly condemn Israeli policies. During the Christmas and Easter seasons of 1987 and 1988, they purposely toned down their traditionally colorful services.

Some Israelis believe that Christian involvement in the Palestinian nationalist cause was the syndrome of a minority bending over backward to accommodate its environment; however, the day-to-day experience of Christian Palestinians was a more likely explanation for their enthusiastic support. The Christian sectors of the Old City of Jerusalem were not spared the humiliation of army and police intrusions into homes, the curfews, or the arrogance of the IDF. The Christian village of Bait Sahur (see Chapter 2) provided one of the most outstanding examples of resistance to the occupation. While in some Israeli and Western Christian circles it is remarked that "however bad the Christians may feel about Israeli rule, they would be far worse off in a Palestinian state which would soon take on the character of an Islamic theocracy. Local Christians tend to reject such a view out of hand," according to *Jerusalem Post* writer Haim Shapiro.

In an interview with the head of Gaza's Greek Orthodox Church, Shapiro was told: "The anguish of the last few months has highlighted that fact that regardless of religious differences, we are all Palestinians. . . . Before the Intifada Moslems may have thought that we weren't as involved in the nationalist effort as they were, but in the last few months we Christians have had more than our share of arrests and beatings."[17] Still, Christians cannot help but be apprehensive about evidence of increasing Muslim fervor since the Intifada began and about the undercurrent of tension between Islamic fundamentalists and secularists in the national movement.

Women have played an increasingly prominent role in Palestinian society during recent decades, a development that was greatly accelerated by the Intifada. With thousands of men in prisons in far larger numbers than ever before, a vacuum was created in many sectors of the community that women began to fill. Not only did they assume leadership roles in political and communal organizations and in the popular committees, but they began to challenge the traditional economic division of labor. The number of women studying medicine, law, journalism, engineering, and other "male" professions has increased, and the number who practice these professions is larger. Women, traditionally required to accept a modest "behind-the-scene" role, have emerged as information officers and organizers while they continue their role as "sustainers" active in a variety of educational, medical, and social work functions. They have organized emergency teams to treat the wounded, child care to deal with pupils during school strikes, and provisions for those unable to shop or whose funds were drained as a result of economic dislocations caused by the uprising. They have also assisted in organizing the strike forces that replaced the police and other government officials who resigned from Israeli service. Women were among the most active in demonstrations, often preparing ammunition for the stone throwers in the Shebab. Many women were also among those killed, injured, and arrested for participating in protests.

Women's activism now reaches into the villages as well as into the more sophisticated urban centers, and their organizations, which are affiliated with each of the principal factions in the UNLU, have begun to mobilize the female half of society in even the most conservative communities. Indicative of this phenomenon is the organization of women by Islamic fundamentalists in emulation of the secular groups.

The emergence of a new feminism is characterized by the relative decline in importance of "charitable" work, which was the province of women from better-off middle-class families who regarded their activities among the poor as noblesse oblige. Their "national" function was to "back up the men." The new feminist movements affiliated with Fatah (Women's Committee for Social Work), DFLP (Association of Women's Work Committees), PFLP (Palestine Federation of Women's Action Committee), and the Palestine Communist party (Association of the Palestine Working Women) perceive themselves to be fully equal participants in the national movement, not mere adjuncts to the male leaders and combatants. Among their services to empower women are literacy training, development of cottage industries, and instruction of women to be economically independent through the acquisition of vocational skills. By exposing village women to such new ways, they hope to change their traditional lifestyles, values, and roles in society.

Many activists are concerned that most women are still not affiliated with any group; as a result, there is no broad women's front and many women are left out of the action. Some activists are also apprehensive about the time in the future when their men return from prison or exile. Will they be prepared to accept women's empowerment; or, as in many similar revolutionary situations, will they expect the female half of the community to return to its traditional places?

ECONOMIC IMPACT

The economic impact of the Intifada on Palestinian society in the West Bank and Gaza has been both negative and positive. Israel has

Woman displaying bruises inflicted by Israeli soldiers when she left home during curfew. She shows the "V" for victory sign of the Intifada, in Beach refugee camp, Gaza. Photo by Deena Hurwitz.

used a variety of economic punitive measures to elicit compliance with its political demands. While these pressures as well as the economic resistance initiated by the Palestinian leadership itself (see Chapter 2) have caused severe dislocations, they have also led to greater emphasis on national self-reliance, willingness to accept austerity, and adjustment to lower standards of living in the cause of Palestinian solidarity.

Merchants, especially those along the tourist routes in the Old City of Jerusalem, were among the first to be affected. The prolonged daily strikes and reluctance of foreign tourists to visit Old Jerusalem nearly brought their businesses to an end. Shopkeepers elsewhere also felt the impact of the strikes. Finally, the UNLU permitted stores to open for a few hours each day, and shoppers concentrated their visits at these authorized times. This procedure prevented the total collapse of the merchant class but caused a major decline in its income.

Between 100,000 and 120,000 Palestinians from the territories have earned their livelihood across the Green Line in Israel. Since 1967 they have made up about half of Gaza's work force and a third of West Bank laborers. Their income became a mainstay of the economy in the territories. With the outbreak of the Intifada and its periodic strike days, many found it difficult to continue regular employment in Israel. Some gave up the daily trek altogether. While certain sectors of Israel's economy were severely hurt by the strikes, they caused a far greater dislocation within the territories. Israeli authorities realized this when, in May 1989, they turned the tables on the leaders of the uprising by banning for several days all Arab labor from Gaza and the West Bank. The officials announced that in the future, work in Israel by Arabs from the territories would no longer be considered a right but a privilege. Only those with individually approved work permits would be allowed to cross the Green Line. The intent was to put economic pressure on the Palestinian working class whose pay in normal times was the largest source of income in Gaza, providing about $1.5 million a day.[18]

The income of villagers who constitute about 70 percent of the West Bank population has been undercut as a result of Israel's punitive measures (see Chapter 2). These include curfews, closures, banning the export of produce such as olives and citrus, uprooting trees, and destroying crops. In May 1989 all citrus imports from Gaza to Israel were cut off, a measure described by the chairman of the region's Citrus Union Association as "a noose around the Gaza Strip's neck." (Citrus exports were the region's second largest source of income.)

Local people's committees and the UNLU attempted to organize a variety of measures to provide for the unemployed. These include soliciting large contributions from wealthy Palestinians in the territories and importing funds from abroad, mostly through the PLO. Although Israel could not undermine local contributions, it imposed severe restrictions of imported funds at all points of entry and on the bridges over the Jordan River (see Chapter 2). Even unhampered, such contributions compensated for only a small part of the economy lost through the various setbacks described above.

Political activists attempted to make a good thing of a bad situation, insisting that austerity would improve the moral fiber of the middle class—that the middle class had become too soft, too accustomed to its automobiles, video-cassettes, and other imported luxuries, especially those made in Israel. A conscious and concentrated effort was made to turn the situation to the advantage of the national movement by making economic hardship synonymous with *sumud*. This led to a boycott of Israeli goods (the West Bank and Gaza were Israel's second largest export market after the United States, as further discussed in Chapter 4) and to an attempt to develop an "alternative" economy. Palestinian women's cooperatives increased their output of pickles and jams to replace those made in Israel, and dairies in Nablus and other towns stepped up production of products as alternatives to those from Tnuva, Israel's largest dairy distributor. Sales of Israeli clothing, cigarettes, soft drinks, soap, and candies greatly declined. The production of many such items was increased in the territories, although it was impossible to replace all of them. Nevertheless, it became a point of honor for shopkeepers to reject stocks of Israeli items and for customers to demand Palestinian replacements for them. Sales of luxury items and durables such as cars, televisions, and video sets nearly came to a halt; merchants either refused to handle them if they came from Israel or, more likely, income so declined that few in the territories could still afford them.

Another aspect of the development of an alternative economy was the increase in the number of home "victory" gardens and small animal husbandry units. People's committees encouraged the inhabitants of towns and refugee camps to grow vegetables and to raise goats, chickens, and rabbits.

The overall effect of such measures is probably more psychological than economic. Their real impact has been to raise morale and national consciousness rather than to develop a long-lasting alternative economy. As shown in Chapter 1, the economies of the West Bank and Gaza are so dominated by Israel that, until the throttlehold of occupation is ended, the territories will find it difficult to develop a genuine Palestinian national economic system. In the meantime, the hope is that the symbolism and slogans of "alternative economy" will, from the Palestinian perspective, counteract the dangers implicit in growing unemployment, enforced austerity, and the restiveness that results from such economic dislocation.

INTERNAL DIVISIONS

Although the Intifada has created a sense of national cohesion and solidarity never before experienced by the Palestinian community, internal divisions persist.[19] They exist even within fairly homogeneous groups such as Fatah, to say nothing of the divisions among Fatah, PFLP, DFLP, and the Communists, and those between these secular factions and the Islamic fundamentalists. While even the most ideologically contradictory factions have been able to paper over their differences temporarily, internecine conflict will very likely erupt among them when the time comes for the Palestinians to determine their political future. Like the Israelis (see Chapter 4), the Palestinians are split on ideological fundamentals concerning future relations between the Jewish and Palestinian communities. Within each community, Jewish and Palestinian, the fundamental division is between those willing to accept the national identity and political existence of the other, and those who still refuse such recognition.

During the 1970s and 1980s, conflicts among and within the diverse Palestinian political factions erupted into open warfare, often on college campuses when student members of fundamentalist groups battled secularists, and when secularists fought among themselves, with make-shift weapons such as chains, iron bars, clubs, and Molotov cocktails. Since the Intifada most of these violent clashes have halted, but ideological tensions continue.

Among Palestinians, the dispute over recognition is, in broad terms, defined by the differences between secular nationalists and Islamic fundamentalists. But even the most militant fringes of the secularist movements have not yet become reconciled to the concept of coexistence between independent Palestinian and Israeli states. On the one hand, some Marxist factions within the PLO, such as PFLP, are reluctant to agree with Chairman Arafat's apparent willingness to accept a Palestinian state within the borders of the occupied territories. On the other hand, the Palestine Communist party proposed such a compromise before it was accepted by the PLO mainstream. The DFLP has been more ambivalent about its position. Though small in numbers and without a broad following among the Palestinian masses, these groups carry much political weight, either because their leaders, such as George Habash (PFLP), have great personal charisma, or because they have a substantial following among students, journalists, and intellectuals who constitute a significant number of the cadres in the people's committees, the UNLU, and the PLO itself.

Fatah is by far the largest nonfundamentalist organization. It organized the Shebab and many women's groups, trade unions, and student, journalist, and other organizations made up of intellectuals. Within Fatah itself there are at least three trends: pro-Arafat, pro–Salah Khalaf (Abu Iyad), and followers of the deceased Khalil al-Wazir, also known as Abu Jihad (see Chapter 2). At times, Fatah leaders abroad have urged their followers in the territories to refrain from altercations with the funda-mentalists if they cannot cooperate with them. During the formative period of the UNLU, its PLO members attempted to persuade funda-mentalist leaders to participate, but they met with only partial success. Initially, members of the Islamic Jihad movement were part of the leadership, but more often than not they have gone their separate way, both in planning and executing resistance tactics and in articulating political objectives. As the fundamentalists gained increasing support, the secularists became apprehensive about the future. Many foresee the possibility of bloody encounters within the Palestinian community, should the fundamentalists decide to convert the movement for national independence into a struggle for an Islamic state.

Islamic fundamentalist groups exist throughout the territories but are strongest by far in Gaza. Both the physical and the political conditions there are conducive to recruitment of the dispossessed and deprived. Since the masses of Gazans, especially those in the overcrowded refugee camps, come from a traditionally conservative Islamic background, they are most receptive to the message of fundamentalism. Such individuals are least likely to be attracted by the PLO slogans of the early 1970s calling for establishment of a "democratic, secular state." Nor are they eager to surrender the "right of return" to their homes within the Green Line. Yet even among the Muslim Palestinian masses there is an ambivalence about their relationship to the PLO and the fundamentalist movements. Although an average Gazan worker from a refugee camp may find solace in the religious message of fundamentalism, he and his family are also Palestinian nationalists and supporters of the PLO, whose heroes are Arafat, Abu Jihad, and Abu Iyad. The Palestinian flag, displayed on pain of arrest, is his symbol. Still, the refinements in terminology developed by the more sophisticated PLO and UNLU leadership in recent years, distinguishing between "Jew," "Zionist," "Israel," and so on, may still be beyond his ken. For the Islamic fundamentalists all these terms are odious, and what distinction, if any, exists among them is irrelevant.

The fundamentalist groups among Palestine Arabs are descendants of the Muslim Brotherhood established in Egypt before World War II and are still powerful there. The Brotherhood was active among Palestinians after the war but was quiescent from the establishment of Israel in 1948 until the conquest of Gaza and the West Bank in 1967. June 1967, the time of the disaster, was a turning point. Since then, conditions have been ripe for a resurgence of militant political activity among the Palestinians. Many, however, were frustrated and disillusioned by the diverse secular nationalist movements and the Marxist and pan-Arab factions. None of these groups succeeded in ending the occupation and attaining justice for the Palestinians. Even the Arab "victory" in the 1973 war failed to restore the homeland. While secular movements seemed to be stymied in achieving their goals, by the late 1970s and early 1980s Islamic accomplishments were on the rise. The Islamic revolution of 1979 in Iran was greeted with great expectations. In 1981 Egyptian President Anwar Sadat, considered a traitor for making peace with Israel, was assassinated by a militant Islamic faction. During 1983 and 1984, attacks by Shiite militants on Israeli troops withdrawing from Lebanon were perceived as heroic acts of Muslim warriors. Within the territories, pious Muslims became increasingly concerned about the outspoken demands of Jewish religious nationalists that Israel take over the Tomb of the Prophets in Hebron and the Haram al-Sharif (Temple Mount) in Jerusalem, both considered holy sites by Islam.

By the 1980s there were at least eight Islamic fundamentalist factions in Gaza, all offshoots of the Muslim Brotherhood. The largest was headed by Sheikh Ahmed Yassin, a figure who was to reappear several times as one of Gaza's most influential religious leaders. He was jailed by the Israeli occupation authorities in 1984 but freed a few months later in an exchange of several hundred Palestinian prisoners for two Israeli soldiers held in Lebanon by a militant Palestinian group.

The changing atmosphere in Gaza and the West Bank was evidenced in the late 1980s by the growing number of men with Islamic-style beards, by women who wore the hijab (a black, cloak-like garment that covered them from head to toe), and by increased mosque attendance. Between 1967 and 1987 the number of mosques in Gaza doubled from 75 to 150. In Hebron and Gaza, universities run according to Islamic tradition were opened; the one in Gaza was affiliated with the world-famous al-Azhar theological institution in Cairo. Many fundamentalists were actively proselytizing and insisted on enforcing Islamic codes. Their zealotry often took the form of vandalization of liquor stores and shops selling video cassettes (considered pornographic), attacks on women wearing "immodest" clothing in public, demands that cinemas be closed, and interruption of weddings at which Western music and dancing were the style. By the mid-1980s fundamentalist militancy had turned against secular nationalists represented by the PLO and its institutions such as the Palestine Red Crescent Society in Gaza.

There were two principal trends among the fundamentalists, especially in Gaza. The largest represented the mainstream Muslim Brotherhood, similar to the Muslim Brotherhood organization now operating in Egypt. Until the Intifada, this group was less involved in politics than in religious and social work: mosque building, organizing prayer vigils, education, and eleemosynary activity. While striving to transform society and to attain an Islamic superstate, it discouraged violence and revolutionary tactics. Its goals were to be attained through peaceful change.

In contrast, the Islamic Jihad, also an offshoot of the Muslim Brotherhood, was militantly activist. Its models were the Islamic revolutionary movement in Iran and the fundamentalist factions involved in Sadat's assassination. Several of its cadres were students at Islamic schools in Egypt; much of the membership was recruited among young men in Israeli prisons. Its militant modus operandi necessitated that it organize secretly in underground cells. Islamic Jihad disagreed that an Islamic society could be attained through peaceful change. As implied by its name, Jihad (struggle), violence was required to change society. The only solution was the Iranian solution, attainable through "martyrdom." Islamic Jihad slogans emphasized its appeal to the "disinherited" of the earth, to the poor and dispossessed.

The intense hostility between fundamentalists and the PLO led Israeli intelligence to support the former as a counterweight to the secular nationalists who were considered potentially far more dangerous. The PLO and Palestine Communist cadres were more sophisticated, university-educated men of the world; therefore, they were less easy to manipulate than the fundamentalists who came from the backwaters of Palestinian society. During an interview with the brigadier general commanding Gaza, the general told *New York Times* correspondent David Shipler that he was providing funds to the fundamentalists to strengthen them against the PLO. Prior to the uprising, Israeli authorities tended to be more lenient in their treatment of the Muslim leaders than those of the PLO, and fewer of the fundamentalists were imprisoned or deported.[20]

Islamic Jihad was the first organization to play an active role in the uprising; it claimed credit for instigating the youth who demonstrated in the Jabalya and Balata refugee camps in Gaza and the West Bank during December 1987 (see Chapter 2). As noted earlier, mosques, especially those in Gaza, were the initial centers for organization and communication of the Intifada. During the first few weeks of the uprising, the Islamic Jihad cooperated with the UNLU but refrained from becoming permanently affiliated because of ideological differences.

Early in January fundamentalist participation in the Intifada took a new form with the appearance of Hamas, an acronym for the Islamic Resistance (or Opposition) Movement. The leaders of Hamas (the Arabic for zeal, ardor, strength, bravery, flame) came from both the Muslim Brothers and the Islamic Jihad. One of the principal leaders was Ahmed Yassin, who became a spokesman for the organization. Another was Sheikh Khalil Qawqa, who was deported half a year after the Intifada began. He made his way to Kuwait, where he became a major spokesman abroad for Hamas.

In August 1988 Hamas published its own covenant, a document of thirty-six articles apparently intended to serve as the fundamentalist answer to the PLO Charter.[21] It was obvious from the document that there could be little long-term collaboration between the Islamic and secular wings of the Palestine nationalist movement, the latter represented by the PLO. The Hamas covenant defined Palestinian nationalism as an Islamic "struggle against the Jews." Hamas was identified as "one of the wings of the Muslim Brotherhood in Palestine," and as "one of the links in the chain" going back to the Muslim leader Izz al-Din al-Qassam. Hamas "strives to raise the banner of Allah [God] over every inch of Palestine." Although under Islam "all religions can coexist in security and safety," their followers must recognize that Palestine is an integral part of the Islamic world. The slogan of the movement is "Allah is its target, the Prophet is its model, the Koran is its constitution, Jihad is its path, and death for the sake of Allah is the loftiest of its wishes."

No part of Palestine may be given up, according to Hamas, because all the land is an Islamic wakaf (religious endowment), "consecrated for future Muslim generations until Judgement Day," like any other land that "Muslims have conquered by force." Nationalism, the charter states, is "part of the Islamic religious creed."

"Initiatives and so-called peaceful solutions, and international conferences, contradict the principles of the Islamic resistance movement." Given the past history of the likely participants in an international conference, and their attitude toward Muslims, it is impossible that such a conference would deal justly with the rights of the oppressed. "These conferences are only ways of getting the infidels into the land of the Muslims as arbitrators." The only solution to the Palestine question is through Jihad; "other means are all a waste of time and vain endeavors."

Jihad for Palestine is "an individual duty for every Muslim wherever he may be." Given "the Jews' usurpation of Palestine, it is compulsory that the banner of Islam be raised." All must participate in the struggle: "scientists, educators and teachers, information and media people, as well as educated masses, especially the youth and sheikhs of the Islamic movements."

The covenant calls for society to "cleanse" itself of "traces of ideological invasion" going back to the Crusades. Education must be reorganized by using a "healthy" curriculum that will include "a comprehensive study of the enemy" so that Muslims will understand his strengths and weaknesses. Women must play an active role in "guiding and educating new generations." The enemy has recognized woman's importance and has attempted to subvert her "through Zionist organizations of various names and shapes, such as Freemasons, Rotary clubs, espionage groups, and others, all nothing more than allies of subversion and saboteurs."

"Islamic art" also plays an important role in the struggle. "The book, the article, the bulletin, the sermon, the thesis, the popular poem, the poetic ode, the song, the play, and others" must be mobilized. The enemy, with his money, has formed secret societies including the Freemasons, Rotary, and Lions, which "took control of the world media, news agencies, the press, publishing houses, broadcasting stations, and others." The enemy was behind the French and Communist revolutions and, again with his money, controls the imperialistic countries. He also was responsible for World Wars I and II, the League of Nations, and the United Nations. His finger is in every war, and he tries to "rule the world," both the capitalist West and the Communist East, says the covenant. "Their plan is embodied in the 'Protocols of the Elders of Zion,' and their present conduct is the best proof of what we are saying." Hamas considers itself the spearhead against the world Zionist conspiracy.

The attitude of Hamas to other Islamic groups and to the PLO is live and let live. Don't slander or speak ill of them, although they should be warned of their errors. As long as other Palestinian movements do not give "allegiance to the Communist East or to the Crusading West," they should be appreciated and Hamas should try to assist them. "The PLO is the closest to the heart of the Islamic resistance movement. It contains the father and the brother, the next of kin or friend. Our homeland is one, our situation is one, our fate is one, and the enemy is a joint enemy to all of us." However, until the PLO "adopts Islam as its way of life," Hamas must have reservations about it.

These descriptions should not lead to the conclusion that fundamentalists control or are about to take over the Palestine national movement. To date, even in Gaza, Fatah has far more adherents than any other organized group. No accurate count of the membership in any of these organizations is yet available, because they are illegal and their cells are underground. Before the uprising, Israeli sources estimated that the largest fundamentalist faction in Gaza had fewer than 2,000 members. Another figure given by an American scholar living in Gaza was a total of 20,000 fundamentalist activists. In discussions between fundamentalists and Fatah during 1987, mention was made that 30 percent of the population in the territories supported the former and 60 percent, Fatah. The fact remains, however, that since the Intifada, fundamentalist political activity has greatly increased and those affiliated with Islamic groups are much more active in the resistance to Israel.

OBJECTIVES OF THE INTIFADA

The Fourteen Demands

Shortly after the first bayanat were issued and the UNLU began to take shape, a group of Palestinians known in the occupied territories and in Israel held a press conference in Jerusalem to inform the public about the demands of the uprising. While those who convened and participated in the conference were not the leaders, it was assumed that the conference had been organized with the approval of the UNLU. The convener was Professor Sari Nusseibeh of Bir Zeit University, who sixteen months later was to be charged by Israel as a leader of the uprising. Others included Gabi Baramke, acting president of Bir Zeit; Murabak Awad (see Chapter 2), director of the Jerusalem Center for the Study of Non-Violence; and the former mayor of Hebron. The IDF prevented notable Gaza personalities from attending the conference and arrested a trade-union leader as well as the director of the Palestine Press Service upon their arrival. In addition to journalists, the audience included some two dozen old-guard representatives of the nationalist movement. The fourteen demands were presented in the name of "Palestinian nationalist institutions and personalities" from the West Bank and Gaza.[22]

The document asserted that the end of the uprising and "real peace" were unattainable without recognition by Israel of "Palestinian national rights, including the right of self-determination and the establishment of an independent Palestinian state on Palestinian national soil." The only way to prevent "further violence and blood-shed, and the further deepening of hatred," would be to convene an international conference that would include the PLO as "the sole legitimate representative of the Palestinian people, as an equal partner, as well as the five permanent members of the Security Council, under the supervision of the two superpowers."

The Jerusalem document specified that, in order to "prepare the atmosphere" for the coming of the suggested international conference, Israel should meet the following demands: Abide by the Fourth Geneva Convention and other international agreements dealing with the treatment of civilians under the occupation, and terminate use of the British Mandate Emergency Regulations; release all prisoners arrested during the uprising; cancel the policy of expulsion and permit all exiled Palestinians to return, free all administrative detainees, revoke house arrest orders, and accept applications for family reunions; immediately lift the siege on Palestinian refugee camps, and withdraw the army from all population centers; initiate a formal inquiry into army behavior in the territories, in jails, and in detention centers; halt all Jewish settlement activity and land confiscation and return land already seized; refrain from interference with or changing the status of Muslim and Christian holy sites; cancel the VAT and other Israeli taxes imposed on Palestinians in Jerusalem, the West Bank, and Gaza; terminate all restrictions on political freedom, and conduct free municipal elections under the supervision of a neutral authority; release and return all monies deducted from the wages of laborers working within the Green Line, a sum estimated at several hundred million dollars; remove all restrictions on permits and licenses for industrial projects, well digging, and agricultural development, and end measures depriving the territories of their water resources; abrogate discrimination within the Green Line against industrial and agricultural products from the territories, or place comparable trade restrictions on Israeli goods transferred into the territories; and, finally, remove restrictions on political contacts between the territories and the PLO so that Palestinians from the West Bank and Gaza may participate in meetings of the Palestine National Council and its decisionmaking process (see Appendix 3).[23]

The fourteen demands became the charter, as it were, of the uprising; they were reiterated in one form or another, in whole or in part, several times within the next year and a half. In a bayan (leaflet) issued by the UNLU during May 1988, most of the demands were repeated; a shorter list of seven was issued in another leaflet in June, and in another in July. Initially, Israel officials' reaction was that "there is nothing to respond to," because there is nothing new in the demands. It took more than a year for the Israeli government to devise an indirect response, and then only after reacting to a variety of international pressures.[24]

One of the first reactions to the political objectives of the uprising came from Jordan's King Hussein. On July 31, 1988, the king abandoned all claims to the West Bank, a territory annexed by his grandfather, King Abdullah, in 1950. For nearly forty years, the inhabitants of the West Bank had been considered subjects of Jordan's king, used Jordanian currency, carried Jordanian passports, and voted in Jordan's elections. The Jordanian parliament, even while inactive, reserved a number of seats for representatives from the West Bank, and many of the King's cabinet ministers were Palestinians. Even after occupation of the West Bank in 1967, Jordan's special ties were recognized despite Israel's rejection of Jordanian sovereignty over the territories.

Jordan continued to subsidize many West Bank institutions such as religious foundations, schools, clinics, and the like; it also continued to maintain on its payroll about 20,000 former Jordanian government employees who now worked for Israel's military administration. Between 1986 and 1988, with backing from the U.S. government and Israel's Labor party, King Hussein floated plans for a $1.3 billion economic rehabilitation project that was intended to be part of the Peres-Shultz scheme to "improve the quality of life" in the territories. The so-called "Jordanian option," in which King Hussein would maintain political authority in the West Bank, under Israeli security supervision, was a solution to the Palestine problem long preferred by many leaders of Israel's Labor party and viewed favorably by the United States.

Despite Jordan's beneficence, only a handful of older-generation leaders such as the mayors of Gaza and Bethlehem could be counted among the Hashemite loyalists. Most of those who benefited from King Hussein's largesse—government clerks, teachers, mosque and waqf officials, former mayors—supported the PLO as the sole representative of the Palestinians, even as they earned their livelihood from Jordanian coffers. As the Intifada gained momentum, it became increasingly clear that there was little love lost between the Jordanian government and its Palestinian subjects. Anti-Jordanian feeling, always latent among the Palestinians, rose to new heights. Not one of the new generation of leaders had a good word to say for the king; and the concept of reunification with Jordan was totally absent from any of the demands put forward by the leaders of the uprising.

In July 1988 King Hussein decided to retaliate. First, he closed down the Jordanian Ministry for the Occupied Territories; next, he slashed salaries and subsidies to the West Bank, except for those to Muslim institutions. The five-year development scheme was abandoned. The lower house of Jordan's parliament, half of whose sixty members were from the West Bank, was dissolved. Finally, the king officially gave up all claims to the West Bank.

In a dramatic televised address on July 31, Hussein proclaimed that "Jordan is not Palestine. . . . The independent Palestinian state will be established on the occupied Palestinian land, after it is liberated, God willing." Although he turned over full responsibility for the occupied territories to the PLO, the king denied that he was deserting the Palestinians. Jordan, he said, remained a principal party to the Arab-Israeli conflict and would continue to stand by the Palestinians in their struggle.[25]

Leaders of the Intifada perceived King Hussein's move as "a tremendous victory," but many worried about the price to be paid. Would the PLO be able to make up the financial loss of Hashemite subsidies? Would the sacrifice of thousands of Jordanian salaries further undermine the economy, already weakened by the Intifada? What kind of travel documents would now be available to West Bank Palestinians traveling abroad? Would they, like their compatriots in Gaza, become "stateless persons"? As Mayor Elias Freij of Bethlehem observed, "This is really a Holocaust. . . . King Hussein has decided to destroy us."[26] However, leaders of the UNLU regarded severance of ties with Jordan as another step toward achievement of the objectives of the uprising. With Hussein's withdrawal from the territories, the position of the PLO was strengthened and the "Jordan option" was undermined, thus frustrating Israeli peace proposals. It now seemed that the goal of an independent Palestinian state was closer than before.

PLO Policy Changes

Indeed, after August pressure increased on the PLO to take a more decisive position on an independent Palestinian state. For more than a decade Palestinian leaders had evaded the issue, largely because of disagreement within the PNC. Over the years the PLO mainstream had moved to more moderate positions, accepting the concept of a two-state solution and recognition of Israel. But it avoided any forthright, clear-cut statement on the subject for fear of alienating the militant fringes of the organization. By August many leaders of the uprising were pressuring PLO chieftains in Tunis to declare a Palestinian state, establish a government-in-exile, and recognize Israel.

In Jerusalem, Faisal Husseini acknowledged that his Arab Studies Society was working on a draft plan for a state. In an unusual move, he appeared before a Jewish audience in West Jerusalem to call for mutual recognition between Israel and the Palestinian state. A few days after his appearance, he was again arrested and imprisoned by Israeli authorities.

After Husseini's arrest, the contents of the draft plan were revealed to the press. It stated that the time had come to move from clashes with stones to a political initiative—an initiative that would not end but escalate the Intifada. After declaration of a Palestinian state, Israel would be subjected to international pressures that would force it to change its policies. Proclamation of the state would divide Israel between those calling for recognition of Palestine and those seeking to strangle it. Popular committees throughout the territories would become leaders of the new state and would implement its program. The UNLU, rather than a government-in-exile, would assume responsibility and establish the capital in Jerusalem. The borders of the new Palestinian state, to be determined through negotiations, would be within those of the 1948 partition plan. Yassir Arafat would become president; Farouk Kadoumi, foreign minister; and the members of the PLO Executive Committee, the new government. It would include the leader of the PFLP, George Habash; and of the DFLP, Nayef Hawatmeh. The UNLU would nominate 152 individuals as a general legislative body to be affiliated with the PNC. An interim body would be established within the territories to deal with administrative affairs, including health, police, agriculture, industry, commerce, construction, electricity, water, municipalities, and press and media affairs. On behalf of the PLO, this interim government would declare readiness to appoint a delegation to negotiate with Israel on matters such as borders, links between Gaza and the West Bank, Jewish settlements, the refugee problem, and relations between the two states.

The new Palestinian state would be a democratic republic, with multiple political parties, an elected president and parliament, freedom of religion, and guarantees for all freedoms stated in the UN Declaration of Human Rights. As the state emerged, residents would exchange their Israeli identity cards for new Palestinian documents distributed by the popular committees (see Appendix 4).[27]

Member of SHEBAB "shooting" at Israeli troops. Photo by *Palestine Perspectives*.

Confronted with such detailed planning from within the territories, PLO leaders abroad were forced to come to grips with issues they had evaded for years. Groups that had opposed such decisive action began to waffle after seeing that the leaders of the uprising and public opinion within the territories favored immediate declaration of a state. Rumors spread that a decision for independence would be taken at the next meeting of the PNC and that Arafat would address the European Community on the subject when its parliament convened in France during the coming September.

As political momentum rose within the territories, Arafat authorized one of his close aides, Bassam Abu Sharif, to float a trial balloon calling for accommodation with Israel. The statement was prepared for publication in the *Washington Post* during May and distributed during the Arab League summit in Algiers; later it was published in the *New York Times* and the *Jerusalem Post*, bringing it to the attention of Israelis as well as the international community.[28]

Abu Sharif noted that despite seventy years of hostility between Jews and Arabs, there were a number of issues on which they had total agreement. Both peoples desired to achieve "lasting peace and security" through "direct talks, with no attempt by any outside party to impose or veto a settlement." The key lay in talks between Israelis and Palestinians, not in outside intermediaries such as the United States. Although the Palestinians would like to choose their Israeli interlocutor (perhaps an organization like Peace Now), they realized that to achieve agreement it would be necessary to deal with representatives chosen by Israelis themselves, even if these delegates were from Likud. Accordingly, it would be futile for Israel to select Palestinians of their choice for negotiations. If a settlement were to be valid, Palestinians would have to choose their own representatives. Let the Palestinians

> express their free will in a manner that will convince doubters: arrange for an internationally-supervised referendum in the West Bank and the Gaza Strip and allow the population to choose between the PLO and any other group of Palestinians that Israel or the United States or the international community wishes to nominate. The PLO is ready to abide by the outcome and step aside for any alternative leadership should the Palestinian people choose one.

Abu Sharif stated that the PLO was prevented from accepting UN Security Council Resolutions 242 and 338, not because of what was in them but because of what they omitted—namely, reference to the national rights of the Palestinian people. The fear that a Palestinian state would be a threat to its neighbor was unjustified, asserted Abu Sharif, because the PLO, the organization representing the Palestinians, would provide a democratic infrastructure for the proposed Palestinian state, and such a state would not likely attack its neighbors. Should Israeli concerns and fears be unappeased by the democratic character of the PLO, Palestinians would accept a transition period "during which an international mandate would guide the occupied Palestinian territories to democratic Palestinian statehood."

Abu Sharif expressed empathy with "the Jewish people's centuries of suffering." No one more than the Palestinians could understand their plight, for the Palestinians also "know what it means to be stateless and the object of the fear and prejudice of the nations. . . . We know what it feels like when human beings are considered somehow less human than others, and denied the basic rights that people around the globe take for granted."

Abu Sharif's emotional appeal received a favorable response outside official circles among many Israelis and American Jewish supporters of Israel; but it was rejected by the Israeli government as a subterfuge disguising the PLO's real intent to destroy Israel, and by the U.S. government as an inadequate response to American demands for a change of PLO policy (see Chapter 5 and Appendix 5). It did signal the coming series of policy changes by the PLO leadership that was to culminate on November 15 with the Palestinian declaration of independence, subsequent statements by Arafat recognizing Israel, and finally

U.S. recognition of the PLO in December 1988 (again, see Chapter 5 and Appendix 5).

IMPACT OF THE INTIFADA

Throughout 1988 the Intifada generated wide support for its objectives, from the fourteen demands in January to the draft proposal for establishment of a Palestinian state in July. The PLO leadership was pushed to move much more rapidly than it wanted; the "Jordan option" was dealt a mortal blow; and the Arab League and individual Arab states were forced to place a high priority on Palestinian issues (see Chapter 5). Even the Israeli government moved from the status quo to an offer, inadequate as it was, of elections in the West Bank and Gaza (see Chapter 4). Although the long-term objective of an independent Palestinian state was still distant, it now had to be confronted as a realistic demand—a demand that no longer seemed remote to the Palestinians, and one that was on the international agenda as the key to settlement of the Arab-Israel conflict.

Palestinian society in the West Bank and Gaza was experiencing greater social and psychological change than had occurred in many decades—perhaps greater than any since the collapse of the community in 1947–1948 or following the 1967 war. Inhabitants of the territories were no longer willing to wait for salvation to come from abroad; they insisted on taking matters into their own hands. They themselves would have to "shake off" the occupation. They realized that they could not rely on the United States, the Arab states, or PLO leaders in Tunis to act on their behalf.

The new self-reliance and spirit of solidarity were forging the human resources for a state, and the leaders, the cadres, and the citizenry had become capable of taking over from the occupation authorities. The activities of the population and their new outlook reversed the process of creeping annexation that had gathered momentum until the end of 1987 (see Chapter 1). Indeed, the uprising restored the Green Line that, five years earlier, Prime Minister Menachem Begin had declared "vanished forever." The popular committees of the Intifada were equated by Meron Benvenisti with "the birth of the Palestine people." Dean Hanan Mikhail Ashrawi of Bir Zeit University described the committees as the "invisible heart of the *intifada* responsible for social restructuring of the community."[29]

Within a year the uprising gave birth to its own "revolutionary" culture, made manifest in scores of poems, fables, and jokes that passed from person to person through the detention camps, markets, and streets of Arab Palestine. Because they were passed by word of mouth, they

In the West Bank village of Taamri, graffiti written by Palestinians ("We mourn the martyrs of the Intifada and dedicate this street to the martyr Salim al-Shair from this corner to the upper Triangle") is covered by graffiti written by Israeli settlers ("IDF" and the star of David). Photo by Deena Hurwitz.

could not be censored by the Israeli authorities; in addition, they were often more biting, more derogatory, and more morale raising than bayanat or wall graffiti. Hundreds of jokes and anecdotes were variants of the underground stories spread among political dissidents in Eastern Europe. Often the censors were more strict with literature and poetry than with political articles; one, for instance, permitted a news story about a boy arrested for throwing a stone but banned a poem on the subject.

The popular culture of the Intifada could be seen in allusory motifs such as the banned national colors (red, green, white, and black) found in the embroidery work of village women, and in the wearing of the kuffiya by young men; it could even be seen in the style with which farmers dressed scarecrows in their fields. During an incident in a Jerusalem neighborhood, a soldier lost his beret one night. When children found it in the morning, they placed it on a stick, stuck it in the ground, and threw stones at it in a performance of street theatre.

After several months, walls in the West Bank and Gaza were covered with layers of multicolored graffiti painted at night. The IDF ordered the slogans painted over, but to prevent repainting, youths scratched deep cracks on the walls. Soldiers then ordered men with axes to chisel out or blur the graffiti. A Palestinian journalist compiled an anthology of these wall writings, but the authorities banned publication.

Hundreds of fables were created with themes about stones, villages defying the army, and women tricking soldiers as they hid young boys from searching patrols; many of the fables became songs and were recorded on cassettes sold under the counter. One Israeli critic described the cassettes as

> perhaps the most authentic expression of the culture of the Intifada . . . [They] tell the story of the Intifada from close-up, intimately, without artistic distance and to hell with aesthetics! Most are nationalist slogans . . . designed to praise and glorify the heroes of the Intifada, the children of the stones. . . . Some children bring the songs home from schools or from the streets and play them to their startled parents.[30]

Many songs come from the prison camps, especially from Ansar III at Ketsiot (see Chapter 2), where dozens of Palestinian poets, writers, and intellectuals were incarcerated. One prison song emphasized Ansar's double significance, as both a desert hellhole and the source of revolutionary esprit: "You, Ketsiot, shall be our tomb; from Ketsiot the sun of freedom will shine!" A new version of the Palestinian anthem "Biladi, biladi" (My country, my country) has also come from Ansar III. The song, originally composed in Egypt during the 1930s, was once the Egyptian national anthem and was later adapted by the Palestinians.

Many songs describe actual events, such as the hanging of the Israeli collaborator from an electricity pylon at Kabatiyeh (see Chapter 2) or the hang-glider incident (see Chapter 1). A song about the gliders describes their pilots as birdmen who crossed the border to the land of their fathers, where they gave their lives in the struggle against the "Zionist colonialist state." Many are unabashed patriotic themes calling on listeners to join the Intifada, telling them that it is "beautiful to die" to save the Holy Land. Some attack Prime Minister Shamir: "Get out of our land. . . . [I]f you fall into our hands, nothing will help you!" Another, written to a well-known children's tune, calls for strikes with the refrain, "Strike, strike! Today and tomorrow, strike!"

There are many examples of well-known, popular folk tunes for which new words have been adapted with themes of the uprising. At Ansar III, guards attempted to drown them out with army and other Israeli pop songs over blaring loudspeakers. Although the authorities attempted to ban the cassettes, the task was impossible and they spread throughout the territories.

The Israeli who wrote about these songs was struck by their resemblance to those of Likud's militant youth group Betar, with their parallel themes of blood and land, the imminent state, and how good it is to die for one's country. They also remind her of a poem by the Hebrew poet Bialik, who wrote: "We are for peace, and you are for battle/ We are few, and you are many/ Woe, know oh strangers/ The power is still with us/ To risk our lives, and our arrows are faithful/ And we shall not budge from this/ We will not budge from this/ forever."

The long-term psychological effects of the uprising were not all beneficial. Family relationships have been severely shaken and may be difficult to restore in the future. Youths have revolted not only against the occupation and Israel but against their parents and teachers as well. Many believe that it could be difficult to direct their energies into constructive channels in the future and to discipline them for the tasks of nation building that lie ahead.

The children have, indeed, experienced psychological trauma, as shown in a survey of dreams undertaken by an Arab and a Jewish psychologist in Jerusalem. Their study of Arab children in several refugee camps indicated that in many dreams they were confronted by Israeli soldiers who broke into homes, smashed windows and furniture, and beat up their parents. A major conclusion was that these children regard themselves as victims of violence initiated by armed men and that the family no longer provides security. The father almost never figures in these dreams; according to the analysis, he has lost his authority.[31]

The impact of the Intifada on the Arabs was akin to arising from a long period of mourning—a mourning for the loss of their land. The first phase of mourning, from 1948 to the 1960s, was denial. The Palestinians did not believe that what had happened to them really did happen; many still kept the keys to their homes in Jaffa, Haifa, or elsewhere, hoping—even believing—that they would return any day, any second.

The next phase was anger, when they began to accept reality. Anger was seen in their support for military attacks and guerrilla raids on Israel. By the late 1970s, there emerged a willingness for dialogue, to find and try the best way possible of living. This, according to the psychologists, was a healthy reaction to mourning. (See Chapter 4 for an analysis of Israeli children's dreams.)

The children who are living today's nightmares will become the leaders of tomorrow. If the Intifada continues for long, their fears of the Israeli intruder may turn to hatred, which will undermine possibilities of dialogue. And, as we have seen, the longer the uprising, the greater the support for Islamic fundamentalists who oppose all compromise. How imminent, then, is the prospect that Israelis will recognize that there is an urgent need to reach a settlement, before it is too late?

NOTES

1. Daoud Kuttab, "A Profile of the Stonethrowers," *Journal of Palestine Studies* (hereafter JPS), no. 67, Spring 1988, pp. 14–16.

2. *Ibid.*

3. *Ibid.*, pp. 19–20.

4. *Ibid.*, p. 93.

5. *Israel Press Briefs*, no. 57, February 1988 (Tel-Aviv: Center for Peace in the Middle East); quote from *Maariv*, 1/17/88.

6. Kuttab, "Beyond the Intifada: The Struggle to Build a Nation," *The Nation*, 10/17/88.

7. Roger Owen, "The West Bank Now: Economic Development," in *Palestine Under Occupation: Prospects for the Future*, edited by Peter F. Krough and Mary C. McDavid (Washington, D.C.: Georgetown University, 1989), pp. 43–56.

8. Kuttab, "Beyond the Intifada," pp. 338–340.

9. *Jerusalem Post International Edition* (hereafter JPI), no. 1,423, 2/13/88 (Yehuda Litani, "How the Protests Are Organized").

10. *New York Times* (hereafter NYT), 5/20/89; *Manchester Guardian Weekly* (hereafter MGW), 4/2/89.

11. Ann Mosley Lesch, "The Palestine Uprising—Causes and Consequences," *USFI Field Staff Reports*, Africa/Middle East, no. 1, 1988–1989.

12. "Intifada: Palestinian Nonviolent Protest—An Affirmation of Human Dignity and Freedom" (Jerusalem: Palestinian Center for the Study of Non-Violence, May 1988), mimeograph.

13. Extracted from a collection of bayanat; also available in *Foreign Broadcast Information Service—Near East South Asia* (hereafter FBIS-NES) at frequent intervals after December 1987.

14. Dov Shinar and Danny Rubinstein, *Palestinian Press in the West Bank: The Political Dimension* (Jerusalem: West Bank Data Base Project and *Jerusalem Post*, 1987), p. 1.

15. Dov Shinar, *Palestinian Voices: Communication and Nation Building in the West Bank* (Boulder, Colo.: Lynne Rienner Publishers, 1987), p. 56.

16. NYT, 5/21/89.

17. JPI, no. 1,448, 6/8/88.

18. NYT, 5/19/89.

19. Yehuda Litani, "Islam as a Political Weapon," JPI, no. 1,387, 6/6/87; Lisa Taraki, "The Islamic Resistance Movement in the Palestinian Uprising," *Middle East Report*, January–February 1989; John Kifner, "Islamic Fundamentalist Group Challenging P.L.O. and Israel," NYT, 9/18/88; Shefi Gabai, *Maariv*, 12/16/88; Glenn Frankel, "Hardline Arab Group Threatens to Take Over Palestine Uprising," MGW, 10/1/88; *Middle East Contemporary Survey*, Vol. VI: 1981–1982, "The West Bank and the Gaza Strip," pp. 371–373; FBIS-NES, 10/13/88, "Hamas Leader Interviewed on Islamic Movement," pp. 3–10.

20. David K. Shipler, *Arab and Jew: Wounded Spirits in a Promised Land* (New York and Toronto: Times Books, 1986), pp. 176–177.

21. *The Covenant of the Islamic Resistance Movement*, 8/18/88 (Arabic and English mimeographed edition, no place of publication).

22. JPI, no. 1,420, 1/23/88.

23. JPS, no. 67, Spring 1988, pp. 63–65.

24. NYT, 6/28/88.

25. NYT, 7/30/88; 7/31/88; 8/1/88; 8/2/88.

26. NYT, 8/6/88.

27. *Jerusalem Post* (hereafter JP), 8/12/88.

28. JP, 6/29/88.

29. Shukri B. Abed, "The Inward Intifada," JPI, no. 1,454, 9/17/88; JPS, no. 69, Autumn 1988, p. 202.

30. Shosh Avigail, "The Voice of Thunder/Rage," *Hadashot*, 12/9/88.

31. Amos Lavav, "Jewish-Arab Psychoanalysis," *Sof-Shavooa*, weekly supplement to *Maariv International Edition*, 12/23/88.

4

THE IMPACT OF THE UPRISING
ON ISRAELI LIFE

The Israeli public, like its leadership, was unprepared for the shock of the Intifada. Israelis had become accustomed to the periodic eruptions of violence in the West Bank and Gaza; this was the price for continued occupation, and occupation, for the person in the street, was a fact of life—albeit for many an unpleasant one. Yet continued occupation was necessitated by what the average Israeli perceived to be the country's perilous situation in a region surrounded by enemies and in a world hostile to the Jewish state. True, public opinion polls indicated that a sizable number of Israeli Jews were willing to give up parts of the occupied territories for peace, but even they regarded as unlikely, if not impossible, the realization of conditions under which they would agree to leave the West Bank and Gaza; only a handful would even consider diminishing Israeli sovereignty over the Arab sector of Jerusalem conquered in 1967.[1]

PUBLIC ATTITUDES AND PERCEPTIONS

Polls conducted since the late 1970s by organizations such as the Israel Institute of Applied Social Research indicated that the first months of the Intifada had "not shaken the decade long pattern of Israeli attitudes toward the occupied territories, despite growing criticism of the government's general handling of security problems" and of the Arabs in the territories.[2] An explanation for the consistency of public attitudes and perceptions was given in a report entitled *Israel's Options for Peace*, published in 1989 by Tel Aviv University's Jaffee Center for Strategic Studies (JCSS).[3] The report observed that the country was "bitterly divided" between those willing to accept territorial compromise—withdrawal from most but not all of the West Bank and Gaza—in return for peace, and those opposed. This division reflected the intense emotional involvement of many segments of Israeli society. It involves not merely a question of foreign and defence policy; it goes to the very heart of Israel's self-image. . . . Since the advent of the *intifada* in late December 1987, the debate has become yet more intense, and with it the growing polarization of Israeli society, to the extent that the question of the territories is now the dominant factor of the Israeli sociopolitical scene. It has already brought about a political stalemate, and is threatening the country with political and national paralysis.[4]

The split in Israeli society was reinforced by the deep mistrust and suspicion among most Jews of Arabs in general and of the Palestinians in particular—a hostility "grounded in a more fundamental Jewish suspicion toward the non-Jewish world in general." These attitudes, according to the JCSS report, derived from such factors as "the Holocaust experience . . . , an essential element of collective subconscious of the Jewish People" and seventy years of conflict with the Arabs. Although many Israeli Jews were willing to return conquered territories for peace, a large number simply did not trust the Arabs to keep their commitments; many assessed the Arab attitude toward a settlement as "not the end of the conflict but rather a ruse aimed at the destruction of Israel in stages. In this sense the term 'in return for peace' does not mean the same thing, from a psychological-cognitive point of view, to all Israelis."[5]

All public opinion surveys conducted in Israel by diverse polling organizations, Israeli and other sociologists, and by the Israeli and foreign press confirmed these basic perceptions, though with varying percentages. Some have been interpreted optimistically to indicate that public opinion is changing and that Israelis might be made more amenable to compromises for peace; other interpretations of identical data conclude pessimistically that the public is too divided to achieve a workable consensus or that hostility is too deeply ingrained to alter government policies.

A survey conducted in March 1989 for the *New York Times* by the prominent Israeli polling concern, Hanoch Smith Research Center, observed that those surveyed believed the Arabs would "commit a holocaust against the Jews in Israel" if they could; yet the poll also showed that 58 percent, the highest number in six years, were willing to open talks with the PLO "if the P.L.O. officially recognizes Israel and ceases terrorist activities." Willingness to negotiate with the Palestinian organization was qualified by deep mistrust of its leader, Yassir Arafat. The poll, conducted several months after Arafat's various declarations recognizing Israel and calling for peace negotiations, showed only 18 percent who believed that the PLO was ready to make concessions for peace.[6]

The ambivalence in Israeli attitudes toward Arabs and Palestinians, toward the future of the territories, and toward a peace settlement was reflected in perceptions of the Intifada and its aims. Most Israelis perceived the uprising only in terms of its violence and were unaware of its nonviolent aspects. Like the world at large, they saw the uprising through television images of petrol bombs, the masked shabab, and the confrontation between Israeli soldiers and screaming, stone-throwing youths. Few were aware that the Palestinian resistance involved nonpayment of taxes, boycott of Israeli products, and mass organization for communal social action. Despite the wide press coverage of IDF actions in the territories, most Israelis believed that the occupation was beneficial to the Palestinians, that it raised their living standards and taught them democracy, perhaps at the cost of some occasional discomfort. The inhabitants of the West Bank and Gaza were ungrateful for all the amenities brought by twenty years of occupation. These perceptions were reflected in the support expressed for the government's rejection of goals outlined in the fourteen points of the Intifada leadership (see Chapter 3). A poll conducted earlier in 1989 found that 77 percent of Jewish Israelis opposed the creation of a Palestinian state, believing that it would endanger Israel's security. Only 17 percent were prepared to give up "all" or "most" of the West Bank and Gaza, and 73 percent said that Israel should resist U.S. pressure to withdraw to modified 1967 boundaries. Eighty-nine percent still did not believe that Arafat was interested in peace.[7]

The Intifada did spark an explosion of public dissatisfaction with the government's handling of security and its policies in the territories. But this criticism also reflected polarization between those who believed that a tougher policy was necessary and those who favored less severe tactics. A poll taken two months after the uprising began showed that fewer than a third of the respondents believed that the government had solved the attendant security problems "very successfully" or "successfully." This was a sharp departure from the usual public approval of government security policies—approval that never before had fallen below 44 percent. All strata regardless of age, sex, ethnic origin, and political or religious identification shared in this increasing decline of confidence. On the eve of the Intifada, another poll showed that only 11 percent believed that government policy in the territories was too harsh; 36 percent felt it was just about right; and 53 percent found it too soft. Two years earlier the percentages were 5 percent, 50 percent, and 45 percent, respectively. A similar poll conducted early in 1988 found that in ten years the percentage of Israelis who believed that the "way we behave toward the Arabs in the occupied territories is not good enough" rose from only 1 percent to 22 percent. The majority, both in the 1970s and in early 1988, were divided between those who believed that Israeli conduct was "exactly as it should be" and those who thought it was "too good." Those who perceived Israeli conduct to be "not good enough" tended to be nonreligious academics of European or native Israeli origin.[8] The latter poll found no correlation between responses to "handling of security problems" and "behavior toward the Arab population in the territories." Even criticism of government occupation policies did not correspond with perceptions of Arab willingness to make peace. Since 1978 a division has persisted between the approximately 40 percent who were willing to return territory for peace and the 60 percent opposed. A 50-50 division of opinion continued over the issue of Jewish settlement in the territories, and an overwhelming 87 percent insisted that all of Jerusalem should remain under the sole jurisdiction of Israel.

The range of attitudes among soldiers sent to quell the uprising reflected the differing public perceptions of the Intifada. Often soldiers serving in the same unit, carrying out identical tasks in a single Arab village, came away with diametrically opposing views of what they saw and of the necessity for their actions.

An illustration of this polarity was seen in the accounts of two soldiers who served in the IDF unit that occupied Kabatiyeh (see Chapters 3 and 4). The diary of one, a young immigrant from England who, while a student at Cambridge, had been the national secretary of a Zionist youth movement, was highly critical.[9] Beginning with training for "life in the territories," he told of being taught how to administer "dry blows" (which don't draw blood). "There was a tremendous callousness all around to the sensitivities of what we were about to face. . . . One sign of things to come—amidst the jokes and nervous laughter there were signs of genuine excitement by some soldiers at the prospect of 'teaching them not to raise their heads.'"

According to this account the troops, upon their arrival in Kabatiya, were told to be "aggressive, purposeful, and don't let them 'take you for a ride.' Does 'take you for a ride' mean that hungry seven-year-olds who break curfew should be beaten?"

According to the diary, the curfew was more like a siege. The troops believed that "we can only speak to them in a language they understand." "They're all liars."

The diary author continued: "The lack of consensus is quite amazing, and people's views and behavior cut across sociopolitical lines.

> There are two separate issues here. Policy is not our business as soldiers. What is our business is how you carry out that policy: with sensitivity, respect, understanding and reasonableness, or with enthusiasm, sadism, glee, etc. . . .

The troops moved into Kabatiya's school to "administer" things. Desks, textbooks, school materials—all are discarded, dumped in a big pile, as the school seethes with sweating bodies. . . . The battalion commander tells us that [the inhabitants] remain under curfew until they are "broken," whatever that means. . . . An obscene situation as I chase down a side road after a nine-year-old who had spotted a piece of bread in the gutter. . . . The roughness of the commands as we scream maniacally at women to shut their curtains. Bear in mind, 11,000 residents, an average of ten people to a family, confined to boiling, cramped living quarters twenty-four hours a day. . . .

I've been branded as soft-hearted, and have been quite ignored by a fair chunk of the unit. Remarkable moment as soldiers steal vegetables from Arab fields, and can't understand when I say that you can't do that. You can't arrest ten-year-olds for picking tomatoes after curfew (their *own* tomatoes), and then laughingly take them yourself.

The biggest disillusion for me are the officers. I think they actually enjoy it: the power, the control and, above all, the humiliation.

The humiliation goes on all the time. . . . Humiliation of old men who are trying to sneak into the fields at night to save two kilos of rotting peppers, caught by my officers and sent to Jenin for "correction."

One reservist, a kibbutznik, carries out his duty as chief prison officer with great joy, and without an ounce of mercy. His philosophy is simple. "They're all liars," he tells me. So when they say they're breaking curfew because their child is ill, they are actually scheming.

One young officer pulled up with a glint in his eye, bringing in two nine-year-old boys strapped to his jeep, in the back seat and on the hood. . . .

The ultimate irony. Amidst a great cheer, an Israeli flag was hoisted to the top of the school by a group of soldiers. Quite sad that a sight which had once filled me with pride brought new feelings of shame. . . .

Tonight my first view of dehumanization. I escorted a group of teenagers to Jenin detention centre. Supposedly they had stepped into their yards during the curfew. On arrival in Jenin the guard asked me, "How many dogs have you brought?" Once the man opposite you is a dog, anything goes. . . .

Among the soldiers, a depressing routine of almost wild abandon. Everybody here makes up their own rules. The younger officers see our job here as some kind of game, and their behaviour ranges from callousness to pure sadism. . . .

Two soldiers: One man is almost ashamed of where he is serving and what he is doing. "The whole curfew is absurd and terribly painful," he says. "When a child of three looks at me with hatred, I feel ashamed at what I'm doing."

Another man feels the patrols shame him. The pain, poverty and disgrace of the residents cause him great distress. . . .

The question of morality troubles the soldiers, and they console themselves by maintaining that any other army would have created a bloodbath long ago. They're divided over whether the "democracy" in the territories is to Israel's advantage. "Only the iron fist will help here," says the first soldier, an interesting contradiction to his policy of dialogue.

Another IDF reservist who served at Kabatiya with the writer of the above diary disputed its version of events a few days later in a letter to the *Jerusalem Post*.[10] He accused the author of "hyperbole, exaggeration, distortion and pure invention." In an attempt to "correct some of the grosser distortions," the letter writer's response was limited to "first-hand knowledge—no hearsay or stories heard second-hand."

During preliminary training, according to the reservist, the soldiers "received lectures on first aid, crowd control, sabotage, communication and the role of the press." Only one passing mention was made of "dry blows" and "I never heard of it again." When troops moved into the Kabatiya school to take over four or five classrooms for their own use, the equipment and supplies were carefully moved into other rooms where they were "all neatly arranged . . . under the eye of the school caretaker." The reservist personally visited each of the rooms vacated "and scrupulously picked up any textbooks, exercise books, etc., that happened to fall out of the desks." He neatly piled all of the material and later personally handed over a few more items to the caretaker.

According to this respondent, children under sixteen were generally not taken away; as for tying a 9-year-old to the hood of a jeep: "I never saw or heard of any other similar incidents." Regarding food shortages: "During the three weeks in Kabatiya I noticed no signs of starvation. In the several homes that we entered, we found tremendous stock-piles of food."

The reservist went on to discuss the insensitivity of IDF soldiers.

Not a day passed without many and heated arguments over our role here and what we should and should not do. Not desensitizing, the opposite in fact. The duty was long and hard. Even if at the start people shouted orders, very quickly it was stopped. It was tiring and ineffective in any case. . . .

There was a general policy not to arrest women. Time, as in Israel, is very elastic. I never heard of anyone being arrested for breaking the curfew by 20 minutes. When I was on patrol we found people breaking the curfew by up to an hour. Apart from hurrying them along no further action was taken.

During one patrol I saw an officer lose his temper and slap a youth of 17 around the head several times. This was the most violent action I ever witnessed. Nevertheless, I made an official complaint to the base commander.

The response was immediate: over the field radio the officer was mentioned by name and explicitly warned not to use any violence. . . .

Again and again we were reminded that only under the most extreme and dangerous circumstances could we use live ammunition. [During a curfew,] the question naturally arose as to what was the policy regarding people we could not physically catch. The answer, with no conditions attached, was that under no circumstances were live bullets to be used. It was possible to use rubber bullets but only at ranges in excess of 10 meters.

As these two contrasting accounts of events at Kabatiya demonstrate, the attitudes and perceptions of observers could differ depending on what they read in the press, saw on television, or heard on the radio. For the average Israeli who did not serve in the regular army or the reserves, life went on as usual. In Tel Aviv, Haifa, and Ramat Gan, and even in most Jewish sectors of Jerusalem, the Intifada affected daily routines very little. Unlike the Palestinians in Gaza, the West Bank and Arab Jerusalem, most Israelis continued their normal employment, went shopping as usual, sent their children to school daily, and even enjoyed vacations abroad or in some part of the country within the Green Line. True, reserve duty was extended and now included some unpleasant tasks; it was no longer advisable and at times forbidden to venture into the West Bank or East Jerusalem; and the Arab street cleaners, waiters, dishwashers in restaurants, and agricultural workers appeared less frequently than before. But, despite occasional shortages of Arab workers, daily life seemed quite normal; cafes and nightclubs were open, and concerts, theaters, and cinemas maintained their schedules. As for events in the territories, reports about the uprising in the press and on radio and television might have been about some distant military campaign.

For many Israelis, it was the media that caused all the trouble. Were it not for the "exaggerated" reports of correspondents in the territories, the IDF would have matters well in hand. Many even accused reporters of organizing demonstrations and stone throwing for the sake of a sensational story. As the Intifada entered its seventeenth month, an IDF spokesman proclaimed that although "Israel has lost the battle for the electronic media . . . it has succeeded in stabilizing the situation in the main battlefield." The problem was, he said, that we cannot make

Israel's political standing and image . . . prettier than it is. We have learned over the last 20 years, starting with Vietnam, that the electronic media will always be on the side of the civilians in confrontation with armed forces.

It doesn't matter if we're right or wrong. That's irrelevant. We didn't learn this basic lesson in the war in Lebanon.[11]

One of Israel's leading mass communication experts, Eliyahu Tal, charged that media treatment of the Israeli response to the Intifada was often absurd and arbitrary.[12] "The very idea of deliberately using women and kids as targets for the camera is one of Arab propaganda's cleverest tricks. . . . They are beating us in the propaganda war." As an example he cited coverage of the uprising in the *New York Times*, where there was "over-exposure and overdose, leading to far greater overkill." The essence of Tal's charge was that small bits of news were "blown up out of all proportion." In contrast to the coverage of other world events, such as Iraq's killing of thousands of Kurds with poison gas, the uprising received far more coverage than warranted. Cases of rioting and bloodshed in Iraq, Iran, India, Italy, Lebanon, San Salvador, the Philippines, Sri Lanka, Kenya, and so on, "were infinitely more horrific than the Intifada." Tal's example of overdose was continuous repetition of the same story over and over again, as happened with the CBS television footage of soldiers beating an Arab (see Chapter 2).

> It was played up as if it were at least the Kennedy assassination and was featured on newscasts six times in one day, as if it were a shattering event of the decade. This is adding malice to injury and this is where you get overkill. . . . The result is character assassination of a nation and an army. . . . Actually, objective observers ought to be impressed that after nine months of riots and after so many thousands of rocks and petrol bombs hurled at innocent Jewish bus and car passengers, only 200 Arabs lost their lives. In any other country, including Britain and the U.S., such goings-on would have elicited a far greater death toll.

Tal and others attributed what they perceived to be media exaggeration of events to anti-Israel and even anti-Jewish sentiment, to Israel's leniency in dealing with reporters, and to the European tendency to expect Indians, Filipinos, Ugandans, and Zulus to murder and mutilate each other but not to accept the use of even limited force when Westerners are caught up "in the confrontation with Third-World populations run amok."[13]

One consequence of this view was the decision by the IDF periodically to close off the territories to both Israeli and foreign journalists. Yosef Goell, one of the principal writers for the *Jerusalem Post*, accused American television reporters of descending to the level of "show-biz," pandering to "our more prurient sides and our sick mesmerization with sights of cruelty, violence, and suffering." Therefore, he urged the government to seriously consider "closing the arena of battle in the territories to a very specific part of media coverage"—namely, television. Meanwhile, the "far less-inflammatory printed press" should be permitted to cover the territories "as a guardian against ever-present temptations in such situations to descend to untrammelled barbarism."[14]

Several Likud cabinet ministers agreed that both the foreign and the domestic media were the true source of the problem. Their very presence incited the Arabs to riot, according to this view. In an editorial on the subject, the *Jerusalem Post* observed that those who blamed the media believed that without it

> there would be no Palestinian rebellion. Or at least, there would be no international backlash to what Israel must do to check it. Without the media, Ronald Reagan, for one, would never have learned what was going on in the territories. . . . What they [Likud cabinet members] would propose, presumably, is that the country, or at least Gaza and the West Bank, be turned into closed military zones . . . for as long as the present emergency lasts. . . . Israel itself, or at least the bleeding hearts in its midst, would be spared the anguish that goes with the discovery of a lost innocence, and the fear of a world-wide backlash calculated to delight the country's worst enemies.[15]

IMPACT ON THE MILITARY

Despite the tendency of many Israelis to perceive the Intifada as a huge media event, it had a traumatic impact on a large number of soldiers who served in the territories. The effect was so serious that it led many officers and observers outside the IDF to be concerned about possible deterioration of military efficiency.

Early in the Intifada, there were enough signs of stress among the occupation troops to warrant recruitment of additional psychologists to deal with the situation (see Chapter 2). A former IDF chief psychologist, Dr. Reuven Gal, now head of the Israel Institute for Military Studies, identified three types of stress: "moral stress, caused by pangs of conscience at being in the territories at all and the methods employed to put down the Intifada; psychological stress arising from the 'stunning' encounter with violence and aggression; [and] operational stress in the field where soldiers are required to carry out duties they were not trained for."[16]

Dr. Gal compared the Intifada with the 1982 war in Lebanon, the other major military operation undertaken by Israel that was racked by controversy. Both operations were regarded as detrimental to the IDF; both were tied to questions of legitimacy. In Lebanon there was controversy over goals and in the Intifada, over the means used to quell the uprising. "Everyone agrees that we must put an end to the riots,

Israeli soldiers on patrol. Photo by *Palestine Perspectives.*

the turbulence. But, should we use plastic bullets, clubs, rubber bullets, the gravel-throwing machine?"

Dr. Gal further observed that the most important asset of a military organization is not its equipment but its personnel. "Soldiers must not have even the smallest doubt about the absolute imperative of the use of the army. They must be convinced that there is no alternative, that they *must* be sent to fight." Given the uncertainty about the situation in the territories, Dr. Gal found it "quite surprising just how well most of the soldiers have coped." They "committed fewer abuses during the Intifada than psychologists might have expected in view of the tremendous stress."

Two other senior researchers at Bar Ilan University concluded that soldiers serving in the territories need not necessarily suffer any "negative psychic changes" as a result of their experiences. "The influence of war on the individual is incomparably smaller than experiences that manifest fear or pain in civilian life, as, for instance, a dog bite."[17]

Given the fact that the IDF reflected the composition of Israel's Jewish population, it was not surprising that soldiers serving in the territories had greatly varying perceptions of their role as occupiers. These differences among the troops were enough, in and of themselves, to cause stress. Furthermore, the army high command perceived the task of suppressing the Intifada as one for which its men were unprepared and untrained, a task in which the army should not have been involved (see Chapter 2). The IDF commanders seemed to be politically neutral and did not speak out on questions about the future of the territories, although some were known to favor return of the West Bank and Gaza for peace and others were opposed. Views of the high command were reflected in the variety of positions taken by former generals during the 1988 election campaign. The overt position of most officers was that the task assigned them in the territories, though unpleasant, was necessary. Even those who favored conditional withdrawal and believed that only a political solution could end the uprising argued that resistance to the occupation had to be suppressed prior to a negotiated settlement. The question was, How much force could or should be used.

Demoralization set in when it became evident that the politicians under whose orders the army operated could provide no answers to questions either about the future or about present policies, such as the use of force. Differences over these questions between the two parties controlling the NUG—Labor and Likud—led to unclear policy directives and frequently made the IDF the focal point of attack by politicians. Some accused its commanders of indecisiveness and of exercising too much restraint; others charged that the army was too brutal and heavy-handed. Technically, the IDF was capable of dealing with civil unrest as harshly as Syria's President Hafez al-Asad in the city of Hama or King Hussein during the 1970 Palestinian uprising in Jordan. In both instances, thousands of dissidents were slaughtered in only a few weeks. The question facing Israel was just how fine a balance should be kept between restraint and the use of force. As one officer commented, the army could put down the Intifada in short order, but "the people of Israel would not allow it."

At times, criticism of the IDF high command from militant nationalists reached a pitch of hysteria. During April 1989 the Likud MK Yehoshua Saguy, a former IDF intelligence chief who quit the service after being criticized for his role in the 1982 Sabra and Shatilla massacre, blamed the uprising on Chief-of-Staff Dan Shomron. "You created the Intifada with your own hands," he accused General Shomron at a Knesset committee briefing. "You did not give the right orders to the army. You bear all the blame for it. Had you done your duty, you would have come to the political leadership with operational proposals which would have done away with the uprising in a matter of days. You hide behind the politician's skirts, and claim that IDF policy was in their hands. You are the first chief of general staff to have come to the cabinet with no operational proposals—empty-handed. . . . You will go down in history as the chief of the general staff of the Intifada." Saguy even held Shomron accountable for the U.S. political pressure on Prime Minister Shamir, who at the time was discussing the situation with officials in Washington.[18]

When questioned further by other MKs about the operational limitations imposed on him, Shomron replied: "There are things you cannot do in a society like ours. If you do them, you would divide the nation."

A Labor MK, also an ex-general who had been a top officer in the military government, defended Shomron and the army, stating that all Israeli governments since 1967 had to bear blame for the uprising because they "had ignored the political problems posed by the territories."

When Shomron attempted to analyze the causes of the Intifada, he was also attacked by Likud MKs. During May 1989, after a shoot-out between Palestinian gunmen and Israeli soldiers, the chief-of-staff declared the incident "an exceptional case of a terrorist group. This is not the Intifada." The Intifada, he stated, was "basically a popular uprising." The general's attempt to disassociate "terrorist" actions from the Intifada aroused the ire of several Likud MKs, who called the distinction "unfortunate." One of them complained: "A chief of staff who treats the Intifada as a civilian uprising can't fight it effectively, and can't inspire his soldiers to put it down."[19]

Politicians constantly attempted to make political capital of the Intifada at the expense of the army, the chief-of-staff, and the defense minister. From the very first days, Likud blamed Labor; and since Defense Minister Rabin was a leader of the Labor party, he was frequently attacked (see Chapter 2 and below). Likud cabinet minister Ariel Sharon, formerly a general and a highly controversial political figure, charged Rabin with "inordinate mildness" in his policies. If Sharon had his way, there would be mass deportations and demolition of all houses belonging to Arab rioters, convicted or suspected. Yet Sharon's recommendations were mild compared to those demanded by the Council of Jewish Settlements representing West Bank settlers. They were supported by Justice Minister Abraham Sharir and Itzhak Moda'i, both Likud MKs who scorned those believing that only political measures could end the uprising. They argued that it could be crushed immediately if the defense minister and chief-of-staff were more determined.[20]

Ironically, while demands for firmer action were descending on the army, it ran into fiscal difficulty. The high command found that the costs of the Intifada were undercutting maintenance and training programs. Unless reimbursed for expenses incurred in the territories, costs such as pay for extended periods of service by reservists, the IDF would have to cut back on procurement programs. Stockpiles of arms and ammunition had been allowed to run down, and the state comptroller criticized the defense ministry for depleting its stores in order to soften the blow of budget cuts.[21]

An important casualty of the Intifada was IDF credibility. Traditionally, the army in Israel has been above public criticism, and its own accounts of activities had been taken at face value. Now, an Israeli correspondent observed: "The vaunted Israeli norm of truthfulness has taken a beating during the *intifada*. . . . Serious questions have been raised about the reliability of reports from the field, and the degree to which IDF guidelines on the use of force and firepower are transmitted and carried out." Correspondent Greenberg noted that on several occasions the IDF's investigation of discipline breaches was hampered by the natural inclination of soldiers and units to gloss over unpleasant incidents, cover them up, and not report them. Despite the appointment of a military police officer to investigate allegations of excesses, "the conclusion to be drawn from all this is that our traditional perception of the IDF, its performance and credibility, have to undergo revision in light of what is happening in the territories." It appeared to Greenberg that senior officers had often lost control of events in the field, "that lines of communication have been blocked, and that communication is lax." Several officers were suspended for failure to report incidents, leading to a loss of credibility in IDF accounts. "The IDF's traditional commitment to reliability and accountability has apparently been subordinated to the fight against the uprising, and news is often given or withheld in accordance with the army's goals." It often seemed as though the army was underplaying the scope of the unrest to project a picture of "relative calm." As a result of this unfortunate situation, the trust that the IDF had earned over the years "must be replaced by a realistic and balanced assessment of what we are hearing from the army, which is sometimes based on incomplete information, or deliberate withholding of facts." Often information about the Intifada from Palestinian sources proves to be "no less reliable than the IDF." The army itself should be concerned, for the situation "means that the era of *a priori* trust in the information delivered by the IDF is over." This, Greenberg believed, was a blow not only to the army's and Israel's public relations but also, "in the end, to the country's security."[22]

The ambiguity concerning the army's role in the territories, and the conflicting perceptions of the country's leaders about such issues, had their inevitable impact on morale. While officers of the high command differed about the extent to which morale suffered, there was a consensus from the defense minister down to platoon-level noncommissioned officers that the Intifada was a blow to IDF effectiveness. Rabin told *Jane's Defence Weekly* of London that "riot control and chasing children who throw stones is not the most effective way of training a combat soldier."[23]

Tension between the IDF and its critics, especially West Bank Jewish settlers, became so great that in June 1989 the country's most unlikely allies, the left-wing Hashomer Hatzair youth group affiliated with Mapam and Gush Emunim, signed a joint statement condemning attacks on the IDF and calling on groups from both left and right "to respect the IDF's impartiality and cease incitement against it."

The number of conscientious objectors increased, although fewer refused service than during the 1982–1983 war in Lebanon. Some 170 soldiers and officers rejected service in Lebanon on grounds of conscience, but fewer than half that number refused to report for duty in the territories. Several groups, most notably Yesh Gvul, organized and assisted conscientious objectors. The military often attempted to negotiate with objectors, to help them avoid difficulties and obviate the long bureaucratic process that would be necessary in dealing with conscientious objection. Officers often took it upon themselves to assign individuals with scruples about serving in the West Bank and Gaza to tasks that did not involve direct contact with Arab civilians, to post them within the Green Line, or to excuse them from reserve duty.

There were more potential COs than the number of those who actually refused duty in the territories. Within the first six months of the Intifada, more than 100 twelfth-grade students about to become eligible for military service signed a letter to Defense Minister Rabin saying that they would refuse to carry out "acts of oppression and occupation" in the territories. A spokesman for the group said that only one of the ten who were later drafted was assigned to the territories. He stood his ground, was jailed and released after a few weeks, and then was reassigned within the Green Line. Many youngsters would have signed the letter but felt that there was no alternative to keeping the territories. One who did sign was undecided until he reached the conclusion that the dilemma he faced in serving in the territories was greater than that he faced by obeying orders. "I would be very angry if they started throwing stones at me and cursing me, and maybe for that second I'd want to put bullets in their heads. But when I ask myself why they're doing it, I realize they have good reasons which we have given them."[24]

Conscientious objectors received much wider moral support than their number would indicate. One of the country's leading intellectuals, Yeshayahu Leibowitz, an octogenarian Hebrew University professor of chemistry as well as a religious philosopher, called for a mass movement of refusal to serve in the territories and lashed out at critics of the government who, although they opposed the occupation, withheld "full moral backing" to those who refused service for reasons of conscience. Leibowitz, an Orthodox Jew, renowned as a curmudgeon and gadfly of the establishment, attacked the left for failing to understand that it was fighting not a legitimate government but, rather, a nondemocratic state, and that continued occupation would lead to "active fascism" and an "all-out war with the entire Arab world."[25]

After more than a year of service in the West Bank and Gaza, disaffection with their assignment began to spread among many reservists. By early 1989 several units demonstrated against what some termed "their illogical and immoral burden of reserve duty in the territories." The wives of a paratroop reserve battalion also lodged a complaint with the high command charging that reserve duty was "not being equitably distributed among the country's army population."[26] Although these protests were far from mass mutiny, they alerted the high command to the deterioration of morale and to the possibility of increasing ineffectiveness of the military machine in the years ahead.

The seriousness of the morale problem was underscored in 1989 at a conference of soldiers attended by reserve commanders from the left-wing Kibbutz Artzi movement and General Amram Mitzna, himself a kibbutz member. The soldiers published a booklet called *Si'ah Lohamim 1989* (Soldiers' Reflections 1989) based on interviews with those who had served in the territories. It was intended to be a new version of *Soldiers' Reflections* published after the 1967 Six-Day War—that is, a candid exposé of fighters' inner feelings, expectations, and fears about battle. Today the situation is much more difficult, many of them said. Now,

there is nothing to be ashamed of if they say about us, "we shoot and we cry." When . . . you are obliged to perform duties which are against your conscience, against your education and your worldview, and when you don't know whether you will accomplish your mission from the military point of view, it is not a disgrace to cry. It's much more honorable than saying "we shoot and we laugh." A spokesman for those participating in the meeting warned General Mitzna: "We have reached a moment of truth, a moment in which the army must listen to us. . . . We are reaching the limits of our abilities.[27]

Experts differed in their evaluations of the impact of the Intifada on the military. In its 1989 edition of *Strategic Survey*, the International Institute for Strategic Studies (IISS) maintained that the IDF's capacity for dealing with external aggression was not "seriously affected." Although repeated riot control assignments had induced a "degree of rot," it was not sufficient "to merit serious concern." However, warned the *Survey*, disruption of normal training routine was "potentially highly detrimental to the country's military readiness—and hence its deterrent image—in Arab (particularly Syrian) eyes." The use of the IDF for police duties in the territories was affecting morale in ways "impossible to quantify." The Intifada was "remarkable" in scope and duration, according to the IISS. Both Israel and the PLO leadership might "find themselves losing control of the Palestinians in the occupied territories" if a solution were not found soon.[28]

Martin van Creveld, an analyst who frequently writes on Israeli and Middle East military affairs, took a more pessimistic view. He was greatly concerned about the IDF's fighting spirit. Because of the questionable legitimacy of operations in the territories and the tremendous disparity between the power of the IDF and that of the Palestinians, attempts to suppress the uprising "put the IDF in a false position. What used to be one of the world's finest fighting forces is rapidly degenerating into a fourth-class police organization. To realize the way such a force will fight when confronted with a real army, we need look no further than the Argentineans in the Falkland Islands."[29]

THE INTIFADA AND ISRAELI POLITICS

As the November 1988 election for Israel's Twelfth Knesset approached, it was clear that the Intifada was one of the most important issues, if not the key one. Debates between Labor and Likud, the two dominant parties, emphasized the uprising, which was also the dominant theme in the campaigns of several smaller factions. The Intifada focused attention on broader issues of national importance, such as peace, security, territory, and relations with the Arabs—issues that had not been so salient in recent elections. As noted previously, Likud politicians castigated Labor for its relatively "moderate" approach to the uprising and for the willingness of many leaders of the Labor party to resolve the Arab-Israel conflict by exchanging territory for a peace settlement. Most militant Likud leaders, such as Ariel Sharon and Yitzhak Moda'i, even blamed Labor for causing the Intifada. If Likud were fully in charge, they blustered, the uprising would be ended in a week. Therefore, vote for Likud!

Many leaders of the Labor party reversed the argument, charging that Likud's desire for territorial aggrandizement and the continued call by several of its militants for annexation exacerbated an already explosive situation in the territories. Likud policies toward the occupation were counterproductive and dangerous, they asserted.

Labor, however, was at a disadvantage in the argument, because its number-two leader, Defense Minister Rabin, was responsible for policy in the territories. Furthermore, the party was split into factions. The most militantly nationalist faction followed a political line on territories and peace not much different than Likud's. Whereas differences among Likud leaders on these issues were not significant, Labor was divided between hawks and doves. Some of the latter would make substantial territorial concessions for peace and would negotiate with the PLO to end the Intifada.

Within Likud, it often seemed that politicians were trying to outbid each other as militant nationalists, using the Intifada to bludgeon those less patriotic than themselves. Prime Minister Shamir constantly reiterated that suppression of the Intifada was a matter of life or death for Israel. He selected incidents, such as Beita or the burning of trees by Palestinians during the summer of 1988, to emphasize that the uprising was not about territory or a Palestinian state but about Israel's very existence. The main efforts of the Arabs "were devoted to ending the Jewish government in Jerusalem," he told a forum in July. Shamir insisted that the Labor party was responsible for splitting the Jewish people and weakening Israel through its support for an international peace conference, one of the fourteen UNLU demands.[30]

Although the Likud mainstream resonated with fervent nationalist rhetoric, a few members joined Moshe Amirav, member of the Herut Central Committee, in a call for negotiations with leaders of the Intifada (see Chapter 2). Amirav, who was expelled from the party for his dovish views, was joined by four other Central Committee members in the call for negotiations. The Likud mayor of Tel Aviv, Shlomo Lahat, another ex-general, sparked controversy in January with his proposal for wholesale Israeli withdrawal from Gaza and the West Bank. In a radio broadcast, he said that Israel should invite Jordan's King Hussein to take over the territories.[31]

According to polls conducted by the Continuing Survey of the Israel Institute of Applied Social Research and the Communications Institute of the Hebrew University prior to the election, the Intifada boosted the right. The public mood since the Intifada had become more pessimistic about the prospects for peace—prospects that garnered "the lowest rating in years." The polls indicated that there was an increase in patriotism and confidence in the army's ability to impose order. Paradoxically, while there was more willingness to relinquish some part of the West Bank in return for peace (from 54 percent of those polled in March 1987 to 62 percent in June 1988), there was also support for continuing Jewish settlement in the territories. Despite the increased willingness to concede territory for peace, "the overall impression is one of self-justification and stoic acceptance of an unending reality that requires 'management.'" On the whole, "it seems fair to say that the Intifada has strengthened the right more than the left."[32] (See Tables 4.1 and 4.2 for additional poll results.)

Small parties on the right took positions on issues related to the uprising similar to those of Likud but without any qualifications. While

Table 4.1: Recent Changes of Opinion on Selected Issues and Direction of Change (%)

		Direction of Change	
Issue	Changed Opinion Recently	% Believe More Than Before	% Believe Less Than Before
Army's ability to bring order to territories	64	66	34
Likelihood of peace with Arabs	62	32	68
Resilience of State	61	57	43
Likelihood of Palestinian State	58	43	57
Need for censorship of radio-TV news	57	68	32
Army's morality	54	67	33
Continue (Jewish) settlements in territories	53	53	47
Arabs in territories have fared well in 20 years of Israeli rule	53	68	32
Credibility of TV news	51	39	61
Trust Israeli leadership	47	21	79

Source: The *Jerusalem Post International Edition*, no. 1,451 (week ending August 27, 1988).

Table 4.2: Direction of Recent Changes by Ideological "Closeness" to Left and Right

	Feel Close to Labor and Parties of Left		Feel Close to Likud and Parties of Right	
	% Believe More	% Believe Less	% Believe More	% Believe Less
Likelihood of peace	42	58	23	77
Likelihood of Palestinian State	55	45	34	66
Resilience of State	52	48	66	34
My party's chances	55	45	67	33

Source: The *Jerusalem Post International Edition*, no. 1,451 (week ending August 27, 1988).

the ideology of Likud leaders was based on territorial unification of the Land of Israel (all of mandatory Palestine), Prime Minister Shamir did not use the term "annexation" during the campaign, implying that this was an option to be determined in the future. The more militantly nationalist Tehiya, Tsomet, Moledet, National Religious, and Kach parties all demanded immediate annexation and tougher measures to suppress the uprising.

The Moledet (Motherland) party, formed during 1988 in response to the Intifada, called for the "transfer" of Arabs from the territories. The concept of "transfer," virtually unmentionable in "respectable" political circles before 1988, became a viable option for many after the Intifada erupted. The founder of Moledet, ex-general Rehovam Ze'evi, argued that "transfer" was a humane and practical solution that would obviate

Israel's need to deal with millions of Arabs within its borders. This resembled the program of Rabbi Meir Kahana's Kach (Thus!) party, which demanded removal not only of all Arabs from the territories but also of those who were Israeli citizens living within the Green Line. Israel's Central Election Committee and the Supreme Court disqualified Kach prior to the election, charging that its program violated an Israeli law against racism. The Moledet party, however, did not take a position against Israeli Arab citizens; it called for a "voluntary transfer" from the occupied territories. "Transfer," stated Ze'evi, is "Zionism by definition"; but out of deference to Holocaust survivors who were shocked by the term, he preferred to speak of "the agreed-upon exchange of populations." The plan, he argued, was humane because it would remove Arabs from the battle zone between the IDF and the enemy armies. Israel's history legitimizes the concept, as shown by disappearance of more than 400 villages since the 1940s and their replacement with Jewish settlements. When questioned about the implementation of the plan, Ze'evi responded that it would be easy to make transfer voluntary as Israel became "unattractive" for Arabs. If they faced unemployment and shortages of land and water, "then, in a legitimate way, and in accordance with the Geneva convention, we can create the necessary conditions for separation."[33]

Tsomet (Land of Israel Loyalists' Alliance), founded by former chief-of-staff Raphael (Raful) Eitan, held its first national convention in May 1988 and was addressed by Prime Minister Shamir. Though not a member, Shamir approved of Tsomet as a part of the "national camp" that "would relay the message that the people of Israel had returned to their former land and would not trade one inch of it away." Raful's followers admired him for his forthrightness. "He can't be bought. He speaks simply," explained a supporter at the convention.

> He's the only one who can raise us up from being a bent and bowed flock, and teach us how to kill, and killing's the only way we'll ensure we stay here. Everyone's done it—the Americans killed the Indians; the Germans killed until they united their country, the British killed in the Falklands, and they weren't ashamed, they were proud to do it. It's the only way, and Raful is the only one![34]

The Israel Institute of Applied Social Research Continuing Survey determined in a June poll that 49 percent of Jewish adults believed transfer would "allow the democratic and Jewish nature of Israeli society to be maintained." Two-thirds of Likud supporters and a third of those in Labor chose transfer in preference to two other options, "Give them equal rights" and "Relinquish the territories," which were supported

Table 4.3: Replies to the questions, "If the territories remain under Israeli rule, what should be done to preserve the (a) democratic and (b) Jewish character of the state?"

	Democratic Character	Jewish Character
Give/deny rights to Arabs	21 (Give)	17 (Deny)
Cause Arabs to leave ("transfer")	49	48
Relinquish territories	28	32
Democratic/Jewish character not important	3	
	100%	100%

Source: The *Jerusalem Post International Edition*, no. 1,450 (week ending August 20, 1988).

by 20 and 30 percent of the population, respectively (see Table 4.3). Questions in the poll were introduced with the statement: "It is sometimes said that the problem of the Arab population in the territories constitutes a threat to the democratic character, and to the Jewish character, of the State." When asked "How important is it to you that the democratic character of the state be maintained, i.e., that every resident . . . have equal rights?" 50 percent replied "very important," 33 percent "important," and 18 percent "not so important." As for preserving the Jewish character of the state, 75 percent answered "very important" and 22 percent "important," a total larger than the 82 percent concerned about the importance of a democratic state.[35]

Small left-of-center parties that qualify as potential allies of Labor, the Citizens' Rights Movement (CRM), Mapam, and Shinui sharply criticized the oppressive character of the occupation. By the end of 1988 all of them were calling for negotiations to end the Intifada along the lines of the UNLU's fourteen points. The CRM had previously been rather reserved about recognition of a Palestinian state; it now urged the government to take the plunge.

The Democratic Front for Peace and Equality, dominated by the Communists, and the Progressive List for Peace, also secular and inter-ethnic, received more than 90 percent of their votes from Israel's Arabs; consequently, both supported the Intifada and its demands. As a result of both Labor's support for IDF actions in the territories and Rabin's "iron fist" policy, the party's only Arab Knesset member, Abd al-Wahab Darwasha, broke away to form his own separate Arab Democratic party (ADP).

Given the major role of rhetoric about the Intifada during the 1988 campaign, it is surprising how little it affected election results. The outcome found the electorate divided as before between two large sectors: the national camp, comprising Likud and its smaller, more militant, territorialist allies on the right, and Labor with support from smaller factions to its left. Because these two blocs have relatively incompatible policies for dealing with the territories, the elections produced another stalemate on issues related to national security and the Intifada. The greatest surprise of the election was the large number of seats won by the religious bloc of four disparate factions. With their eighteen seats, these parties could have held the balance in a new coalition, but their demands for entering the government were too high. Instead, Likud and Labor formed a new National Unity Government (NUG), with Likud gaining slightly more power than in the previous unity coalition between 1984 and 1988. Because three of the four religious parties were indifferent to foreign affairs and territorial issues, they would probably not have affected policy regarding the Intifada even had they obtained a significant role in the new cabinet.

THE EMERGENCE OF NEW PEACE GROUPS

The number of organizations in Israel concerned with peace is prodigious. Although their total membership is not large, these groups have high visibility and are often influential beyond their numbers. In April 1988 the Hebrew daily *Ha-Aretz* published a list of 46 groups. Another account by Myron J. Aronoff estimated that some two dozen emerged after the Intifada began.[36] One of the most influential was the Council for Peace and Security formed in 1988 at the initiative of the JCSS director in Tel Aviv University, ex-general Aharon Yariv, a former chief of military intelligence. By mid-1988 the Council included 36 retired or reserve major-generals, 84 retired brigadiers, and more than 100 retired colonels. The organization's secretary was Moshe Amirav, the former Herut member expelled for his dovish views. The new Council argued that "Israel is strong enough to risk conceding territory. This is preferable to holding onto it with the palpable continuing harm that it does to national security." In an article explaining the Council's rationale, Amirav emphasized that while "strategic depth" was an asset, continuing occupation was eroding the strength of the IDF, draining its power, and inviting a new and bigger war. Politically, continued occupation undermined the national consensus and threatened to sabotage the "central theme of Zionism—the establishment of a Jewish state—because of the large number of Palestinians who would be incorporated under Israel's control." The group called on the government to negotiate with any representative body of the Palestinians (including the PLO) willing to recognize Israel and enter peace talks. Few could dispute this group's loyalty, question its motivations, or accuse its members of compromising national security. Its views corresponded with those of several leading Labor MKs, some of whom joined the Council.[37]

The Intifada had a profound effect on Israel's largest and one of its oldest dovish groups, Peace Now, established more than a decade ago. Peace Now was perceived by more radical groups as being establishment oriented because many of its members were affiliated with Labor and, before the Intifada, had refrained from expressing overt support for a Palestinian state and negotiations with the PLO. The leaders had argued that "a rash radicalization of its slogans might push the movement to the fringe of the Israeli body politic and thus decrease its impact."[38] Rather than attacking the army or the officer corps from which many in the organization had come, Rabin became the chief target of criticism. While Peace Now did not go as far as Yesh Gvul had done in urging and supporting conscientious objection, it demanded "a clear-cut and humane definition . . . of the moral norms and limitations on the use of force." Soldiers were urged "to refrain from actions and even to disobey orders which were blatantly illegal and unnecessarily cruel."[39] By the end of 1988 several Peace Now leaders were taking a much more direct and overt position on political issues. Most now called for Israel's evacuation from the territories and recognition of the PLO. Peace Now successfully organized several public protests against government policy toward the uprising—meetings that were attended by tens of thousands of people, the largest since those in 1982 against the war in Lebanon.

Peace Now's relative caution in dealing with many controversial issues made it suspect in the eyes of more radical critics. Whereas it sought to enlist support from mainstream Israel—that is, mainstream as represented by the Labor movement—groups such as Ad Kan (Till Here), Dai l'Kibbush (End the Occupation), Hal'ah Ha-Kibbush (Down with the Occupation), Kav Adom (Red Line), Yesh Gvul (There's a Limit) (see Appendix 12), and the Twenty First Year were far more confrontational toward both the Likud and the Labor governments. Some of these, and a few of the forty other peace groups, were established to protest against the war in Lebanon; several were formed after Lebanon but before the Intifada to protest the occupation, and a few were created in response to government policies after the uprising began. Most were formed by university faculty, writers, and other intellectuals.

The Twenty First Year, founded in January 1988, had the broadest perspective and adopted the most far-reaching program. Its *Covenant for the Struggle against the Occupation* declared that after twenty-one years of occupation, Israel was losing its democratic character and that the situation was not only deplorable for the Palestinians but had a pernicious effect on all aspects of Israeli society. According to the Twenty First Year covenant, "The occupation has become an insidious fact of our lives." Its impact was felt on Israel's economy, the educational system, the civilian judiciary, and on culture, language, and political thought.

The Hebrew language, for instance, was being contaminated because it was "harnessed to the imperatives of the occupation. It has been called upon to provide a misleadingly benign vocabulary to anesthetize the repression and flagrant violations of human rights."[40] The Twenty First Year sought to alert Israelis to the process by which government policies in the territories were being widely accepted; the public was unaware of subtle changes in their own attitudes and perceptions. In teaching about the occupation, schools referred to the West Bank as Judea and Samaria; maps no longer showed the Green Line separating Israel from the territories; patriotic events such as Independence Day emphasized Israel's military might rather than its cultural achievements; and Jewish industries received tax rebates for their operations in the territories. The Twenty First Year supported Yesh Gvul in assisting soldiers who refused to serve in the West Bank and Gaza; its members advocated a "strategy of refusal" to collaborate in any aspect of the occupation; and it established seminars for youths of military age advising them as to how to challenge the status quo. Education committees met with teachers to diffuse information in the schools. Meetings with Palestinians were arranged so that the members could "witness the occupation" and learn of the Palestinians' problems, travails, and hopes. Protest demonstrations, such as the sit-in of several days outside Ansar III, were organized against the government. The organization also planned to boycott products made by Jewish settlements in the territories and to arrange mock trials of conscientious objectors.

In October 1988 the Israeli newspaper *Hadashot* published a satirical note on how the Intifada distorted everyday language. When the deputy chairman of the Israel Broadcasting Authority suggested that the term "collaborators" be replaced by "Arabs who desire peace," MK Yossi Sarid of the CRM mocked the proposal with the suggestion that the following changes also be adopted: curfew—an evening at home with the family; plastic bullets—sedatives; demolition of homes—neighborhood rehabilitation; deportations—sabbaticals; sealing homes—remodeling homes; and Intifada leadership—chiefs of gangs.[41]

Several women's groups formed to protest against the occupation, to assist soldiers who refused service and Palestinians injured by IDF actions, and to raise public consciousness about events during the uprising and their consequences for Israeli life. These included Israel Women Against the Occupation, Women for Women Political Prisoners, and Women in Black. The last group was formed during January 1988 in Jerusalem and was modeled on the actions of protesting mothers in the Buenos Aires Plaza del Mayo. Later, identical groups were formed in Tel Aviv and Haifa. The Women in Black held weekly protest vigils in each of these cities at a prominent place in the center of town. The

The weekly vigil of the "women in black" in Paris Square, West Jerusalem. The sign says "Dai-le kibush" ("End the occupation"). Photo by Deena Hurwitz.

demonstrators remained silent but were frequently taunted with sexual comments by males.

Some organizations were created for a very specific purpose like the Committee for Beita established in May 1988. Its members sought to rebuild houses damaged or destroyed by the IDF during its punitive attack on this West Bank village (see Chapter 2). The Committee undertook a legal and financial campaign to aid Beita residents and oppose the influence of extremist Jewish settlers on government policy.

A small group of Orthodox Jews actively opposed the occupation. They were organized in Oz v'Shalom (Courage and Peace)/Netivot Shalom (Paths of Peace), formed in 1975 to counteract the growing influence of Gush Emunim. Members placed major emphasis on pre-serving Jewish values and Torah principles, which they perceive to be, "above all, peace and justice." Some members of Oz v'Shalom were active in Meimad (Religious Center Camp), a politically moderate Or-thodox party formed prior to the 1988 election to counter the militant nationalism and religious zealotry of other Orthodox parties. However, Meimad failed to win sufficient votes for even a single Knesset seat.

The more than forty peace groups varied on the basis of function and degree of radicalism. Before the PLO publicly recognized Israel, some groups were reluctant to establish contact with the organization or to support a Palestinian state. On occasion, several groups collaborated in demonstrations or other protest activities. Some of the most radical groups appealed to Israel's friends abroad to pressure their governments to intervene against brutality in the territories and to initiate negotiations with the PLO.

While these groups represented but a fringe of Israeli society, they raised public consciousness about the Intifada and Israeli-Palestinian relations. They included many of Israel's leading scholars, writers, artists, musicians, scientists, soldiers, and politicians. Consequently, their messages were listened to and reported in the media. Their role in Israeli society was similar to that of the anti–Vietnam War protesters in the United States during the 1960s and 1970s—a vanguard role that could profoundly affect the nation's policies in the future.

Among the notable "converts" to the peace camp were former Foreign Minister Abba Eban and Dan Almagor, the colorful television personality. Almagor, a performer and song writer who composed the anthems of several famous IDF units, had become an Israeli institution—"the symbol of everything Israelis are proud of, the personification of the sentiments expressed in the early Israeli folk songs." After years as the darling of Israel's elite combat units, Almagor experienced a sudden conversion; on the first anniversary of the Intifada, he appeared at a demonstration against the occupation held in Tel Aviv. To the surprise of all, he held forth on the "war crimes" of the IDF in the territories and called for negotiations with the PLO. For days, the Israeli press commented on this amazing turnabout. In interviews, Almagor told of his initial hesitation to confront Israel with the painful truths that had pricked his conscience for some time. "No longer to please and to lead a comfortable life; no longer to be silent." Now he was prepared to burn all bridges behind him. "When people like me already speak out," he said, "things are really going too far." After several weeks of his new persona, he was discussed in the Knesset. Defense Minister Rabin announced that Dan Almagor would no longer be called for reserve duty in the IDF Education Corps, because "a person who is accusing our soldiers of murdering children is not fit to educate them."[42]

THE INTIFADA AND THE ISRAELI ARABS

Israel's 800,000 Arab citizens, about 18 percent of the total population within the Green Line, have been greatly affected by the Intifada. As many Israeli Arabs had relatives living in the occupied territories, they naturally sympathized with the plight of those under occupation. Many were more than merely sympathetic, taking an active role in the uprising or giving material support—food, clothing, blankets, money, etc.—to help besieged towns, villages, and refugee camps. Though citizens of Israel, most did not feel that assisting their compatriots compromised their loyalty—an attitude much like that of the Diaspora Jews toward the Jewish State. To a large extent, the role of Israeli Arabs in the Intifada reflected resentment against the position to which they were relegated in Israeli society, a position of second-class citizens. Rebellion against this status was intensified and strengthened by the uprising. In effect, the Intifada crossed the Green Line, from the Palestinians in Gaza and the West Bank to the Arab citizens of Israel. The result was mutual reinforcement. Whereas Arabs in the territories were fighting to end the occupation and for independence, the Israeli Arabs were demanding full integration and equal rights with other Israeli citizens.

The economic and social discrimination against Israeli Arabs was underscored in the 1988 report *Conditions and Status of the Arabs in Israel* funded by the Ford Foundation and sponsored by the International Center for Peace in the Middle East. Research for the document was undertaken by an Arab-Jewish team directed by Haifa University Professor Henry Rosenfeld. The researchers concluded that Israeli Arabs, though equal in theory, were secondary citizens in practice.

Since the 1980s, the report noted, the incomes of more than 40 percent of Arab households were below the poverty line. Attempts by the National Insurance Institute to compensate for the erosion of income among Israel's impoverished people favored Jewish families over their Arab fellow citizens. During the 1970s and 1980s Arab housing problems became acute. The number of Arab families living in extremely crowded conditions increased, whereas in the Jewish community it decreased. More than a quarter of all Arab families lived in highly crowded conditions compared to 1.1 percent of Jewish families. In some areas within Israel, Arab families were crowded into shacks and huts; in the vast majority of Arab villages there were severe sanitation problems caused by poor— or nonexistent—sewage networks. There were no housing projects for Arabs, only minimal mortgage assistance and very limited availability of land for construction. The Arab educational system in Israel was underdeveloped, short of classrooms, and overcrowded; it also lacked equipment and trained school personnel. Large numbers of Arab children suffered from malnutrition and poor health. Employment prospects for Arab youth were dismal, with many working in menial, low-paid jobs. Consequently, most youngsters spent free time in cafés, on the street, and in gambling establishments; the result was a constantly rising rate of delinquency and criminal behavior. The gaps between the facilities and services provided to the Arab and Jewish communities were enormous. Jewish local municipal councils secured budget allocations three times those received by Arab councils of the same size.[43]

The Israeli Arab community, much like the Arabs in the territories, had significant reasons for being dissatisfied with their status. Only a spark was needed to ignite this explosive situation. After December 1987 the number of incidents revealing unrest sharply increased. In many villages Israeli Arabs, too, joined the stone and petrol bomb throwing, protest demonstrations, and other manifestations of hostility toward the authorities. Palestinian flags were flown in solidarity with the Arabs of the territories; and many feared that the strong-arm tactics used in the territories would be employed against Israeli Arabs. Less than two weeks after the uprising started, on December 21, Israeli Arabs organized a general strike to demonstrate solidarity with the Palestinians in the territories.

Israel's Arab community was divided among anti-Israeli radicals, Palestinian nationalists loyal to Israel, and traditionalists; the latter opposed overt protests against the authorities for fear of reprisals. Sammy Smooha of Haifa University divided the community into four principal categories: (1) Accommodationists, who conformed in their views to the Zionist establishment and believed that they could best extract concessions by working within the system; (2) Reservationists, positioned between the Zionist establishment and Communist opposition, who believed that by organizing independently they could achieve their goals through negotiations; (3) Oppositionists, guided by the ideology and politics of the Israel Communist party (Rakah), who accepted the state of Israel but opposed its Zionist character and believed they could attain their goals only by challenging the Zionist establishment from the outside; and (4) Rejectionists, who totally negated Israel and desired to replace it with a secular, democratic, Palestinian state in all of mandatory Palestine. The percentage of the Arab public in each category, according to Smooha, was as follows: Accommodationist—11.3 percent; Reservationist—45.9 percent; Oppositionist—38.3 percent; and Rejectionist—6.5 percent. Although Smooha's categories were established before the Intifada, it is likely that all Israeli Arabs but those in the first category sympathized with the Intifada and were influenced by it.[44]

A second country-wide strike was organized by Israeli Arabs on March 30, 1988, to commemorate Land Day. This became an annual event, following the demonstrations in 1976 protesting against government expropriation of Arab land when Israel security forces killed six Arab citizens. On Land Day in 1988 and 1989, the demonstrations acquired a special significance against the background of Intifada. Both Arab traditionalists and Israeli authorities were apprehensive about the Land Day demonstrations, fearing that they might get out of hand and lead to violent altercations between the security forces and Arab citizens.

However, the Arab organizers succeeded in disciplining the demonstrators and maintaining peaceful protests.

A third major Israeli Arab strike was organized in November 1988 to protest against government destruction of illegally built Arab houses. Because the strike coincided with the Palestine National Council meeting in Algiers and the PLO declaration of an independent state, many Israeli officials again anticipated trouble. About 90 percent of Israeli Arabs observed the strike; only some Druze and Bedouin did not participate. The demonstration, again, was peaceful.

Israeli authorities denounced the strike. The deputy director general of the Interior Ministry proclaimed: "I cannot remember any other incident of such magnitude where a section of the population went on strike in support of people who broke the law. It was nothing less than a slap in the face for democracy and the rule of law." He asserted that of some 6,000 illegally constructed houses, only 300 were demolished because they were in "problematic spots." Furthermore, he insisted, the government had done much to help Arab localities with plans for housing development, although he made no claims about large-scale financial assistance.[45]

The militancy of Israel's Arabs demonstrated during the Intifada was, according to Smooha and others with intimate knowledge of the community, not a sign of disloyalty to the state of Israel. Rather, it was an expression of dissatisfaction with their status as second-class citizens and with government policies, as well as an expression of sympathy for a Palestinian national state. Like many loyal Israelis who were Zionists, even many who were part of the establishment, Israeli Arabs perceived no conflict between their support for a Palestinian state and loyalty to Israel. Many compared their outlook to that of American Jews toward Israel.

The new assertiveness of Israeli Arabs was viewed by many Israeli leaders and much of the public with alarm. The prime minister's adviser for Arab affairs interpreted the reaction to the Intifada "as only a catalyst—the ongoing process of Palestinianization, pressure for autonomy, a dissociation from Israel . . . a new dangerous situation." Ariel Sharon accused Israel's Arabs of joining the enemy and seeking "to destroy us" instead "of fighting together with us as loyal Israeli citizens." Even several Israeli journalists and public figures critical of the government's harsh policies in the territories were worried about the danger; they, too, feared that the Arabs might soon demand separation from Israel. The fact that the November strike against demolition of homes occurred on the same day as the PNC declaration of independence was perceived as a thinly disguised indication of solidarity with the PLO, an organization still regarded by most Israeli Jews as terrorist. In an article by Meron Benvenisti, "Israel's Apocalypse Now," he asserted that "Belfastization" of the country was well under way, and that unity between Palestinians on both sides of the Green Line was now a solid fact.[46]

Prime Minister Shamir's Arab affair's adviser believed that the problem was a "national emergency." His advisers warned him: "On the day the idea of a Palestinian state starts gaining legitimacy, the Arabs inside Israel will start campaigning for autonomy, and then they will ask to be integrated into the Palestinian state."[47]

The backlash of anti-Arab public sentiment resulting from the Intifada and the outpouring of criticism from public officials only embittered the Israeli Arabs and underscored their status as second-class citizens. Many believed that politicians were using Arab demands for equality to justify militant nationalist positions, such as "transfer."

Israeli Arab political consciousness was demonstrated by participation in the 1988 Knesset election. Nearly 76 percent voted (compared to 79 percent of Israeli Jews). About 59 percent voted for parties considered to be Arab—34 percent for the Democratic Front for Peace and Equality (DFPE), 14 percent for the Progressive List for Peace (PLP), and 11 percent for the Arab Democratic Party (ADP)—and the others voted for a variety of Zionist parties. The major effect of the Intifada was to greatly diminish Arab support for Labor, as evidenced by the decrease from 31 percent in 1984 to 17 percent of the Arab vote in 1988. Probably most Arab voters who abandoned Labor voted for Darwasha's ADP, which was formed early in the year when he left Labor in protest against Rabin's policies in the territories.

Smooha has pointed out that the Intifada was "the hardest test of loyalty Israeli Arabs have ever had," and that after the first year they successfully passed the test. Although they supported the Intifada, they did not join it. Their struggle was not for an end of occupation or for independence, but for democratic rights within Israel.

> The key concepts for understanding Israeli Arab patterns of behavior are militancy, not radicalism; opposition, not resistance; acceptance, not rejectionism; integration, not separation; and institutional autonomy, not irredentism. By the same token, the change in their behavior is conveyed by politicization, not radicalization; and [by] an increase in political activism, not a rise in rejectionism."[48]

THE INTIFADA AND ISRAEL'S ECONOMY

The economy of Israel within the Green Line suffered far less than the economies of Gaza and the West Bank (see Chapters 2 and 3).

Initially, the Intifada did cause dislocations in several sectors dependent on Arab labor, mostly in textiles, footwear, construction, agriculture, restaurant, and sanitation jobs. In these enterprises, Palestinians from the territories provided cheap labor in jobs that most Jewish workers rejected, even when unemployed. The West Bank's per capita productivity and consumption were only about a third of Israel's; Gaza's were only a sixth.

The first indications of this economic impact were apparent during December 1987 and January 1988 when 40–60 percent of the Arabs in the above occupations failed to appear for work in Israel. Because the Arab strike began at the height of the citrus season, Jewish students were released from school to help with the harvest. Even members of the Histadrut (Labor Federation) Central Committee, including the secretary general, Yisrael Kessar, volunteered to spend three days a week working in citrus groves.[49]

At the end of January, Labor and Social Affairs Minister Moshe Katsav told the cabinet that turmoil in the territories "has thrown the economy out of gear to a considerable extent." In the previous weeks, he added, only 57 percent of the industrial workers and 42 percent of those in services showed up for work. As a result, the minister admitted, there was no alternative but to import labor from abroad. Nevertheless, he warned, the country must learn not to rely on these workers.

The slowdown of business in the territories caused by strikes and other dislocations also affected Israeli commerce. During the first year of the Intifada, sales of Israeli products in the West Bank and Gaza fell from $928 million in 1987 to $650 million in 1988, as a result of the boycotts and the steep decline of Palestinian income. Early in 1988, the Israel Association of Chambers of Commerce predicted that a series of bankruptcies would occur as the impact of declining sales filtered through to Jewish enterprises.[50]

By the end of 1988 citrus growers were warning the government that unless they were permitted to bring in 2,000 foreign workers, mostly from Portugal, Turkey, and the Philippines, they stood to lose $20 million a week. About 12,000 workers were needed immediately to harvest the country's 90,000 acres of fruit. Despite increasing unemployment in Israel, citrus farmers were still almost totally dependent on workers from the territories. According to the Citrus Growers Association, "There are virtually no Jewish workers willing to do this kind of work."[51]

After a year, the construction industry also was unable to adjust to the loss of Arab labor. An estimated two-thirds of those employed in building were from the territories. Because the industry relied on day labor, it was difficult to determine how many Arab workers were absent; absentee rates varied from one section of the country to another. The

Arab strike hit construction when it was most vulnerable, just when the number of housing starts was beginning to pick up after a two-year slump. An indication of the decline was the precipitous drop in the sale of building material. Koor, the largest single provider of construction materials, estimated that sales dropped by 20–30 percent during the first three months of the uprising. During 1988 it was faced with bankruptcy because of inability to pay its debts.

Contractors also demanded that the government permit them to import foreign workers. The Labor Ministry allowed 200 foreigners to work in the industry, but this total was a mere drop in the bucket compared to the 40,000 to 50,000 Palestinians employed before the uprising. In May 1989, when the IDF imposed new rules restricting Arab departure from the territories, many construction firms warned that they would have to suspend operations and furlough their Jewish employees. Because of housing shortages caused by the slowdown in construction, it was estimated that apartment prices rose nearly a third during 1988–1989.[52]

Some contractors perceived the shortage of Arab labor as an opportunity to modernize Israel's construction industry which many judged was forty to fifty years behind Europe and the United States. Now, they said, was the time to raise standards, introduce new equipment, and start training programs for Jewish workers. Rehabilitation of the industry would make it more efficient and less dependent on unskilled labor. If the industry were modernized, they argued, the remaining Arab workers would be sufficient. As one contractor put it, "What we don't have is enough Israelis who are trained to manage and supervise and thus utilize what resources are available."[53]

The textile and shoe industries were also victims of the Intifada. Many small textile and shoemaking firms depended on workshops subcontracted in the territories, especially in Hebron and Nablus. Loss of contact with them caused many Israeli shops to close. Although large factories were relatively unaffected, many small plants sold much of their output in the territories. Within the first four months of the uprising, sales of Israeli textiles fell by nearly 30 percent. To assist smaller companies during the crisis, the government provided funds to help boost export sales. Larger textile plants that employed Arabs were advised to modernize—that is, to introduce new machinery that would lead to more efficient production.[54]

By mid-1988 the bias against importing foreign workers was broken. As the director of the government employment agency observed, "Before the riots, it was taboo to talk about foreign workers." By mid-1988 some 3,500 were legally employed and another 9,000 worked under tourist visas, many of them from Portugal. The head of a London-based firm, European Manpower Services, announced plans to bring in up to 10,000 blue-collar workers on short-term contracts of up to a year. To discourage these employees from staying in the country, most of their pay was withheld until after they returned home.[55]

The tourist industry also suffered a significant decline. Many of the most visited sites, such as the Old City of Jerusalem and Bethlehem, were at the center of the uprising and thus either shut off or perceived by tourists as dangerous. Reports abroad of the continuing unrest discouraged many, although Israel within the Green Line experienced almost none of the action. After a pre-Intifada boom of more than a year in duration, the tourist industry seemed to have run out of steam. Tourist centers that depended on large numbers of visitors for the Passover, Christmas, or Easter seasons were especially hard hit.[56]

By the end of 1988, it was estimated that the Intifada had boosted average hourly labor costs by 2.5 percent because of Arab absenteeism. The number of hours worked by Palestinians fell 22 percent, with the result that wages in Israel increased automatically. Jews who replaced Arabs were paid more for the same work. But this situation was usually accompanied by improved productivity per worker. The former minister of economics, Gad Ya'acobi, estimated that the total cost of the Intifada to Israel's economy during 1988 exceeded $900 million, approximately 1.5–2 percent of gross domestic product. Bank of Israel Governor Michael Bruno observed that the loss included $650 million in exports and $250 million in tourist dollars. The output of the business sector declined by 1.5 percent, exports by 4.2 percent, and tourism by 15 percent during 1988, according to Bruno. Although the total number of Palestinians working in Israel rose from 103,000 to 109,000 during the previous two years, frequent absenteeism caused a 25 percent decline in the effective supply of labor from the territories. To prevent continued deterioration, the Bank recommended greater mechanization of industry, the shutdown of production largely dependent on unskilled labor, and the temporary importation of limited numbers of foreign workers.[57]

Other costs of the Intifada included a rise in insurance rates resulting from a large number of fires, attributed to "nationalist arson" and "built-in" damage to new building by workers from the territories. In one case a contractor discovered that each of the twenty-three baths installed in a new building had been damaged by hammer blows the next morning.[58] The increase of reserve duty from forty-five to sixty days cost an estimated $100 million to $200 million. In addition to the extra time served, the number of soldiers in the territories was increased up to five times, according to some estimates. At the end of June 1988, the army asked for an extra $450 million to cover the expenses incurred by its assignment in the territories. Government revenue from the territories dropped as a result of tax strikes by the inhabitants and because of their declining income. In addition, direct costs resulted from altercations between the army and the civil population, and from demonstrations. Egged, one of Israel's largest transport cooperatives, reported that during 1988, 1,260 of its buses were damaged; of these, 41 were destroyed by fire.[59]

By mid-1989 some gaps in the economy caused by the uncertainty of Arab labor were being filled with Jewish workers. Unemployment in Israel had reached 8.2 percent by June, the highest rate in years. As a result, many of the more than 60,000 Jews who were without work began to take the places of Arabs from the territories. Some 9,000 Israelis took jobs left by Arabs in construction, and the government began to track down some of the 10,000 foreigners with tourist visas who had "disappeared" into low-paying jobs. Furthermore, workers began to return from the territories. By June 88 percent of the Palestinians had returned, an increase of ten percent over the May figure. Among construction workers, 78 percent appeared for work; the figure for industry was 90 percent. About 90 percent of Palestinians from Gaza were working in June 1989, in contrast to 56 percent from the West Bank.[60]

Some observers believed that if the territories were sealed off, the 112,000 unemployed Israelis could replace the approximately 110,000 Palestinian laborers. Unemployment would disappear, and potentially hostile Arabs would be kept out of the country. However, this did not happen. The total number of Jews who replaced Arabs was relatively small. In the construction industry, the number of Jews employed increased by about 11 percent to 68,000. According to the government employment service, about 13,000 Israelis joined the work force in the restaurant and hotel industries.

Despite the import of foreign workers, the increased employment of Jews in jobs previously worked by Arabs, and the army's attempts to confine Arabs to the territories, Palestinian labor remained an important element in the economy. If Arab workers from Gaza and the West Bank suddenly disappeared, "the economy would find itself in chaos, short of seven percent of its work force," according to one expert. Over the long run, there could be adjustments—substituting capital for labor and training skilled workers.[61] However, while the Intifada continues, the climate for investment from abroad is not inviting. According to cabinet minister Gad Ya'acobi, a diplomatic breakthrough is a prerequisite of economic growth; it is "the essential key to all progress." Ya'acobi believed that costs attributed to the Intifada "simply ate up most of the economic growth for the entire year [1988–1989]. Had this not happened, we could have saved the educational and health systems and the farming movements from their crises, while maintaining a lower level of inflation and increasing exports."[62]

THE INTIFADA AND ISRAEL'S FOREIGN POLICY

Although at least half of the Israeli public recognized that only a political resolution would end the disturbances, the NUG seemed little aware of this. When the new NUG was formed in December 1988, its Basic Policy Guidelines reiterated those of the previous four years regarding the territories. The Guidelines again referred to the Camp David formula (part of the Israel-Egypt peace settlement), stating that "the Arabs of Judea, Samaria, and the Gaza District will participate in the determination of their future, as stipulated in the Camp David accords." Palestinians in the territories would be granted local autonomy only. There were no provisions for independence. The Guidelines emphasized that "Israel will oppose the establishment of an additional Palestinian state in the Gaza District and in the area between Israel and Jordan." No change would be made "in the sovereignty over Judea, Samaria and the Gaza District, except with the consent of the Alignment [Labor] and the Likud." An indication of Likud's determination to prevent any change in the status quo was a provision in the Guidelines for establishment of five to eight new Jewish settlements in the territories during the following year and for additional settlements after that (see Appendix 2).[63]

As the Intifada gained momentum, pressures from abroad (see Chapter 5) as well as within the country increased, and a new political strategy had to be devised for dealing with the crisis. The EEC, the United Nations, the Soviet Union, American Jews, and, most important of all, the U.S. government were becoming impatient with the NUG's concentration on forceful measures to confront the uprising. They all called for a new political initiative. Following the PNC's declaration of independence, Arafat's plea for peace negotiations and his recognition of Israel, and the U.S. recognition of the PLO (see Chapter 5), international consensus demanded an Israeli response. The time had come for Israel to publicize a peace initiative of its own.

The first official reaction was Defense Minister Rabin's four-stage plan in January, which called for (1) cessation of Palestinian violence, (2) a three-to-six month period of quiet prior to elections among the Palestinians, (3) negotiations with elected Palestinian leaders and with Jordan for an interim form of autonomy, and (4) negotiations leading to final disposition of the territories. Rabin specifically excluded the PLO from participation. Since the plan differed little, if at all, from the Camp David scheme, it was unacceptable to the leadership of the UNLU. In their leaflet number 34, they rejected elections before withdrawal of Israeli forces from the territories and insisted on exclusive leadership of the PLO. It was clear that they would accept nothing less than an independent Palestinian state.

As the time approached for Prime Minister Shamir's April visit to Washington, where he was to meet President George Bush and members of the administration, rumors spread that he would present a new peace plan to end the Intifada. The scheme that eventually emerged was Shamir's version of elections, leading to still another type of autonomy. This was an innovative approach for Shamir because he had adamantly opposed autonomy for years; one of the reasons for his taking a firm stand against the Camp David agreements with Egypt in 1978 was his fear that provisions for autonomy would eventually lead to an independent Palestinian state. Now, however, he seemed willing to take the risk, believing (according to some in his party) that the Palestinians would never accept the proposal. The actual implementation of the proposal would thus be obviated. During the rest of the year, attention focused on proposals for the election of Palestinian representatives to negotiate an interim agreement—merely a first step in a lengthy process with an inconclusive end.

After bitter infighting within both Labor and Likud, and following behind-the-scene debates between the two parties in the inner cabinet containing the leaders from each, the government in May formally adopted a "new peace initiative" by a twenty to six vote in the cabinet and forty-three to fifteen in the Knesset. The first step was to be "free and democratic elections among the Palestinian Arab inhabitants of Judea, Samaria, and the Gaza District" for representatives to conduct negotiations. The proposal categorically opposed "establishment of an additional Palestinian state in the Gaza District and in the area between Israel and Jordan," and rejected negotiations with the PLO. The only change to be permitted in the status of "Judea, Samaria, and Gaza" would be in accord with the Basic Guidelines of the NUG; in effect, the maximum concession anticipated was some form of autonomy (see Appendix 8).[64]

A two-stage process was envisaged, involving a transitional period for interim agreement and a permanent solution. During the proposed five-year transition, Palestinians in the territory would be "accorded self-rule, by means of which they will themselves conduct their affairs of daily life." Israel would remain in charge of security, foreign affairs, and all matters concerning Israeli citizens in the West Bank and Gaza. As soon as possible, but not later than three years after beginning the transition period, negotiations for a permanent solution would start. Moreover, Jordan and Egypt would be invited to participate in all stages of the negotiations, "if they so desire."[65]

Although the proposal stated that "the elections shall be free, democratic, and secret," controversy arose over procedures for conducting the balloting. Would elections take place under Israeli occupation? Would Israeli troops withdraw from places where the voting was conducted? Would international supervision occur? Would Arabs in pre-1967 Jordanian Jerusalem participate?

Although the principle of "free elections" was accepted by all parties to the conflict—the Israeli government, the Palestinians, and the United States (see Chapter 5)—disagreement over implementation became the major obstacle to further progress. It seemed that years of discussion would be needed before this first of many steps toward peace would be taken.

Within Israel, many in influential positions adamantly opposed even this first step. The prime minister was opposed by a powerful bloc within Shamir's own party led by Ariel Sharon, Deputy Prime Minister David Levy, and Yitzhak Moda'i, leader of the Liberal party wing of Likud. They complained that the election plan did not exclude Jerusalem Arabs and did not demand termination of the Intifada before any further concessions. Sharon and some of his colleagues insisted that elections would inevitably lead to the creation of a "PLO state." Shamir indicated that he would compromise with his critics by modifying the plan, such that Jerusalem Arabs could not vote, outside supervision would not be permitted, and Israeli law would apply in heavily populated Jewish areas. His true intent was revealed when he told a Likud meeting prior to the Knesset debate on the plan that "we shall not give the Arabs one inch of our land, even if we have to negotiate for ten years. We won't give them a thing. . . . We have the veto in our hands. . . . The status quo of the interim arrangement will continue until all the parties reach agreement on the permanent arrangement."[66]

The Labor party, too, was divided on the peace proposal. The mainstream approved, but the left wing, although it sympathized, doubted Shamir's intent to implement it. Ezer Weizman, who voted against, believed that Israel should take a more direct approach and open immediate negotiations with the PLO. Rabin also proposed compromises with his party's critics such as permitting Arabs from Jerusalem to vote—but in the neighboring West Bank, not in the city itself.[67]

The plan was rejected in a statement by eighty well-known West Bank Palestinians. Their counterproposal called for elections free of Israeli occupation and under international supervision. Rabin's response was to warn inhabitants of the territories that he would order the military to deal more harshly with them if they rejected his offer. "We are not just offering elections," Rabin stated; "we are offering a political solution in two stages to come to a permanent solution. . . . We want to convince them [Palestinians] mainly along positive lines." To reinforce support for the plan, Rabin decided that several steps were necessary: (1) reduction of Israel's dependence on Arab labor and other economic measures against Palestinians in the territories; (2) interference with their freedom of movement between Israel, the West Bank, and Gaza by putting the entire Gaza area under an indefinite curfew; and (3) suspension of some laws, such that Palestinians are, for instance, denied the right to appeal military orders to Israel's Supreme Court. Rabin asserted that "he would have no qualms about significantly increasing the military pressure if the Palestinians refused even to consider Israel's plan—the only one Israel intends to offer."[68]

By late 1989 the Shamir-Rabin plan, Israel's diplomatic answer to the Intifada, was still the only official response other than the use of force. But even this approach relied on the power of the IDF. As Rabin and Shamir stated, they would go no further; it was a "take-it-or-leave-it" proposal, a proposal in which the leaders of Labor and Likud were determined to hold all the cards. Shamir believed that the Palestinians would reject the plan and, therefore, that it was not dangerous; Rabin, who was willing to implement it in his own way, did not regard it as a threat, even if implemented, for it would leave Israel and the IDF in control of the West Bank and Gaza.

Early in 1989 a lengthy and detailed report on Israel's options for peace was released. It was the result of an extensive study group project undertaken during the latter half of 1988 by the Jaffee Center for Strategic Studies, headed by Reserve Major General Yariv and including a number of scholars and other retired officers associated with the Center. The study observed that six major options were available to Israel for determining the future of the West Bank and Gaza: (1) continuing the status quo; (2) autonomy; (3) annexation; (4) a Palestinian state; (5) withdrawal from Gaza only; and (6) a Jordanian-Palestinian federation. The study rejected immediate implementation of any of these options, thus undercutting the "peace plan" of the NUG. Instead, it concluded that, contrary to government policy, eventual establishment of a modified Palestinian state and qualified negotiations with the PLO were measures least likely to harm Israel's interests over the long run. However, the process envisaged was lengthy—ten to fifteen years during which there would be no Palestinian state and Israel would maintain its "comprehensive" security arrangements in the West Bank and Gaza.[69]

The Israeli press gave extensive coverage to the report—coverage that was mostly favorable but still critical. As one commentator noted, "I ask the strategists: Do you not understand that the Intifada obliges you to provide a final answer today for what you have avoided answering since 1967? Could you end the Intifada today in exchange for a promise to talk to the PLO in another fifteen years?" Likud members of the NUG dismissed the study; Foreign Minister Moshe Arens called it the "work of a bunch of leftists"; and Premier Shamir said he refused to read it.[70]

ISRAEL'S MOOD

After nearly two years of the Intifada, what was the mood in Israel? Because of its ineffable quality, opinions and perspectives differed. As we have seen, the economic or material consequences were marginal, affecting certain sectors but only to a relatively small degree, certainly far less than they affected the Arab inhabitants of the territories. Few Israelis were displaced from their work. There were no serious shortages of commodities and no major price increases. The principal economic impact was suspension of economic growth and shortages of Arab labor in some areas. But ways were found to make up for these shortages through mechanization and modernization, through the importation of small numbers of foreign employees, and through the gradual reintroduction of Israelis to work that many had come to regard as "fit only for Arabs." The length of time served by reservists, although it increased considerably, was more an annoyance than a serious economic loss.

The army leadership, which was greatly discomfited by the tasks imposed upon it, lost much of its credibility and the high regard with which it had been held. It became the focus of controversy among politicians, accused of being too lax by some and of brutality by others. The indecision of the country's political leaders, which left the army high command with uncertain directives about its long-term role in the territories, caused morale to suffer in many units. Some pessimistic observers argued that the IDF had become a fourth-rate military establishment and others, that its capacity to wage a "real" war was only slightly affected; all the experts, however, agreed that the Intifada had had a deleterious impact on IDF efficiency and morale.

The soldiers serving in the territories, often in the same units, had diverse perceptions of their role. Their differences reflected those of the public at large. Most, by far, regarded duty in the West Bank and Gaza as an unpleasant but necessary task—a task imposed by Arab obstinacy or fanaticism, or by outside agitators. Most were ambivalent about the political aspects of the Intifada; only a few, like those in the Israeli peace groups, sympathized with the goals of the uprising. Still, most would be willing to leave the territories if they could be assured of Israel's security.

Few Israelis had any social or political contact with Arabs outside their military duty, even with their fellow Arab citizens within the Green

The Israeli military presence in Jerusalem has been much increased since the Palestinian uprising in 1988. UNRWA photo by George Nehmeh.

Line; yet a common response to outsiders, during discussions of the situation, was "We know the Arabs," or "We know how to deal with them." Those most perturbed by the tragedy of the situation were found among intellectuals, writers, academicians, musicians, artists, mental health workers, even potters. Despite the wide coverage of the Intifada in the Israeli press, the extensive reportage of atrocities, and the criticism in editorials and columns of most newspapers, the majority of the population supported the "iron fist"; many thought it should be applied even more severely.

In short, while the Intifada had its costs, they were relatively small for most Israelis—in terms of Jewish lives, far smaller than those in any of Israel's five or six wars. After nearly two years of confrontation with the inhabitants of the territories, barely a score of Israelis had lost their lives, fewer than in any month of traffic accidents and fewer than a twentieth of the Arab lives lost. The fact that few had suffered led to acceptance of the situation, reinforced by persistence of the national self-image: Israel as the only democracy in the Middle East; "purity of arms" in the IDF; equality of all citizens; the Arabs against peace and the Jews for it. One critic described this as the "psychology of self-deception," in which many Israelis find it literally impossible to believe that their *own* people—sons, brothers, husbands, friends—could do something like drag a fifteen-year-old boy from his home, blindfold him, line him up against a wall and break his arms and legs. This information is threatening, so it slips into the black holes [of the mind]. Or else, it is repackaged in a more acceptable way, so that we insist that these cases are few and isolated; that they are being stopped now; that the media always emphasize and exaggerate these sorts of occurrences; that the army is being provoked beyond all endurance . . . or that (a repackaging I heard recently) "it's only the Sephardi soldiers who are doing this sort of thing." The point of neutralization or repackaging is not to deny responsibility, but to deny reality.[71]

The psychologists referred to in Chapter 3 who analyzed the dreams of Arab and Jewish children believed that the Israelis had adjusted to the daily violence in the territories and were thus diminished in their ability to relate to the suffering of others. The Israelis were indifferent not only to Palestinian suffering but also to economic problems, to people injured in road accidents, to the troubles of other sectors of the economy. Dr. Hanoch Yerushalmi, one of the psychologists, believed that, more seriously, violence was becoming an acceptable way of settling disputes. It was "a natural and legitimate outlet for frustration." Because suppression of the Intifada was not a war for Israel's existence, it created ambivalence. "The enemy has no definition and is unfamiliar. Anyone can be the enemy. . . . In a situation like this, people have no choice but extremism. Either withdraw from a difficult decision, or identify in a decisive manner with the assignment and make everyone the enemy." The question is, who will be the enemy tomorrow: striking workers, Israeli Arab citizens, peace demonstrators, or one's own wife?[72]

Early in 1989 many parents began to be concerned about a new, lethal "game of chicken" that seemed to be spreading among Jewish children in Israel. Some variations follow: (1) Boys would lie in the street until a car approached, and the last one to leap up and run away as the car came close was the winner. (2) Boys would place an object in the street and dash out to grab it as a car approached; the one who had the closest call won. (3) An Israeli candy called "krembo" would be placed in the road for a child to dash out and seize as a car approached; the one closest to being hit won. (4) A group would stand by the roadside and shove a companion in front of an oncoming car. (5) A boy would jump in front of a car to see if the driver would stop. This new game became so popular among 11 to 17 year olds that the Minister of Education ordered an investigation and demanded a stop to it. A variety of psychological explanations was offered: Violence had become endemic; the constant threat of war or terrorist attack had bred frustration, leading to bizarre outlets; because society demanded bravery, children played the game to demonstrate their own courage; boys had to outdo the daring of Arab youths confronting Israeli tanks, a scene they frequently viewed on television. Likud Justice Minister Dan Meridor believed that there was too much emphasis on psychological analysis of the problem; he advised that the main way to deal with it, "if not the only one, is harsh punishment for the children involved and, if they were under age, for their parents."[73]

One casualty of the situation was Israeli satire. It is in the doldrums and the satirists are "filled with despair," observed a Tel Aviv University professor of the subject. According to his account, most satirists were overcome by feelings of ineffectuality, believing that they could no longer change anyone's opinions. "Satire does not move the masses." A columnist for *Ha'aretz* opined that "there is great despair. We always knew intellectually that satire has no effect. Now we know it in our blood, in our gut. This has led to a certain tiredness. Everything has been said and it has affected nothing." The professor noted that sharp political satire "that sinks its teeth into its subject flourishes here during wars or in their immediate aftermath." But a satirical poem about the Intifada by Ephraim Sidon, "The Burning Home," was cut by the Israel Broadcasting Authority lest it "provoke[s] questions in the Knesset." Although the Intifada sparked many protests and demonstrations, it failed to generate satire. After almost two years, there were no plays about the subject. Many who had satirized the occupation for twenty years felt that they had had no effect. Satire, one writer claimed, "is often preaching to the converted." It can even be counterproductive; it angers a few people, offers a few jokes; and people laugh and go home. "You have enabled them to let off steam, then they forget the object of their anger." It was acceptable to satire discrimination in other places, against blacks in South Africa or Jews abroad. "But writing about discrimination of Arabs in Israel does not go over so well." One writer envied Bertold Brecht, who was "able to write about the evil of war and oppression. Today, we can't write about these things. They are clichés and we suffer from a grotesque reality—a reality which often is more absurd than anything you could write."[74]

Because so few Israelis have suffered from the Intifada, because for most, other than the military, it is like a war on a distant continent, decisions about the future of the territories, about the terms for ending the uprising will be made by a few and be accepted by the majority. It matters little whether the decision is annexation, a Palestine state, or any of the various proposed intermediate solutions. But no matter what the decision, there will be powerful fringe groups that oppose it: the settlers who reject withdrawal from the territories, and the peaceniks who oppose annexation. Some Israelis have feared that polarization at the fringes of society could push the country to the brink of civil war. The zealotry of the extreme right and its resistance to anything short of annexation was demonstrated in numerous outbreaks, reaching a pitch of hysteria when they attacked Prime Minister Shamir as a traitor and labeled his administration "the Intifada government."

NOTES

1. *The West Bank and Gaza: Israel's Options for Peace* (Tel-Aviv: Jaffee Center for Strategic Studies, 1989) (hereafter JCSS 89), Appendix 2; Sammy Smooha, *Arabs and Jews in Israel, Vol. 1: Conflicting and Shared Attitudes in a Divided Society* (Boulder, Colo.: Westview Press, 1989), Preface and passim; Gloria H. Falk, "Israeli Public Opinion on Peace Issues," in *Israeli National Security Policy*, edited by Bernard Reich and Gershon R. Kieval (Westport: Greenwood Press, 1988); *New York Times* (hereafter NYT), 4/2/89 (Joel Brinkley, "Majority in Israel Oppose P.L.O. Talks Now, a Poll Shows"); *Near East Report*, cited in *Broome County Reporter*, 3/9/89.

2. *Jerusalem Post* (hereafter JP), 3/25/88 (Shlomit Levy, "Ingrained Israeli Attitudes to the Areas").

3. JCSS 89, Appendix 2.

4. *Ibid.*, pp. 184–185.

5. *Ibid.*, p. 185.

6. NYT, 4/2/89 (Brinkley).

7. *Near East Report*, cited in *Broome County Reporter*, 3/9/89.

8. JCSS 89, p. 189; JP, 3/25/88 (Shlomit Levy).

9. *Jerusalem Post International Edition* (hereafter JPI), no. 1,455, 9/24/88.

10. JPI, no. 1,456, 10/1/88.

11. JPI, no. 1,485, 4/22/89.

12. JPI, no. 1,457, 10/8/88.

13. JPI, no. 1,428, 3/19/88 (Joseph Goell, "The Case Against TV").

14. *Ibid.*

15. JPI, no. 1,427, 3/12/88.

16. JPI, no. 1,476, 2/18/89; no. 1,470, 1/7/89 (Kenneth Kaplan, "The Book and the Sword").

17. JPI, no. 1,433, 4/23/88.

18. JPI, no. 1,484, 4/15/89.

19. JPI, no. 1,490, 5/27/89.

20. JPI, no. 1,444, 7/9/88.

21. JPI, no. 1,445, 7/16/88.

22. JPI, no. 1,447, 7/30/88 (Joel Greenberg, "The IDF's Credibility Is Under Strain").

23. JPI, no. 1,493, 6/17/89.

24. JPI, no. 1,432, 4/16/89.

25. JPI, no. 1,479, 3/18/89.

26. *Ibid.*

27. JPI, no. 1,486, 4/29/89.

28. JPI, no. 1,491, 6/3/89.

29. JPI, no. 1,476, 2/18/89.

30. JPI, no. 1,444, 7/9/88.

31. JPI, no. 1,420, 1/23/88.

32. JPI, no. 1,451, 8/27/88.

33. JPI, no. 1,426, 3/5/88; no. 1,429, 3/26/88.

34. JPI, no. 1,434, 5/7/88.

35. JPI, no. 1,450, 8/20/88 (Elihu Katz, "49% Lean Towards 'Transfer' of Arabs from Areas").

36. *Ha-Aretz*, 4/1/88; Myron J. Aronoff, *Israeli Visions and Divisions: Cultural Change and Political Conflict* (New Brunswick: Transaction Press, 1989), pp. 148–158.

37. JP, 9/2/88.

38. Mordechai Bar-On, "Israel's Reactions to the Uprising," *Journal of Palestine Studies* (hereafter JPS), no. 68, Summer 1988, p. 55.

39. *Ibid.*

40. *The 21st Year—Covenant for the Struggle Against the Occupation* (Jerusalem).

41. *New Outlook*, vol. 31, no. 10, November–December 1988, p. 14.

42. *The Other Israel*, vol. 1, no. 35, January–February 1989, pp. 4–5.

43. JPI, no. 1,438, 5/28/88 (David Rudge, "Second-Class Citizens").

44. Sammy Smooha, *Arabs and Jews in Israel*, Chapter 18 ("Arab Orientation Types").

45. JPI, no. 1,464, 11/26/88.

46. Smooha, *Arabs and Jews in Israel*, pp. xiv–xv.

47. NYT, 6/18/89 (Joel Brinkley, "Pride and Resentment Rising Among Israeli Arabs").

48. Smooha, *Arabs and Jews in Israel*, p. xvii.

49. JPI, no. 1,421, 1/30/88.

50. NYT, 2/13/89; JPI, no. 1,423, 2/13/88.

51. JPI, no. 1,466, 12/10/88.

52. JPI, no. 1,428, 3/19/88; no. 1,466, 12/10/88; no. 1,494, 6/24/89.

53. JPI, no. 1,430, 4/2/88.

54. JPI, no. 1,431, 4/9/88; no. 1,445, 7/16/88.

55. JPI, no. 1,438, 5/28/88; no. 1,422, 2/6/88.

56. JPI, no. 1,434, 4/30/88.

57. JPI, no. 1,435, 5/14/88; no. 1,447, 7/30/88; no. 1,450, 8/30/88; no. 1,479, 3/18/89; no. 1,492, 6/10/89.

58. JPI, no. 1,469, 12/31/88.

59. Azmy Bishara, "Israel Faces the Uprising: A Preliminary Assessment," *Middle East Reports*, no. 157, March–April, 1989.

60. JPI, no. 1,442, 6/28/89; no. 1,456, 10/1/88.

61. JPI, no. 1,490, 5/27/89 (Jeff Black, "If the Arab Workers Were to Disappear").

62. JP, 6/7/89; JPI, no. 1,490, 5/27/89.

63. JP, 12/23/88 ("The Coalition Documents—Guidelines and Agreement").

64. Department of Academic Affairs, Consulate General of Israel, *Newsletter* (New York, May 18, 1989).

65. *Ibid.*

66. JPI, no. 1,490, 5/27/89; no. 1,494, 6/24/89.

67. JPI, no. 1,490, 5/27/89; NYT, 5/15/89.

68. NYT, 5/16/89 (Joel Brinkley, "Israel Says Army Will Get Tougher If Palestinians Reject Offer of Vote").

69. JCSS 89, pp. 17–24.

70. *Israel Press Highlights* (New York: Institute of Human Relations, American Jewish Committee, 3/13/89).

71. Stanley Cohen, "Criminology and the Uprising," *Tikkun,* September/October 1988, p. 62.

72. Amos Lavav, "Jewish-Arab Psychoanalysis," *Sof-Shavooa,* weekly supplement to *Maariv International Edition,* 12/23/88.

73. JPI, no. 1,481, 3/25/89; NYT, 4/3/89 (Joel Brinkley, "Lethal Game of 'Chicken' Emerges for Israeli Boys").

74. JPI, no. 1,481, 4/1/89 (Benny Morris, "Laughter in the Dark").

INTERNATIONAL REPERCUSSIONS
OF THE INTIFADA

THE UN, THE EEC, AND EUROPE

From the very start of the uprising, in December 1987, Israel was the target of international criticism. The first in a spate of UN condemnations was passed within two weeks of the outbreak, on December 22. In an unusual move, the United States did not veto the Security Council resolution but abstained, allowing it to be passed by the Council's fourteen other members. The resolution, like many previous ones, "strongly" deplored Israel's violation of human rights in the territories. Now, however, there was specific condemnation of the IDF for the "killing and wounding of defenceless Palestinian civilians." Israel was called on to provide the inhabitants of the occupied territories with protection "guaranteed civilians in time of war under international conventions." The UN Secretary General was asked to examine the situation and report back in a month with recommendations to "improve the safety of Palestinians living there." Although the United States abstained because it found the resolution unbalanced, it too joined the criticism of IDF measures as "unnecessarily harsh." The demonstrations and riots, said the U.S. representative, were "spontaneous expressions of frustration and not externally sponsored."[1]

In June 1988 the United States first supported, then abstained when the fourteen other Security Council members passed two resolutions calling on Israel to cancel plans for deportation of Palestinians and to permit those already expelled to return. Although the United States took an unusually severe tone in objecting to the deportations (see Chapter 2), it abstained on the second resolution because "repeatedly raising the issue does not help the process of restoring order." Israel's UN delegate complained that the organization was so biased that, "even if we threw rose petals at the Molotov-cocktail throwers, this body would find a way to condemn us."[2]

Within the next year and a half the United States continued its policy of vetoing similar Security Council resolutions, not because it was uncritical of Israeli policies in the territories but because it opposed the "harsh rhetoric," or the resolutions failed to "take into sufficient account the context [of Israeli policies and practices] . . . or the excesses of the other side," or the resolutions were "unbalanced."[3]

Nearly a score of resolutions were passed condemning Israel during the 1988 session of the General Assembly, a UN body in which the United States has no veto. These included criticism of Israel for "arming settlers . . . in order to commit acts of violence against Palestinian[s]"; demands that Israel comply with the Geneva Convention on the Protection of Civilians in time of war, deploring the "arbitrary detention or imprisonment" of thousands of Palestinians; and a request that member states cut off all diplomatic, trade, or cultural ties to Israel in order to "isolate it in all fields." The Assembly reiterated the assertion that the Palestine question was at the root of conflict in the Middle East and again voted to endorse an international peace conference with the PLO as an equal participant. In several votes there was a substantial number of abstentions, up to forty or forty-five, mostly by Western European and Latin American nations that declared several resolutions unbalanced because they failed to condemn "Arab violence against Israel." In many instances, only Israel and the United States voted against some 150 other members, and at times Israel was left alone in its opposition while the United States abstained.[4]

In compliance with the Security Council call for an investigation of the situation, the UN under-secretary general, Marrack Goulding, visited the occupied territories in January 1988. Although he met with Foreign Minister Peres, Prime Minister Shamir refused to see him because he "was interfering in Israel's internal affairs." Goulding reported that he had witnessed the use by Israel of "unduly harsh" measures in the territories and that, although the IDF had the right to maintain order, it had "over-reacted" to the demonstrations.[5]

After Goulding submitted his investigation results, Secretary General Javier Perez de Cuellar issued a report that Israelis found "not as bad as expected." He concluded that the only way to safeguard the Palestinians in the territories was to use a political solution. He called on nations with diplomatic ties to Israel "to use all the means at their disposal" to persuade it to abide by the Fourth Geneva Convention, which concerns occupied territories during war. The Israelis were relieved that the secretary-general had not called for the introduction of foreign observer troops, a measure he said was "not practicable at present."[6]

Relations between Israel and several of its European friends also began to unravel within the first months of the Intifada. After a visit to Gaza during January, the British minister of state for foreign affairs, David Mellor, stirred up a storm of outrage among Israeli officials because he upbraided the IDF for its actions. "Conditions here" in Gaza, Mellor protested, "are an affront to civilized values. It's appalling that a few miles up the coast there is prosperity and here there is misery on a scale that rivals anything anywhere in the world."[7] Although Foreign Secretary Sir Geoffrey Howe fully supported Mellor, the incident became a cause célèbre in both Israel and London when the minister was accused of butting into matters that were none of his concern.

The European Parliament joined the chorus of criticism when it called on Israel to halt reprisals against Palestinian protestors and an executive of the EEC accused it of "scandalous" acts of repression. The 518-member parliament urged Israel to abide by the international treaties concerning conduct of occupation forces. The climate of opinion in the EEC was so hostile that the organization decided to postpone ratification of its vote on three vital trade agreements with Israel, a delay that Prime Minister Shamir labeled "blackmail." The most important of these agreements would have provided lower tariffs to compensate Israel for the entry of Spain and Portugal into the Common Market.[8]

In October 1988 the EEC modified its position when the European parliament voted 314 to 25, with 19 abstentions, to ratify the trade pacts with Israel. Parliament members who supported the measure believed that "sufficient protest had been registered" by blocking the agreements during the previous ten months. But approval of these treaties did not signify a European carte blanche. Early in 1989 the European Community launched a major diplomatic offensive perceived as hostile by Israel. A series of "fact-finding missions" was launched by foreign ministers and other top diplomats of the Community with the intent of devising a European solution to the conflict. Israel was apprehensive that the "Mediterranean coalition" of France, Spain, and Greece would renew the 1980 Venice declaration that called for PLO "association" in peace talks and recognition of Palestinian rights to self-determination.[9]

By the end of 1988 diplomatic fallout from the Intifada had spread across Europe. Poland scuttled its plan to raise the level of diplomatic representation from the existing Interests Section to a higher level. Greece reneged on a promise to raise diplomatic representation to an ambassador when it took the chair of the European Community. The Soviet Union delayed issuing visas to Israel's Moscow consular delegation. Ireland continued to refuse to accept an Israeli ambassador. Portugal decided not to open a chancery in Tel Aviv. One of the most severe reprimands came from a long-term ally of the Israel Labor Alignment, Britain's

Labour party. At its 1988 annual conference in Blackpool during October, members defied the National Executive Committee, which had called for support of Israel's Labor party in the forthcoming election. This support was intended to replace a resolution censuring Israel for "indiscriminate use of ammunition, tear gas and beatings" and urging withdrawal from the territories. While the conference did vote to support the Labor party, it refused to withdraw the censure motion, which passed by 4 million to 2 million votes.[10]

Even the Vatican seemed to join the chorus. In December, Pope John Paul II appointed a Nazareth Arab priest to be Jerusalem Patriarch of the Latin Catholic Rite, the first Palestinian appointed to the post since it was established 800 years ago. Although the pope called for peace in the territories, the Vatican denied that the appointment was related to unrest in the Holy Land, a disavowal regarded with skepticism by many.

In Denmark, supermarket chains imposed an unofficial boycott on Israeli products. There was a reversal of public opinion in many countries previously noted for strong pro-Israel sentiments, such as Norway and Holland, where protests and demonstrations erupted against events in the West Bank and Gaza. When Norway's foreign minister visited Israel early in 1989, he told journalists: "Frankly, we cannot understand your policies. We cannot understand your handling of people in the occupied territories." He reminded Israelis that Norway and other Nordic countries had long demanded from Arafat and the PLO that they recognize Israel and denounce terrorism. Now that these demands have been met, Israel should respond accordingly.[11]

It seemed that the damage to Israel caused by the Intifada hit where it hurt the most, in the countries of Western Europe and North America. After visiting several West European countries, President Haim Herzog diagnosed the outbreak of anti-Israel sentiment to the media, which, he maintained, were carriers of "a certain strain of latent anti-Semitism."[12] Although Third World countries, other than Arab states, in Asia and Africa usually gave scant attention to events in the territories, the Arab-Israel conflict acquired a prominent place in the media there, too. Perhaps the most notable of the outspoken African critics was Archbishop Desmond Tutu, winner of the 1984 Noble Peace Prize. Tutu's sharp criticism came as he accepted a grant from the Institute of Black-Jewish Relations, affiliated with the Reform Jewish movement in the United States. He was deeply indebted to the Jewish people for his own spiritual heritage and supported Israel's right to security; but its treatment of Palestinians nevertheless reminded him "of the South African government's treatment of blacks." Until the Palestine question is settled equitably, he warned, Africans and American blacks would remain alienated from Israel.[13]

THE INTIFADA AND U.S.-ISRAELI RELATIONS

While the United States abstained from, or vetoed, many of the UN resolutions condemning Israel for its policies in the territories, there were several sharp exchanges between the two countries resulting from Washington's disapproval of events during the Intifada. Eventually, the uprising caused a sea change in U.S. policy toward the Arab-Israel conflict, culminating in recognition of the PLO as a legitimate party in the negotiations.

For the first time since the invasion of Lebanon in 1982, large numbers of U.S. representatives and senators openly expressed concern about Israeli policies. But this concern was not reflected in their continued support for aid to Israel or their backing of its stance on larger issues related to the conflict. The Intifada sparked interest in and sympathy for the Palestinian plight at the state and city political levels, as expressed by resolutions introduced in several local elections. It also caused tremors within the American Jewish establishment, leading many of its leaders and organizations to raise questions about Israeli policies for the first time since 1982.

As it became clear to U.S. government officials that the uprising was not a passing phenomenon and that its implications could reach far beyond the territories, thus affecting larger U.S. interests in the Middle East, the Reagan administration began to take notice. The Arab-Israel dispute again received high priority, removed, as it were, from the back burner where it had been placed since the failure of President Reagan's peace plan in 1982. Attempts had been made to organize an international peace conference with Jordan representing the Palestinians, but these efforts were stymied, principally because of disagreement about the Palestinian representatives in the Jordanian delegation and because Likud leaders opposed the whole idea. Secretary of State George Shultz again became personally involved, visiting Israel and the surrounding countries several times during 1988 to devise still another peace initiative.

After parleys with Prime Minister Shamir and King Hussein in March, Shultz sent them identical letters outlining his new scheme for a comprehensive peace procedure that would provide "for the legitimate rights of the Palestinian people." Negotiations between Israel and its Arab neighbors would begin by May 1, 1988. Discussions between Israel and a Jordanian-Palestinian delegation would initiate talks that were to last some six months, leading to a three-year transition period. And it was hoped that "final status negotiations," beginning before the transition period, would be completed within a year. The United States would offer the parties a draft agreement for their consideration. All these negotiations would be preceded by an international conference under the auspices of the UN secretary general. Palestinian representatives would be part of the Jordanian-Palestinian delegation, and the Palestine issue would be negotiated between Israel and Jordan. According to this procedural scheme, peace would be in sight in four years or less (see Appendix 9).[14]

The major obstacle to progress remained the question of Palestinian representation in the negotiations and Shamir's opposition to an international conference. Foreign Minister Peres was more receptive to the Shultz initiative and was lavishly praised by Reagan's spokesman for his "vision of the future," his creativity, and his "courage and wisdom to say 'yes' when real opportunities arise." But Shamir, according to the United States, had "yet to demonstrate such boldness or willingness to explore new ideas." In what seemed an oblique criticism of the prime minister, the White House denounced "those leaders who are negative," consistently reject new ideas and fail to exploit realistic opportunities to bring about negotiations." They make progress "impossible" and, "in the end, they will have to answer to their own people for the suffering that will inevitably result."[15]

The overwhelming majority of Palestinians, within the territories and outside, continued to insist that the PLO was their sole representative. Israel, backed by the United States, objected to any direct contact with the organization. The U.S. position was based on a commitment given to Israel during the Nixon administration by Secretary of State Henry Kissinger that the United States would not deal with the PLO until it recognized UN resolutions 242 and 338, recognized the state of Israel, and ceased all terrorist activities. Although the PLO had gradually moved toward accepting these conditions, and Chairman Arafat with several of his associates had made statements indicating nuanced recognition of the U.S. requirements, they were still vague and indirect enough to justify the continued boycott of the PLO. Consequently, Shultz's 1988 visits to the area bore no fruit. It was not until the last weeks of the Reagan administration that the United States changed its position, largely as a result of the decisions made by the PNC at its meeting in Algiers during November.

By the end of 1988 the new outlook of the PLO and the Reagan administration's increasing exasperation with Shamir's reluctance to accept the Shultz initiative had caused serious strains in Washington's relations with Israel. As early as June, Shultz was cautioning that continued occupation of the West Bank and frustration of Palestinian rights were "a dead-end street." In August, when Deputy Secretary of State John

C. Whitehead told Israel's representative in Washington that his government should reconsider deportation of Palestinians or the result would be "damage to our bilateral relations," there was a furor in Israel and its government angrily rejected the criticism. In September, Washington issued another harsh condemnation of the use of plastic bullets by the IDF. "We have consistently opposed the use of lethal force in controlling the situation in the occupied territories," the White House spokesman asserted. One of the most severe indictments by the U.S. government was published in February 1989 as part of the State Department's annual report on human rights practices around the world. The report charged that Israeli troops had caused "many avoidable deaths and injuries" by firing on Palestinians in the West Bank and Gaza, and that their response to the Intifada had led to "a substantial increase in human rights violations." Israeli officials saw "no merit in the report," but they perceived it as a blow to the special relationship with the United States.[16]

The traditional unqualified bipartisan support for Israel in the U.S. Congress began to erode as many Democratic and Republican representatives openly questioned policies in the territories. In February 1988 a dozen members of Congress met in private with Israel's ambassador to voice concern over the beatings and shootings. They made it clear that the more than $3 billion in aid to Israel was not endangered; however, they warned, "the time is drawing nearer when [Israel] will have to do something" about its policy toward the protesters. In March thirty senators from both parties, many of them among the staunchest supporters of Israel, sent Shamir a letter criticizing his rejection of the U.S. peace proposals. The letter supported Shultz's strategy, which "can be summarised in three words: land for peace. . . . We were dismayed . . . that Prime Minister Shamir had said that 'this expression of territory for peace is not accepted by me.'" The senators did not expect Israel to leave all the land captured in 1967, but "peace negotiations have little chance of success if the Israel government's position rules out all territorial compromise." In response, Shamir blamed the Arabs, except Egypt, for failing to "prove in deeds that they are willing to negotiate peace with us." His own approach was to put forward the Camp David accords, which he had originally voted against.

When discussion of the U.S. foreign aid bill came before Congress early in 1989, key representatives warned that Israel's "unacceptable" treatment of the Palestinians could weaken support for U.S. assistance. Although the $3 billion 1988 allocation was not endangered, the lawmakers cautioned that if the IDF continued to deport, detain without trial, shoot at, and blow up the houses of Palestinians, Israel could not count on receiving the same amount in the future. The Israelis would get their money in 1989, warned Senator Patrick J. Leahy, but "they build up enormous resentment in the United States, and in the future it would hurt them." The congressional panel approved the State Department's human rights report, noting, however, that Israel "was not the world's worst violator . . . by any means." Still, the United States had "a higher visible responsibility" to investigate Israel's human rights practices because it received more U.S. aid than any other country, as Representative David D. Obey, a panel chairman, explained. The congressmen opposed cutting aid in 1989 because Israel needed reassurance after having been shaken by the U.S. decision to talk with the PLO. In the absence of such reassurance, Israel would be unlikely to make concessions in peace negotiations, according to the congressional estimates.[17]

The Intifada raised political consciousness about the Palestinian question during the 1988 U.S. presidential campaign, when candidate Jesse Jackson's supporters brought it to the floor of the Democratic convention in Atlanta during July. It was the first occasion on which the issue was openly debated at such length and with such intensity by either party at a national convention. Since the 1950s all major party platforms relating to the Middle East had been formulated by ardent Israel supporters, with no mention of self-determination or the national rights of the Palestinians. During 1988 mention of these rights in the Democratic platform was adamantly opposed by the Israeli lobby, whereas Jackson's delegates struggled to include it. His supporters were a strong minority, but they failed to persuade the convention to mention Palestinian rights as equal to those of Israel. Nevertheless, the minority plank brought the question to the forefront among the delegates and in the national media.

In ten states, Democratic party conventions passed resolutions calling for Palestinian statehood and self-determination. These states were California, Illinois, Iowa, Maine, Minnesota, New Mexico, Oregon, Texas, Vermont, and Washington. Ballots in several cities included measures supporting the Palestinians. In San Francisco, proposition "W" asked voters to support establishment of an independent state in the territories, side by side with Israel; it received 31.5 percent of the vote. Question "5" in Cambridge and Sommerville, Massachusetts, demanded an end to Israel's violations in the territories, cessation of U.S. government expenditures for Israel's occupation of the West Bank and Gaza, and an independent Palestinian state; it won by 52.7 percent. In Berkeley, measure "J" called for establishing a sister-city relationship with the Jabalya town and refugee camp in the Gaza district. The Berkeley vote culminated a dispute that began in January 1988, when the city council defeated a resolution of concern about violence in the territories. The dispute split the local Jewish community between supporters, including organizations such as the New Jewish Agenda and the International Jewish Peace Union versus the Jewish Community Relations Council and the local Jewish establishment.[18]

Public opinion polls generally indicated division in the American public on issues related to the Arab-Israel conflict and the Palestinians. According to a Roper poll conducted in April 1989, there was little change in support for Israel after the Intifada began. From April 1988 to April 1989, the decline was only 1 percent in preference for Israel over the Arab states—that is, from 37 percent to 36 percent. Support for the Arabs increased from 11 to 13 percent. However, there was a marked difference after 1986, when 53 percent favored Israel and only 8 percent favored the Arab states. In 1989, 23 percent said they were not sympathetic to either side, 11 percent were equally sympathetic, and 17 percent did not know. Another poll conducted by two American professors showed that 28 percent of Americans had become more favorable to Israel and 20 percent more favorable to the Palestinians after December 1987. A Gallup survey in February and March 1988 found that 35 percent of the American public favored an independent Palestinian state and 23 percent were opposed, although among the "aware" public 41 percent favored the state; among college graduates the figure was 31 percent. In January 1989 a *New York Times* CBS poll revealed that 64 percent favored contacts with the PLO, whereas 23 percent were opposed. Only 24 percent thought "Yassir Arafat and the PLO want peace in the Middle East enough to make real concessions to the government of Israel," whereas 56 percent did not think so. Twenty-eight percent believed Israel was willing to make "real concessions" for peace, and 52 percent thought it was not. The major conclusion to be drawn from these diverse and rather inconsistent polling results was that the American public was divided, like the public in Israel, on issues related to the Arab-Israel conflict, Palestinian independence, and the Intifada—a division that made it feasible for the U.S. government to devise innovative proposals in the peace process.[19]

The combination of changing international perceptions of the Arab-Israel conflict, the PLO's new stance, shifts in American public opinion, and the administration's growing impatience with the failure by the Israeli government to respond to these changes caused a turnabout in U.S. policy during the final weeks of the Reagan administration. After much haggling between the United States and the PLO over phraseology in the new Palestinian position, Secretary of State Shultz announced on December 14, 1988, that Washington would open a "diplomatic dialogue" with the PLO and the American ambassador to Tunisia was designated the only "authorised channel" for the new talks.

Despite Israel's strenuous objections to the new U.S. policy and its repeated unsuccessful attempts to persuade Washington to break off the talks, they became the principal channel in a new initiative by the Bush administration. Since the United States was unable to advance proposals for either the international peace conference or the 1988 Shultz scheme, the next tactic was to use Shamir's own plan for elections in the territories as the point of departure (see Chapter 4 as well as Appendix 8). The plan, approved by the Israeli cabinet and Knesset, included elements of the Shultz proposal and the Camp David agreements. It was based on the concept of "free and democratic elections," a principle that even the PLO and the UNLU had accepted. The only problem was that Shamir attached conditions to the scheme that were unacceptable to the Palestinians. Consequently, the next step of the new administration would be to convince both Israel and the Palestinians that the United States was an honest broker in negotiations. Secretary of State James Baker attempted to establish this role with the PLO through the U.S. ambassador in Tunis and in direct contact with Israel. To demonstrate his even-handedness, Baker addressed the American Israel Public Affairs Committee, a powerful pro-Israel lobby in Washington, during its annual meeting in May 1989. Attempting to establish credibility with the Palestinians, Baker spoke in what was perceived as unusually blunt tones calling on Israel "to lay aside, once and for all, the unrealistic vision of a greater Israel." He noted that for negotiations to be successful, the outcome would "in all probability involve territorial withdrawal and the emergence of a new political reality." At the same time, to give his statement balance, Baker reiterated that the U.S. government "does not support the creation of an independent Palestinian state" but, rather, supports "the reasonable middle ground to which a settlement should be directed." The secretary's statement reinforced an earlier call to Israel by President Bush to end the occupation. The Bush plea was made in conjunction with a visit to Washington during April by Egyptian President Hosni Mubarak. While these were not particularly new or innovative positions, they seemed to present the U.S. stand in blunter terms than usual to Israel and its supporters. Certainly, they were much more direct than the statements on the subject made during the previous eight years of the Reagan administration. This directness could be attributed to the growing urgency with which the Bush administration perceived the instability caused by the Intifada (see Appendix 10).[20]

Prime Minister Shamir's reaction to the Baker speech was to call it "useless," and to assert that he could not agree with the references to greater Israel or to ceasing Jewish settlement in the territories. "I don't think these issues on which we differ are anything to do [sic] with our proposed peace initiative." A number of Israel's supporters in the Congress and in national Jewish organizations severely criticized Baker's comments because of their blunt tone.[21]

Despite the hostile reception to Baker's speech from supporters of Shamir in Israel's government and in the United States, the Bush administration continued to promote the Rabin-Shamir election proposal. U.S. diplomats even convinced the PLO at their parleys in Tunis to seriously consider the scheme. But the project was brought to a halt during July 1989, when Prime Minister Shamir—at the insistence of militants within his own Likud—publicly announced the restrictions he would place on any elections to be held in the occupied territories. Although these were previously known, Shamir's acceptance of them at the Likud party convention promoted them to doctrine, thus binding him in the event of negotiations. The four basic restrictions were exclusion of Jerusalem Arabs from participation; termination of the Intifada before elections; continued establishment of Jewish settlement in the territories; and no surrender of any territory by Israel. In addition, Shamir made it clear that he would not negotiate with the PLO, nor would he ever accept the establishment of a Palestinian state.

Public articulation of these conditions by Shamir seriously threatened continuation of the National Unity Government because the Labor party maintained that they undermined the peace effort. In July, a Labor party convention denounced Likud for subverting the election plan and threatened to leave the government. Likud's demands also threw into jeopardy the delicate negotiations between the United States and the PLO; the demands derailed the whole election scheme—a result probably intended by Likud militants who insisted that Shamir publicly and officially proclaim his restrictions and conditions for the election process.

THE AMERICAN JEWISH REACTION
TO THE INTIFADA

Initially, the leaders of the American Jewish establishment were cautious in their response to the uprising and to Israel's attempts to cope with it. When the Reagan administration criticized Israel's riot control tactics, several of the sixty-odd agencies affiliated with the Conference of Presidents of Major American Jewish Organizations, the overarching body of establishment agencies, denounced the criticism as premature and overly harsh. At the local level, professionals reported far less condemnation of Israel than during the 1982 invasion of Lebanon. Many, however, were worried about the continued use of "iron-fist" tactics. Some local rabbis reported "ambivalence"; others, "frustration." Jewish leaders, though concerned about the loss of life, were reluctant to speak out on Israeli security issues. When Rabbi Alexander Schindler, a leader of the Reform Jewish community, observed that Israel's continued occupation of the territories was "a time-bomb, ticking away at Israel's vitals," he was reprimanded by several right-wing Knesset members. Some in Likud were shocked; Tehiya leader Geula Cohen said the rabbi's comment "armed the terrorists with grenades to destroy the state."[22]

Confusion was created in the Jewish community and among the professional leaders by conflicting reports about events in the territories. Initially, when officials of the Israel embassy briefed American Jewish leaders in "closed-door" sessions, they said that Israel's intelligence had intercepted PLO communications. These communications revealed that the Intifada was instigated from abroad, principally by Palestinian terrorists. Following such a meeting with the Israeli consul general in New York, Morris Abram, chairman of the Presidents' Conference, wrote an article in the *New York Times* making this charge. Within a few weeks, however, Defense Minister Rabin acknowledged that the uprising had been spontaneously generated—led and organized from within the territories, not from abroad.[23]

When the United States in an unusual vote supported the first Security Council resolution, in January 1988, censuring Israel for deporting Palestinians, evidence of a split in the leadership began to emerge. Many were chagrined about the fact that when Jordan deported thousands of Palestinians in 1970, the United Nations was silent. Abram issued a statement expressing disappointment over the U.S. vote, complaining that it would not advance the cause of peace. "Calling on Israel to refrain from punishing the ring-leaders of the violence will only encourage further violence," he said. Another of his colleagues complained that "it is certainly disturbing to see the PLO calling the shots in the Security Council." When still other leaders began to be indecisive about defending Israel, or about criticizing the U.S. position, they were privately reprimanded by Israeli officials who insisted that the Reagan administration would have been much more reluctant to support the Security Council resolution if the American Jewish community had been solid in backing Israel.[24]

Within a month, it was no longer possible to conceal the divisions in the Jewish community. Several prominent rabbis, leaders of rabbinical groups, and former chairmen of the Presidents' Conference were sending messages to Israeli leaders and making public statements about their concerns. Rabbi Schindler sent a telegram to Israel's President Herzog calling Rabin's policy of beating demonstrators "an offence to the Jewish spirit [that] violates every principle of human decency." He was "deeply troubled and pained" to send such a message, but could not "remain silent." The ex-director of the prestigious American Jewish Committee also condemned Rabin's policy. "Using brute force evokes other times and places when it was used against us," he observed. The President of Hadassah, the largest women's Zionist organization, was "appalled" by Rabin's stand. It "is not the Israeli way and it is not the Jewish way," she warned. Jacob Stein, another former chairman of the Presidents' Conference and a prominent Republican, said that he was "rather appalled by the reports of random beatings of Palestinians."[25]

Events in Gaza and the West Bank aroused the concern of well-known American Jews who usually stood aloof from developments in Israel and the Arab-Israel conflict. One was the actor and writer Woody Allen, whose op-ed article appeared in the *New York Times* stating that "Israel's policy defied belief." Allen pointed out that there had been "few times that I have taken a public stance" on political issues of the day. He had been so infuriated by South Africa's treatment of blacks that he refused to permit his films to be shown there. Although a firm supporter of Israel, he was now "appalled beyond measure by the treatment of the rioting Palestinians by the Jews. . . . Am I reading newspapers correctly?" he asked. "I can't believe it. And I don't know exactly what is to be done, but I'm sure pulling out my movies is not the answer." Perhaps, he stated, it was time "for all of us who are rooting for Israel . . . to speak out and use every measure of pressure—moral, financial, and political—to bring this wrongheaded approach to a halt."[26]

Allen's protest sparked a flurry of correspondence in the New York and Israeli press. Some commentators supported him; others took him to task for failing to understand Israel's difficulties. One Israeli professor at Tel Aviv University criticized Allen for not taking a stand earlier, "when we needed him." Where was he during the previous twenty years of occupation when the homes of Arab suspects were bulldozed away, or during the war in Lebanon? the professor asked.[27]

By February the divisions in the American Jewish community had begun to annoy Prime Minister Shamir. Those who criticize "are people who want to see us defeated and massacred," he thundered. At a Jerusalem meeting of the Presidents' Conference, he demanded a clamp-down on Jewish criticism from abroad. "It is inconceivable that, God forbid, any American Jews would permit themselves to be used in campaigns against us, even if they have criticism or doubts of their own regarding some of Israel's policies and practices." It is just what the Arabs want, he argued. Jewish criticism must end because "every critical statement of a Jewish leader does much more harm than many violent demonstrations in Gaza and elsewhere." It is "absolutely un-Jewish and very dangerous to join an anti-Israel front with non-Jews," he warned.[28]

In responding to Shamir, Morris Abram cautioned that "there is a danger of serious erosion" in the support of the American public "if the status-quo continues indefinitely"; however, after visiting Israel, American Jewish leaders were assured by the prime minister and President Herzog "that the policy of restraint continues." The American Jewish leaders, Abram argued, should not air their criticism of Israel in public, because it "ill serves our purpose. . . . It is unwise to disagree in public with the Israeli government's policy on matters of life and death," for it could create the impression that American Jews were divided in their support.[29]

When Shamir visited the United States in March, he successfully rallied Jewish leaders to his side. After addressing some 3,000 members of the United Jewish Appeal Young Leadership, a principal American Jewish fundraising organization, he received a foot-stamping ovation while the audience rose to cheer him. Despite this reaction, a survey by Steven M. Cohen of Queens College in New York a year before the Intifada showed that only 22 percent of American Jews agreed that they "should not publicly criticise policies of the Israel government." Sixty percent disagreed, and 15 percent were not sure.[30]

During March and April 1988 the *Los Angeles Times* conducted a poll comparing the views and perceptions of American Jews and non-Jews. Jews strongly supported the U.S. proposal for an international peace conference and more autonomy for the Palestinians, but they opposed by 61 percent negotiations with the PLO. Forty-one percent of the Jews and 65 percent of the non-Jews felt "that there is an element of racism involved in attitudes of Israelis toward Arabs." Perceptions of media coverage also differed among Jews. Eighty percent of the Orthodox Jews, 62 percent of the Conservative Jews, and 53 percent of the Reform Jews felt that it was distorted, compared to 42 percent of the non-affiliated Jews. Fifty-seven percent of the Jews polled had a favorable impression of Shimon Peres, compared to the 49 percent who favored Shamir. U.S. Secretary of State George Shultz was favored by 70 percent. *New York Times* reporter Robert Sheer concluded that the survey demonstrated "a profound dismay over the recent months of violence in the occupied territories. This feeling has, in turn, produced views that are far more nuanced by a sense of contradiction and complexity than most analysts have thought. Moreover, Jewish Americans are neither so preoccupied in their thinking nor so different from non-Jews as usually is thought."[31]

In a few months it was clear that the divisions inside the Jewish community about Israeli policies in the occupied territories could no longer be kept "within the family." The dispute brought to the fore an even more fundamental question than whether Israel's policies were wise: Should "loyal" Jews be permitted to criticize Israel publicly at all? Henry Siegman, ex–vice president of the American Jewish Congress, pointed out that disagreements over Israel's policy between Labor and Likud were aired publicly and exposed to the world's media. If Israeli Jews are deeply divided on such crucial issues, why shouldn't these differences be reflected among Diaspora Jews? Israeli right-wingers who so vehemently denounced American critics of Israel "would not hesitate for even a fraction of a moment to seek Diaspora Jewry's intervention including that of U.S. congressmen, if they thought it would prevent the return of the territories and the dismantling of Jewish settlements," he asserted. This certainly would constitute outside interference in Israel's affairs, so why should their unwillingness to permit those who disagree with them about Israel's security be the prevailing standard? These rightists claimed for themselves the exclusive prerogative of criticism. American Jews could "no longer enjoy the luxury" of avoiding policy debates about Israel that might detract from their preoccupation with maintaining a united front, Siegman believed.[32]

An opposing view was presented by Joseph S. Sternstein, a prominent leader of the Jewish National Fund, the Zionist Organization of America, and the American Zionist Federation. He believed that "in issues involving political and military security—hence, physical survival—a line must be drawn" beyond which Diaspora Jews should not intervene. Those who, for example, denounced the responses of the Israeli army and police to events in the territories as being brutal were giving aid and comfort to Israel's enemies. The enemy was equally gleeful about terms such as "intransigent" when applied to Israel's leaders. Even the U.S. State Department had taken to "quoting with satisfaction the words of Jewish leaders" who criticized Israel. "Intervention by self-righteous Diaspora Jews" was transforming "responsible and constructive cross-fertilization of thoughts [between Israel and the diaspora] into palpable political injury for Israel."[33]

Whereas the great majority of the American Jewish community were mere spectators in the controversies over support for Israel, activists at either end of the spectrum reflected the views of both the militant nationalists and the doves of Israeli politics. Gush Emunim not only had supporters in the United States but included among its activists in Israel a large percentage of American Jews. When the Intifada began, the head of the World Zionist Organization's Immigration Department reported that "more than half the immigrants from the U.S. in recent years" settled in the West Bank, whereas only 15 to 20 percent from other countries settled in the region.[34] American Jewish supporters of Gush Emunim took the lead in attacking fundraising organizations such as the Jewish National Fund (JNF) and the United Jewish Appeal (UJA) for not underwriting Jewish settlement in the West Bank and Gaza. The issue arose when the fundraisers became concerned that the U.S. Internal Revenue Service might not approve of such aid. They also feared that it might be questioned by the U.S. State Department. Supporters of the settlers who demanded philanthropic funding for the territories persuaded New York senators Alphonse D'Amato and Daniel Patrick Moynihan to intervene on their behalf. The senators found out that the U.S. government does not prohibit such investment but considers it unwise, whereupon the American Jews who had demanded the aid decided to sue the JNF in a New York court hoping that the fundraising organizations would eventually be compelled to subsidize their favored projects.

Israel's peace groups also had their partisans among the hundreds of American Jewish organizations. These included American Friends of Peace Now, Friends of Yesh Gvul, the New Jewish Agenda, Americans for Progressive Israel, and dozens of others. In April 1988 some twenty of these groups formed a coalition to demonstrate in New York City against Likud's rejection of territorial compromise. A similar mass protest against policies in the territories was convened in 1989. Characteristic of these factions was the Committee for Judaism and Social Justice formed in 1989 in association with the Jewish monthly magazine *Tikkun*. Its purpose was to form a Jewish peace lobby as an alternative to the American Israel Public Affairs Committee (AIPAC) and the Presidents' Conference, with views supporting "peace for territories" and recognition of Palestinian national aspirations. Among the prominent American Jews associated with it were Woody Allen, Arthur Miller, Philip Roth, Betty Friedan, Abbie Hoffman, Norman Lear, and Irving Howe. One of its first newspaper ads published in the *New York Times* began "No, Mr. Shamir . . . don't assume that American Jews support your policies toward the Palestinians."[35]

It should be noted that the political clout of Jewish "peaceniks" was never as great as that of supporters on the right. The "hawks" were far more influential among American politicians and members of Congress, probably because their views were closer to those of AIPAC, established in 1954 as one of the most effective lobbies in Washington congressional circles.

Although AIPAC presumed to represent the prevailing consensus of organized American Jewry on matters relating to Israel and the Middle East, it was challenged in 1988 by the leaders of three other Jewish establishment groups—the American Jewish Committee, the American Jewish Congress, and the Anti-Defamation League of Bnai B'rith—for several of its positions on legislation pertaining to the Middle East pending in Congress. The leaders of the three organizations asserted that AIPAC was out of step with "the consensus of the organized Jewish community on some Middle East issues. More significant than the issues themselves, however, was the willingness of several establishment groups to take independent and diverse positions on matters relating to Israel. This new stance was prompted by awareness that the American Jewish community was not solidly behind Israel, especially in its policies toward the Intifada.[36]

More than 150 Jewish publications (35 in Greater New York) made coverage of the Intifada a major theme at the 1988 annual meeting of the American Jewish Press Association. Participants observed that the Jewish press "is caught between a rock and a hard place. On the one hand, they felt obliged to correct the "biased reporting" about the uprising (see Chapter 4); on the other, they were obligated to reflect the divisions within the community. "We can't be apologists." One editor was astounded at "the intensity of the anger . . . encountered because of our coverage." The number of articles in *Tikkun* about the Intifada and Israeli policies in the territories was unusual. The monthly was established in 1986 as an alternative to *Commentary*, one of the magazines published by the American Jewish Committee. Over the years *Commentary* had come to represent the views of the U.S. conservative establishment in general and positions close to those of Likud on matters related to Israel and the Middle East.[37]

Most worrisome to the Israeli establishment and its supporters in the United States was the decision by increasing numbers of prominent American Jewish personalities to break the U.S. government and Israeli boycott of contacts with the PLO. For a decade or more, delegations of American Jews representing the establishment had traveled to Arab countries surrounding Israel, especially to Egypt and Jordan, where they parleyed with Arab leaders, in effect acting as unofficial intermediaries. More recently, many seemed to take seriously the statements by PLO officials about their changing policies toward Israel. Stirred by events in the territories, several of the Jewish leaders now urged the U.S. government to reconsider its position toward the PLO, much to the chagrin of Israel's leaders. Several important American Jews, much concerned about the Intifada, concluded that contact with the PLO was a prerequisite to ending unrest in the territories. During 1988 several meetings were arranged between them and PLO representatives, culminating in a visit by a small Jewish delegation to Stockholm, Sweden. There the delegation received assurances from Yassir Arafat that the PLO would recognize Israel and UN resolutions 242 and 338, and that it would cease terrorist activities. Arafat's assurances were instrumental in the subsequent recognition of the PLO by the U.S. government. As was to be expected, reaction in the official Jewish community was divided. Leaders who had unwaveringly supported Israeli government policies condemned the Stockholm meeting and labeled those Jews who participated as deviant nobodies who represented only themselves. Others, who were less staunch backers of current Israeli policies, perceived the parleys with Arafat as a development of paramount importance, indicating a fundamental change in the PLO; few, however, publicly acclaimed the event.

Prime Minister Shamir resolved that preemptive measures were required to prevent continued erosion of American Jewish support and decided to convene a Conference on Jewish Solidarity with Israel during March 1989. The meetings would demonstrate world Jewish "togetherness" and rally support for his peace plan (see Chapter 4 and Appendix 8). To ensure the bipartisan nature of the conference, Shamir solicited Peres's support. A prominent member from each party was designated as a coordinator and sent to the United States to obtain cooperation from American Jewish establishment leaders. The conference was carefully orchestrated to minimize any public dissent; however, enough discussion was permitted to avoid the appearance of rubber-stamping Shamir's policies. With only a few exceptions, the 1,580 delegates from 42 countries (730 from the United States) endorsed the Israeli course of action. Pounding the podium, Shamir demanded unity and solidarity to show the world that "the Jewish people is not divided, the Jewish people is not weakened, the Jewish people is responding to Israel's call." Many of the delegates urged Israel to reconsider its opposition to negotiations with the PLO, but Shamir remained adamantly opposed. Foreign Minister Arens explained that although the Intifada would not "destroy" Israel, if it created the impression that Jews are isolated and have lost the support of Diaspora Jewry, then "mortal danger will be lurking in the shadow for Israel and the Jewish people." Therefore, it was necessary for world Jewry to show their solidarity with the Jewish state.[38]

After nearly two years, it was clear that the Intifada had been, if not the cause, then a catalyst in creating new relations between Israel and American Jews. The 1982 war in Lebanon, too, had loosened these ties, but events there ended in one summer; after 1982 Lebanon seemed to disappear from the consciousness of American establishment Jews. But the Intifada continued; it seemed to be lasting indefinitely, a situation that would be difficult to forget in a month, or two, or three. Every day for nearly two years, Jews in the United States were reminded of the uprising, of the embarrassment caused by Israeli policies in the territories, and of the changing U.S. government and PLO positions. Many American Jews eventually became convinced, like many Israelis, that the time had also come for Israel to change its outlook. By the end of 1989, those advocating change were no longer merely fringe elements within the community; the Intifada had created a fundamental division between Jewish supporters of the status quo and those who believed in the need for greater flexibility.

THE ARAB STATES AND PLO REACTIONS

The Intifada refocused the attention of the Arab world after a period when priority had shifted to other issues, such as the Iraq-Iran War. At the November 1987 Arab League summit in Amman, Palestinians were disappointed by the secondary place their concerns had been assigned on the agenda. Indeed, many believed that one of the causes of the uprising was despair among the population in Gaza and the West Bank over the indifference to their fate shown by other Arabs, especially during the Amman meeting. But the courage of Palestinians in resisting Israeli occupation after December 1987 could no longer be ignored, and every Arab country joined in, giving at least verbal support to the Intifada. The uprising warranted a new "extraordinary" Arab League summit convened during June in Algiers and attended by seventeen chiefs of state from the twenty-one member nations. (The PLO was recognized as the twenty-second member.) This was the League's second summit in seven months, one of the best-attended in a decade. Even Libya's Muammar al-Qaddafi participated, after boycotting other recent meetings. The PLO requested a $300–400 million "insurrection fund" to support the uprising and to provide assistance for those in the territories unable to work because of strikes and other labor stoppages. Instead of providing this sum, however, the League established a joint committee of the PLO and six other members to make political decisions and direct international support for the uprising. The PLO charged in a pamphlet distributed at the meeting that Arab officialdom was derelict in its duty to the Intifada. The final communiqué dealing with the Intifada criticized the United States for its pro-Israel bias and its antagonism to "Palestine national rights." It characterized Secretary of State Shultz in his efforts to negotiate a settlement as "slow, ineffective, and incapable of standing up to the Israeli position." The League insisted that settlement could be attained only through an international conference under UN auspices.

Most Arab governments did little about the Intifada after the Algiers conference, probably because they were incapable of taking any tangible action. As a result of their special relationship with the United States, Egypt and Jordan attempted to persuade the Americans to intervene on behalf of the Palestinians and to ameliorate their plight. Other countries with American ties, including Tunisia, Kuwait, and Saudi Arabia, joined with the Arab League representative in Washington to request greater U.S. pressure on Israel to alter its policies in the territories.

Ties between Israel and Egypt were severely strained by the uprising. Because Egypt was the only Arab country with which Israel had a peace agreement and diplomatic relations, this strain was a serious matter. Within the first weeks of the uprising, Egypt summoned Israel's ambassador in Cairo to protest "the brutal, oppressive measures . . . against the Palestinian people," a protest that they repeated several times. Cairo's statements indicated that relations with Israel were at their lowest ebb since Mubarak withdrew his ambassador from Israel in protest against the 1982 invasion of Lebanon. The uprising led to a wave of popular sympathy by Egyptians for the Palestinians, expressed in demonstrations on campuses and in the streets, statements issued by professional organizations, and escalating demands that the government break all ties with Israel. President Mubarak resisted these pressures, attempting to revive the Middle East international peace conference. At a meeting with President Reagan in Washington during January 1989, the two leaders urged Israel and the Palestinians to accept a six-month truce— a cooling-off period during which political issues could be discussed. Mubarak also added a plea to Israel urging it to suspend further Jewish settlement activity during the moratorium, while steps would be taken to guarantee Palestinian political rights and plans would be made for the international conference.

Mubarak's role as regional peace-maker was demonstrated again in October 1988, when he became the intermediary between Yassir Arafat and King Hussein, following their two-year estrangement. The three leaders met in Jordan, where King Hussein once again recognized the PLO as the "sole legitimate representative of the Palestinian people" during discussions on the international peace conference. Mubarak offered to visit Israel if it "would lead to solving the problem"; but because his conditions included suspending Jewish settlement activity in the territories, the visit did not occur. During June 1988 Mubarak sent his minister of state for foreign affairs to Jerusalem to discuss the Rabin-Shamir election plan and to offer mediation between Israel and the PLO—an offer that Shamir strongly rebuffed.

Mubarak made still another attempt to reconcile the differences between the Israeli government and the Palestinians toward the end of 1989 with a ten-point compromise plan. The plan proposed that

1. All Palestinians in the West Bank, Gaza, and East Jerusalem would be permitted to vote in local elections and to run for office.
2. Candidates would not be subjected to interference from Israeli authorities.

3. International supervision of the election process would be permitted.
4. Construction of new Jewish settlements or expansion of existing ones in the occupied territories would be suspended during the election period.
5. The IDF would withdraw its forces from polling areas on election day.
6. All Israelis except those who live or work in the territories would be banned from entry on election day.
7. Egypt and the United States would help to form an Israeli-Palestinian committee to prepare for the elections within a two-month period.
8. During the negotiation process, Israel would agree to discuss the exchange of occupied land for peace, giving full consideration to its security needs.
9. The United States and Israel would publicly guarantee Israel's adherence to these proposals.
10. Israel would agree publicly in advance to accept the outcome of the election.

Although King Hussein withdrew all Jordanian responsibility for the West Bank in July 1988 (see Chapter 3), he continued to play a highly visible role in the peace process. Parleys continued among King Hussein, Mubarak, and Arafat. Hussein supported Mubarak's activity as intermediary between the Palestinians, other Arab states, and the United States. The Egyptian and Jordanian leaders consulted each other before and after their respective visits to Washington, maintaining positions that would be perceived as "moderate" by the United States. A moderate position involved continued backing of the international peace conference, recognition of the PLO as the primary representative of the Palestinians, and appeals to Israel through the United States to ease its policies in the territories. Neither Egypt nor Jordan rejected the Rabin-Shamir election scheme out of hand; each country commended the idea of elections but requested greater clarification of how the plan would be implemented without emasculating Palestinian rights to self-determination. Egypt, as the senior partner in this unofficial alliance of "moderates," undertook to persuade Arafat not to discard the plan without further examination; at least that was the case until Shamir himself undermined the plan with the series of restrictions imposed on it by the Likud party in July 1989.

The Intifada galvanized the PLO into speedy political action and forced the organization to confront many of its own internal contradictions, which had prevented timely response to political opportunities during the previous decade. True, there had been nuances of change in PLO policy since the early 1970s, but to detect them required a keen political sense and an ability to decipher and interpret many of the organization's rather obscure or convoluted pronouncements. These "hints" about accepting coexistence with Israel and giving up violence were insufficient either to elicit change in U.S. policy toward the PLO or to convince Israeli moderates that the organization had abandoned terrorism and was no longer determined to eliminate the Jewish state.

There were objectively valid reasons for the reluctance of the leadership to surrender its "constructive ambiguity"—primarily the deep divisions within the PLO between moderates willing to accept political compromises and militants who clung to ideological formulations that made peace negotiations irrelevant. Although Yassir Arafat's home base, Fatah, was by far the largest and strongest of the six key guerrilla factions affiliated with the PLO, it was not strong enough to overcome the opposition from smaller Marxist or militantly nationalist groups without totally disrupting the movement. Furthermore, there was the danger of at least another half-dozen Palestinian factions outside the PLO, many of whose leaders were terrorists in the true sense of the word. They had already assassinated several key aides to Arafat who dared to initiate dialogue with Israel. To complicate matters even further, several factions within and outside the PLO received material aid and political support from various Arab governments—Syria, Libya, and Iraq. Beyond the spectrum of nationalist factions, there were several Islamic fundamentalist groups that also had to be considered if any sort of Palestinian consensus were to be achieved.

Palestinian leaders outside the occupied territories were not subject to the same daily pressures as their compatriots living under occupation for twenty years. For those outside, the choice was between taking risky political initiatives and disrupting the semblance of cohesion within the PLO, or continuing to issue vague statements, maintaining political ambivalence, and keeping the PLO intact, free of internecine conflict. Throughout the twenty years of occupation, PLO leadership and the individual leaders of the diverse factions maintained regular contact with their cadres in the occupied territories (see Chapter 3). The PLO steadily increased its standing and influence among the Palestinians in the West Bank and Gaza, despite competition from Islamic groups and from supporters of Jordan's King Hussein. Whereas the Islamic factions also increased in numbers and influence, supporters of the king steadily lost ground as Palestinians became increasingly restive under the occupation.

After twenty years, the patience of those living in the territories had worn thin; they were determined to take overt political action despite the ambivalence of the outside leadership. As the uprising gained momentum, visibility, international sympathy, and support, the PLO leadership was forced to choose between new decisive and unambiguous action or becoming irrelevant to their constituencies in the territories. There was serious danger that the leadership of the UNLU in Gaza and the West Bank would preempt the outside PLO directorate. The UNLU had already issued a number of clear-cut, straightforward political pronouncements, such as their fourteen demands in January 1988 (see Appendix 3). In August Faisal Husseini's draft of a plan for an independent Palestinian state supplied to the public in greater detail the goals of the Intifada (see Appendix 4). These initiatives from within the territories finally convinced Arafat that the PLO itself must respond with more decisive political action. An initial step was the position paper distributed by Bassam Abu Sharif, special adviser to Arafat, at the Arab League summit in Algiers during June 1988 (see Appendix 5).

The Abu Sharif statement opened discussion about PLO moderation, both within the organization and among the parties that Arafat was seeking to influence, such as the U.S. government, American Jews, and Israeli peace advocates. It also created the anticipated uproar among militant factions within the PLO, evoked criticism from Syria and Libya, and made Arafat the center of a political storm among Palestinian nationalists.

By the summer of 1988 plans were under way for a meeting of the 448-member Palestine National Council (PNC), also known as the Palestine parliament in exile. Rumors abounded that the organization would issue a declaration of independence in conjunction with a number of political changes, including recognition of Israel and renunciation of "violence" (terrorism) outside the territories. However, internal disagreements loomed so large that the leaders of the organization feared a full-scale meeting would disrupt the PNC, causing irreparable damage. After several postponements, the PNC was finally convened in an emergency session in Algiers during November 1988. In a speech on November 15 to the nineteenth session of the Council, called the "Intifada meeting," Arafat proclaimed "in the name of God, in the name of the people, of the Palestine people, the establishment of the state of Palestine on our own Palestine nation, with its capital in the holy Jerusalem."

The PNC also issued a political program calling for a solution to the conflict based on UN Security Council's resolutions 242 and 338; it declared willingness to negotiate with Israel in the context of an international peace conference, provided that Israel recognized Palestinian rights. The PNC rejected the use of violence outside the territories, and it paid respects to the special relationship between the Palestinian and Jordanian peoples. Plans were to be prepared for a confederation of the two countries approved in a referendum following Palestinian independence (see Appendix 7).

Analysts have found a number of striking similarities in the phraseology used in the Palestinian, U.S., and Israeli independence declarations. Both the Palestinian and Israeli documents opened with references to the country as the birthplace of their respective peoples. The Israeli declaration read: "The land of Israel was the birthplace of the Jewish people. Here their spiritual, religious and national identity was formed"; and the Palestine declaration read: "Palestine, the land of the three monotheistic faiths, is where the Palestine Arab people was born, on which it grew, developed, and excelled." Both documents emphasized the "everlasting union" (Palestinian) or "historical association" (Israeli) of the people with the land and the deep attachment they retain. Like the Israeli declaration, which proclaims that the Jewish state is "open to the immigration of Jews from all countries of their dispersion" and calls "to the Jewish people all over the world to rally to our side," the PNC document declares that "the state of Palestine is the state of Palestinians wherever they may be . . . to enjoy in it their collective national and cultural identity." Like the American Declaration of Independence, the Palestinian charter reaffirms "inalienable rights" and the right to "independence."

The PNC document also emphasizes the importance of the Intifada, referring to it several times and ultimately paying respect to those "sainted martyrs" who gave their lives, were wounded, or were prisoners or detainees in the uprising.

In an unusual departure from the modus operandi of the PNC, the declaration and its accompanying political statement were debated and voted on item by item rather than by acclamation. After lengthy discussion in committees, the declaration and policy statement were adopted with 253 voting for, 46 against, and 10 abstentions. Not all of the approximately 380 members who attended the conference were present for the voting. Strong objection came from George Habash, leader of the PFLP, who opposed the acceptance of resolutions 242 and 338 because they recognized the Palestinians not as "a people" but merely as "refugees." He also felt that the new program's implicit recognition of Israel was premature, that such recognition should be a concession emerging from peace negotiations. Despite his negative vote, Habash, like other PNC members who opposed the documents, declared that he would accept the majority decision (see Appendixes 6 and 7).[39]

Ten Arab League members as well as Turkey, Malaysia, and Indonesia immediately recognized the Palestinian state. Eventually, only Syria and Lebanon (occupied by Syria) among the Arab states failed to fully acknowledge the new nation. The Europeans were initially more hesitant.

The British Foreign Office called the declaration "premature"; Norway said that it was a step forward but would require a territory that the Palestinians controlled before they received recognition; and Spain's foreign minister regarded the move as "of enormous importance," obliging the United States and Europe "to review their policy stand on the Middle East peace process." Palestinian militants who opposed the whole idea of negotiations and political compromise—like the Fatah dissidents, Saiqa, the Popular Struggle Front, and Ahmad Jebril's PLFP–General Command, all backed by Syria—adamantly opposed the declaration. The Fatah Uprising in Damascus asserted that the whole series of events leading to the declaration was a "catastrophe" that would "deal a blow to the unity of the Palestine land."[40]

Israel immediately dismissed the declaration and its accompanying statements as irrelevant and unimportant. Foreign Minister Peres believed that much of the Western world was "fooled by moderate-sounding voices in Algiers . . . under a headline of moderation" and that the PNC had adopted an even "more extreme position." Lest Palestinians in the territories be taken in by the events in Algiers, Israeli authorities clamped a curfew on Gaza and the West Bank for several days to prevent any unruly celebrations (see Chapter 3).[41]

The peace movement in Israel, particularly Peace Now and parties to the left of Labor, considered the Algiers meeting a significant positive move. PNC acceptance of the 1947 UN partition plan was the first unequivocal and open recognition of a two-state solution. Even though renunciation of terrorism was perceived as ambiguous, acceptance of UN resolutions 242 and 338 indicated willingness to consider a peaceful approach to the conflict, according to these Israelis.

The U.S. government believed that the PNC meeting in Algiers probably had "gone too far in raising public expectation" about PLO acceptance of resolution 242. Furthermore, as a State Department spokesman observed, it was "extraordinary that a convicted murderer" would continue to serve on the PLO Executive Committee. She was referring to Abul Abbas, convicted in absentia by an Italian court for his role in the murder of an American during the hijacking of an Italian passenger ship. Despite these reservations, the U.S. government considered the declaration and the accompanying political resolutions as "progress, though insufficient."

By 1989 more than 100 nations recognized the Palestine declaration of independence, although the degree of recognition varied from establishment of full diplomatic ties to mere acknowledgment of the move. In April 1989 the seventy-member PLO Executive Committee gave further substance to the declaration by unanimously electing Yassir Arafat as the first president of the state of Palestine. He was to remain in office until democratic elections could take place in the independent state. At the same time, representatives of dissident Palestinian factions opposing the PNC met in Tripoli, the capital of Libya, to denounce Arafat and the Algiers decisions. They declared that they would establish their own PLO to replace the movement led by Arafat.

During the month following the Algiers meeting, there was a flurry of international activity aimed at getting the U.S. government to end its diplomatic boycott of the PLO. The independence document, the PNC political statement, and Arafat's journeys through Europe attracted world attention and became a focus of diplomatic discussions. One after another barrier to recognition fell as Western statesmen, political analysts, and several leaders of the American and Israeli Jewish communities called for opening channels of communication with the PLO. Several of the United States' European allies and Middle East leaders, including President Mubarak of Egypt, King Hassan of Morocco, and King Hussein of Jordan, urged Washington to reconsider its policy toward the organization.

At first, Secretary of State Shultz resisted these pressures. He demonstrated to those who opposed a change in U.S. policy that he was a staunch defender of Kissinger's conditions for recognizing the PLO by refusing to grant Arafat a visa when he was invited to address the UN General Assembly in New York. Shultz still considered Arafat a "terrorist" and maintained that he had not demonstrated a willingness to engage in peaceful dialogue. Various intermediaries intervened with Arafat to elicit a statement from the PLO that would satisfy Washington's interpretation of its conditions for recognition.

The next step was Arafat's speech to the UN General Assembly in Geneva during December. The meeting, originally scheduled for New York, was shifted to Geneva when Shultz refused to grant the visa. Arafat's UN statement came closer to meeting the conditions for U.S. recognition but still did not satisfy Shultz. The PLO leader concluded with a direct appeal to Israel for negotiations: "I come to you in the name of my people, offering my hand so that we can make true peace, peace based on justice. I ask the leaders of Israel to come here under the sponsorship of the UN, so that, together, we can forge peace. . . . Come, let us make peace. Cast away fear and intimidation. Leave behind the specter of the wars that have raged continuously for the past 40 years."[42]

The State Department responded that, as positive as the appeal had been, Arafat was still ambiguous on three key points and still failed to meet U.S. conditions for direct talks. Unless Arafat addresses "clearly, squarely, without ambiguity" the PLO's recognition of resolutions 242 and 338, of Israel's right to exist, and rejection of terrorism, the United States will maintain its boycott.

A few days before Geneva, Arafat met in Stockholm with a delegation of five prominent American Jews under the auspices of Sweden's foreign minister. Following the two-day meeting, the foreign minister issued a statement signed by the conferees that strengthened Arafat's commitment to the U.S. conditions (see Appendix 11).

At a press conference on December 14, Arafat further "clarified" his Stockholm and UN pronouncements, appearing to fulfill all of the U.S. demands; this final statement, however, was nearly identical to previous "pre-clarifications." Shultz now announced that he was satisfied: The PLO had complied with U.S. conditions for direct talks, and Washington was "prepared for a substantive dialogue with PLO representatives." The Reagan administration explained that the sudden shift in U.S. policy resulted from elimination of the "background noise" in earlier PLO statements; the latest was "clear" and "not encumbered." Sweden played a significant role as intermediary in eliciting the "right words" from Arafat and in clearing up the "background noise." Egypt and the Saudi ambassador in Washington also helped to coordinate the statement with the United States' demands. The apprehension of U.S. allies in Europe about the continued Intifada and its impact on Middle East stability and growing divisions within the U.S. government were also influential factors culminating in the Reagan administration's decision to at last begin a direct dialogue with the Palestinians.

Had it not been for the Intifada, however, neither the PLO nor the United States would have altered their policies by the end of 1988. The insurrection convinced Washington that negotiations with the PLO were inevitable if any credible new peace initiatives were to be realized. The PLO was forced to abandon its policy of "constructive ambiguity" on the key issues of recognizing Israel, the UN resolutions, and renunciation of terrorism. Insistence by the UNLU within the territories on independence as a condition for ending the uprising forced the PNC to confront the issue—one it had avoided for years. The independence declaration was initially a morale builder, but it did strengthen the PLO's diplomatic position and forced several nations to confront the relationship of the Intifada to Middle East stability.

Israel's Prime Minister Shamir was more angry than ever at the new U.S. policy; he called it a "blunder" that would "not help us, not help the United States, and not help the peace process." But he now had to react with some "positive" response. Israel was more isolated than ever; even the American Jewish Presidents' Conference refused to take up cudgels against the new U.S. policy. Aside from the Israeli left, there was one cabinet voice that took heart from the U.S. turnabout—that of the Labor party's Ezer Weizman. A few other Labor party leaders agreed with him that "we've started a new era. . . . The pressure of the U.S. has brought a change in the PLO. I certainly don't think it's a sad day."[43]

By early 1989 Shamir's "positive response" was to accept the 1978 Camp David proposals for Palestinian autonomy in the territories, recasting them in the Rabin-Shamir peace plan adopted by the cabinet and the Knesset during May. Later, in July 1989, when Shamir attached four qualifications to the Palestinian elections in the territories, the proposal was converted from a Rabin-Shamir to a Sharon-Shamir scheme that lost all credibility (see Chapter 4).

It should be kept in mind that from the beginning of the Intifada the UNLU supported, even demanded elections. This demand was included in its fourteen points, in subsequent statements, and in several of the bayanat issued by the leadership. It was the subject of dialogue between American and PLO representatives in Tunis following the U.S. policy changes in December. Arafat responded to the Shamir proposals by saying that he, too, favored elections but with conditions of his own—quite different from those imposed by Likud. His included (1) Israeli withdrawal from Palestinian population centers in the territories, to be overseen by an international force (Israel, however, could temporarily maintain a military presence in those areas); (2) elections would be held for representatives in the territories to join the PNC; (3) five of those elected would be designated by Arafat to negotiate a two-year interim period prior to an international peace conference; (4) in the last stage of the process Israel and the PLO would negotiate the final status of the territories in the international peace conference. Throughout this whole process, Israel would be bound by a written guarantee to the United States that it would remain engaged and that it was committed to Palestinian self-determination (see Appendix 13).[44]

CONCLUSION

After nearly two years it appeared that the Intifada was unlikely to end in the near future. Its final objective—an independent Palestinian state—was still opposed by powerful forces, principally Israel's two dominant parties, Labor and Likud, and the U.S. government. Indeed, as Palestinians became more resolute in their efforts to obtain their goal, Israeli militants became more determined in their opposition to it.

The Intifada did bring the Palestine question to the forefront of world politics, and it again raised the Arab-Israel conflict in public consciousness as a critical and urgent item on the international agenda; but the divisions between mainstream Israeli and Palestinian leaders were so wide that there seemed little prospect for quickly resolving their differences. Rather, the uprising—by forcing all parties concerned to again confront the issue directly—deepened these differences, not only between Palestinians and Israelis but within each society as well.

The Palestinians, united in their determination to obtain independence, were likely to become increasingly divided over the tactics and strategies for achieving their goal. For nearly two years, the UNLU within the territories and the PLO leadership outside had successfully maintained the discipline required to keep the uprising relatively nonviolent. Nevertheless, small but influential factions such as the Islamic fundamentalists in the West Bank and Gaza, and the rivals of Fatah within the PNC, were becoming increasingly impatient with strategies of restraint. The younger-generation Palestinians were also restive, their anger waxing at Israeli occupation and frustrated by the limitations of nonviolence. The major deterrent to the use of more violent strategies and "hot weapons" was awareness of Israel's military might—of its capacity to uproot villages and to deport hundreds or thousands of Palestinians—and the growing acceptance of the "transfer" concept by ever-larger numbers of credible Israeli politicians.

Israel's society was becoming polarized between advocates of greater force versus those urging political compromise as the way to end the Intifada. While the uprising was a dominant theme in political discourse and in the media, there were sufficient numbers of other critical issues to distract public attention. The economy remained in ill repair, with unemployment and inflation out of control (both were more than 10 percent by mid-1989). Some argued that ending the Intifada would improve the economic situation, but the causes of economic crisis were much deeper; ending the Intifada would bring only marginal relief. Public opinion on issues related to the uprising was so divided, it appeared, that any strong political leader would have his way in coping with it.

Within Labor, the leadership was divided; no single politician had the charisma or enthusiastic popular following found among the several politicians on the right. Labor was so torn within its ranks that it failed to devise a coherent and credible program for dealing with the uprising or the complex issues related to it. Likud, too, was divided, but less so; its program for dealing with the Palestinians was clear-cut, straightforward, and generally more to the liking of the "man-in-the street." Likud's leaders included such figures as Ariel Sharon, who had simplistic answers that were easily understood by the public at large when they recommended ending the Intifada by "eliminating" Yassir Arafat and other Palestinian leaders. Without such action, Sharon asserted, there was no possibility of peace.

The maximum that most Israelis, certainly those who dominated Labor and Likud, were likely to concede was far less than nearly any Palestinian leader was willing to accept. On each side the parameters within which acceptable political solutions could be found were fairly well-defined: for Palestinians, an independent state; for Israelis, autonomy with IDF security controls. The differences within each camp had more to do with strategies and tactics for achieving solutions. For Palestinians the choices were active or passive resistance to occupation; for Israelis, the use of military force or political negotiations to end the uprising. It was disagreement over these measures that polarized both Palestinians and Israelis. Divisions within each society were such that the possibility of civil war was not inconceivable. As the intensity of internal debate escalated, there were increasing incidents of violence within both the Israeli and the Palestinian societies.

The ramifications of the Intifada extended far beyond the borders of Israel and Palestine. It was not an isolated conflict like that of the Kurds against the government of Iraq. The struggle involved, on the one side, Israel and its constituencies in the diaspora and the Jewish communities in the Western world, supported by the U.S. government, versus twenty-two Arab nations on the other, particularly the so-called confrontation states, immediately bordering Israel.

The Arab-Israeli conflict began as a struggle for Palestine between the indigenous Arab and Jewish populations, although most Jews at the time were immigrants from Europe. It became a conflict involving the new state of Israel and the surrounding Arab countries, with Palestinians playing a secondary role. The Intifada led to re-Palestinization of the conflict—confrontation between the inhabitants of the West Bank and Gaza and Israel. Now, the Arab states were the secondary participants, with Palestinians again in the lead. Although the Palestinians, especially those under the occupation, were again the primary actors, the Intifada affected most other Arab states and their relations with the United States. Consequently, neither the United States nor the international community could ignore the larger implications.

Though smaller in scale, with many fewer casualties and less violence than similar ethnic conflicts—the Kurds versus Iraq, Northern Ireland, Cyprus, the Turks in Bulgaria, the Algerian revolution, and others—the Intifada captured far more attention in the Western media. It was perceived as a greater threat to peace by many in the West, because of U.S. involvement and the special relationship between the U.S. government and Israel. Because the Arab-Israeli conflict caused at least five wars, each leading to tensions between the United States and the Soviet Union, there was apprehension that the Intifada, too, could spark still another international crisis. It therefore received extensive media coverage and was a topic of prime importance in the chanceries of the West and the Soviet Union.

Prospects for ending the Arab-Israeli confrontation seemed remote, as remote as ending the conflicts in Northern Ireland, Kurdistan, or Cyprus. The Intifada, too, it appeared, would continue but in new forms: in cycles with periods of repression by the Israel army followed by renewed outbreaks. As Palestinians and Israelis wearied of the confrontation, it would lapse into inactivity, only to erupt again when tensions escalated and energies were revived. Inherent in this situation has been the danger that the restraints observed by both Palestinians and Israelis during the first two years of the uprising would erode: that the Palestinians would be provoked or become impatient enough to use "hot weapons," and that the IDF would in turn retaliate with measures like those used by the French in Algeria or the Americans in Vietnam— mass resettlement, large-scale expulsion, and severe economic pressures. If events take this turn, the Arab-Israel conflict could again become the catalyst for international crisis: The Israeli-Egyptian peace treaty could crumble away, Syria could intensify its confrontation with Israel, and the region could again become a diplomatic battleground between the Soviet Union and the United States. For these reasons, the Intifada cannot be ignored or assigned a minor place among U.S. foreign policy priorities.

Perhaps the search for solutions in the Arab-Israeli conflict, the attainment of conflict resolution, is too much to expect. Perhaps a more modest approach would be conflict management, with measures on a less grandiose scale than a peace treaty, or an international conference. Intermediate measures that would not jeopardize Israel's security but could deescalate tensions include President Mubarak's truce, suspension of Jewish settlement during negotiations, IDF withdrawal from heavily populated Palestinian areas, lifting the ban on nationalist symbols, reopening schools and universities, and a halt to stone throwing and other violent manifestations. While conflict management along these lines would satisfy neither the Palestinian nor the Israeli militant nationalists, it could provide time for devising new alternatives and diminish many of the harsher aspects of the Intifada that both Palestinians and Israelis now suffer.

NOTES

1. *New York Times* (hereafter NYT), 12/23/88.
2. NYT, 1/15/88.
3. NYT, 2/18/88; 6/10/89.
4. NYT, 10/4/88; Jewish Telegraphic Agency (hereafter JTA), 12/23/88.

5. *Jerusalem Post International Edition* (hereafter JPI), no. 1,420, 1/23/88.

6. JPI, no. 1,421, 1/30/88.

7. JPI, no. 1,419, 1/16/88.

8. JPI, no. 1,421; no. 1,428, 3/19/89.

9. JPI, no. 1,459, 10/22/88; no. 1,414, 1/14/89.

10. JPI, no. 1,444, 7/9/88; no. 1,458, 10/15/88.

11. JPI, no. 1,484, 4/15/89.

12. JPI, no. 1,458, 10/15/88.

13. JPI, no. 1,475, 2/11/89.

14. NYT, 3/10/89.

15. NYT, 5/18/89.

16. NYT, 6/16/88, 8/25/88, 9/29/88, 2/8/89; *Country Reports on Human Rights Practices for 1988*, submitted by the U.S. Department of State to the 100th Congress (Washington, D.C.: U.S. Government Printing Office, February 1988), pp. 1376–1387.

17. NYT, 2/14/88, 3/10/88, 2/12/89, 3/15/89.

18. *Middle East Report*, November–December, 1988, no. 155, pp. 4–11 (Micha Sifry, "Jessie and the Jews: Palestine and the Struggle for the Democratic Party"); *Middle East Report*, March–April, 1989, no. 157, pp. 40–41 (Marianne Torres, "Berkeley's Sister-City Initiative"); *The Washington Report on Middle East Affairs*, March 1989, p. 20; *Journal of Palestine Studies* (hereafter JPS), no. 72, Summer 1989, pp. 71–83 (Andrea Barron, "Referenda on the Palestine Question in Four U.S. Cities").

19. NYT, 1/18/89; *Los Angeles Times*, 3/14/89; *Washington Report*, April 1989, p. 13 (Fouad Moughrabi, "American Public Opinion Far Ahead of U.S. Policy"); JPI, no. 1,496, 7/8/89.

20. U.S. Department of State, Press Release, no. 96, 5/22/89 (James A. Baker III, "Principles and Pragmatism: American Policy Toward the Arab-Israel Conflict").

21. NYT, 5/24/89.

22. JPI, no. 1,417, 1/2/88.

23. JPI, no. 1,421, 1/30/88.

24. JPI, no. 1,419, 1/16/88.

25. JPI, no. 1,422, 2/6/88.

26. NYT, 1/28/88.

27. JPI, no. 1,423, 2/13/88.

28. JPI, no. 1,427, 3/12/88.

29. *Ibid.*

30. JPI, no. 1,430, 4/2/88.

31. JPI, no. 1,433, 4/23/88.

32. JPI, no. 1,469, 12/31/88.

33. JPI, no. 1,477, 2/25/89.

34. JPI, no, 1,414, 12/12/87.

35. JPI, no. 1,484, 4/15/89.

36. NYT, 10/18/88 (Robert Pear, "Leaders of 3 U.S. Jewish Groups Take Issue with Pro-Israel Lobby").

37. JPI, no. 1,455, 9/24/88.
38. Jewish Telegraphic Agency, cited in *Broome County Reporter*, 3/30/89.
39. *The Nation*, 12/12/88 (Edward W. Said, "Palestine Agenda").
40. NYT, 11/16/88.
41. NYT, 11/18/88; 11/16/88.
42. NYT, 12/14/88.
43. NYT, 12/16/88.
44. NYT, 4/15/89.

Appendix 1

TEXT OF UNITED NATIONS SECURITY COUNCIL RESOLUTION 242 OF NOVEMBER 22, 1967

Adopted unanimously at the 1382nd meeting

The Security Council,

Expressing its continuing concern with the grave situation in the Middle East,

Emphasizing the inadmissibility of the acquisition of territory by war and the need to work for a just and lasting peace in which every State in the area can live in security,

Emphasizing further that all Member States in their acceptance of the Charter of the United Nations have undertaken a commitment to act in accordance with Article 2 of the Charter,

1. *Affirms* that the fulfillment of Charter principles requires the establishment of a just and lasting peace in the Middle East which should include the application of both the following principles:

(i) Withdrawal of Israeli armed forces from territories occupied in the recent conflict;

(ii) Termination of all claims or states of belligerency and respect for and acknowledgement of the sovereignty, territorial integrity and political independence of every State in the area and their right to live in peace within secure and recognized boundaries free from threats or acts of force;

2. *Affirms further* the necessity

(a) For guaranteeing freedom of navigation through international waterways in the area;

(b) For achieving a just settlement of the refugee problem;

(c) For guaranteeing the territorial inviolability and political independence of every State in the area, through measures including the establishment of demilitarized zones;

Source: U.S. Department of State, *The Camp David Summit September 1978*, pub. no. 8954, N.E. and South Asian Series 88.

3. *Requests* the Secretary-General to designate a Special Representative to proceed to the Middle East to establish and maintain contacts with the States concerned in order to promote agreement and assist efforts to achieve a peaceful and accepted settlement in accordance with the provisions and principles of this resolution.

4. *Requests* the Secretary-General to report to the Security Council on the progress of the efforts of the Special Representative as soon as possible.

TEXT OF UNITED NATIONS SECURITY COUNCIL RESOLUTION 338

Adopted by the Security Council at its 1747th meeting, on 21/22 October 1973

The Security Council

1. *Calls upon* all parties to the present fighting to cease all firing and terminate all military activity immediately, no later than 12 hours after the moment of the adoption of this decision, in the positions they now occupy;

2. *Calls upon* the parties concerned to start immediately after the cease-fire the implementation of Security Council Resolution 242 (1967) in all of its parts;

3. *Decides* that, immediately and concurrently with the cease-fire, negotiations start between the parties concerned under appropriate auspices aimed at establishing a just and durable peace in the Middle East.

APPENDIX 2

BASIC (POLICY) GUIDELINES OF THE GOVERNMENT'S
PROGRAMME, DEC. 22, 1988
(Translated by the Government Press Office)

At the centre of the activity of the National Unity Government presented to the 12th Knesset are the following tasks:

1a. Recognition of the shared fate and common struggle of the Jewish people in the homeland and the Diaspora of exile.

b. A sustained effort to create the social, economic and spiritual conditions to attain the State of Israel's central aim: The return of Diaspora Jews to their homeland.

c. Boosting immigration from all countries, encouraging immigration from Western countries, and consistently struggling to save persecuted Jews by bringing them to safety and realizing their right to immigrate to Israel.

2. The central policy objectives of the Government during this period are: Continuing and expanding the peace process in the region; consolidating the peace with Egypt; and ensuring the security of the northern settlements.

3. The Government will act to cultivate friendly relations and mutual ties between Israel and all peace-loving countries. . . .

4. Israel's foreign and defence policies will aim to ensure the country's independence, to strengthen its security, and to establish peace with all its neighbours.

5. The Government will strive to increase the strength, deterrent capability and endurance of the IDF against any military threat, and will take firm action against terrorism, regardless of its source. The IDF and the other security forces will continue to ensure the safety of all the residents, and will act forcefully in order to curb the riots, prevent the violence, and restore order.

6. United Jerusalem, Israel's eternal capital, is one indivisible city under Israeli sovereignty; free access to their holy places and freedom of worship will continue to be guaranteed to members of all faiths.

7. The Government will continue to place its desire for peace at the head of its concerns, and will spare no effort to promote peace.

Source: Israel Government Press Release 12/22/88.

8. The Government will work to promote and strengthen the mutual ties with Egypt in accordance with the peace treaty. The Government will call on Egypt to fulfill its part of the peace treaty with Israel, and to give it substance and content in keeping with the spirit of the treaty and with the intentions of its signatories.

9. The Government will work to continue the peace process in keeping with the framework for peace in the Middle East that was agreed upon at Camp David, and to resume negotiations to give full autonomy to the Arab residents in Judea, Samaria and the Gaza District.

10. Israel will call on Jordan to begin peace negotiations, in order to turn over a new leaf in the region, for the sake of [the region's] development and prosperity. The Israel Government will consider proposals for negotiations.

11. The Arabs of Judea, Samaria and the Gaza District will participate in the determination of their future, as stipulated in the Camp David Accords. Israel will encourage representatives of Judea, Samaria and the Gaza District to take part in the peace process.

12. Israel will oppose the establishment of an additional Palestinian state in the Gaza District and in the area between Israel and Jordan.

13. Israel will not negotiate with the PLO.

14. During the term of office of the Unity Government, no change will be made in the sovereignty over Judea, Samaria and the Gaza District except with the consent of the Alignment and the Likud.

15a. The existence and development of settlements set up by the governments of Israel will be ensured. . . .

b. Between five and eight settlements will be established within a year. . . .

16. The Government will do everything necessary to ensure peace for the Galilee. . . .

22. The Government will act to continue the development of the Arab and Druze sectors, in accordance with Cabinet decisions in these spheres, and to complete ordnance plans for the Arab and Druze settlements in order to facilitate future construction in accordance with the ordnance plans.

23. Special efforts will be made to integrate educated minority group members into the civil service and into various public institutions, in order to advance their participation in state and public responsibility.

24. The Government will look into the issue of the Moslem religious trusts.

25. The principle of national ownership of the land will be preserved. A ministerial committee will be established to deal with exceptional cases.

APPENDIX 3

THE PALESTINIANS' FOURTEEN DEMANDS

The following document was presented at a press conference held in Jerusalem on 14 January 1988 by Professor Sari Nusaybah of Birzeit University. Also present at the session were Mustafa al-Natshah, former mayor of Hebron; Gabi Baramki, acting president of Birzeit University; and Mubarak 'Awad, director of the Jerusalem Center for the Study of Non-Violence. . . . It was presented in the name of "Palestinian nationalist institutions and personalities from the West Bank and Gaza."

During the past few weeks the occupied territories have witnessed a popular uprising against Israel's occupation and its oppressive measures. This uprising has so far resulted in the martyrdom of tens of our people, the wounding of hundreds more, and the imprisonment of thousands of unarmed civilians.

This uprising has come to further affirm our people's unbreakable commitment to its national aspirations. These aspirations include our people's firm national rights of self-determination and of the establishment of an independent state on our national soil under the leadership of the PLO, as our sole legitimate representative. The uprising also comes as further proof of our indefatigable spirit and our rejection of the sense of despair which has begun to creep to the minds of some Arab leaders who claim that the uprising is the result of despair.

The conclusion to be drawn from this uprising is that the present state of affairs in the Palestinian occupied territories is unnatural and that Israeli occupation cannot continue forever. Real peace cannot be achieved except through the recognition of Palestinian national rights, including the right of self-determination and the establishment of an independent Palestinian state on Palestinian national soil. Should these rights not be recognized, then the continuation of Israeli occupation will lead to further violence and bloodshed, and the further deepening of hatred. The opportunity for achieving peace will also move farther away.

The only way to extricate ourselves from this scenario is through the convening of an international conference with the participation of all concerned parties

Source: *Journal of Palestine Studies*, No. 67, Spring 1988, pp. 63–65.

including the PLO, the sole legitimate representative of the Palestinian people, as an equal partner, as well as the five permanent members of the Security Council, under the supervision of the two superpowers.

On this basis we call upon the Israeli authorities to comply with the following list of demands as a means to prepare the atmosphere for the convening of the suggested international peace conference, which conference will ensure a just and lasting settlement of the Palestinian problem in all its aspects, bringing about the realization of the inalienable national rights of the Palestinian people, peace and stability for the peoples of the region, and an end to violence and bloodshed:

1. To abide by the Fourth Geneva Convention and all other international agreements pertaining to the protection of civilians, their properties and rights under a state of military occupation; to declare the Emergency Regulations of the British Mandate null and void, and to stop applying the iron fist policy.

2. The immediate compliance with Security Council resolutions 605 and 607, which call upon Israel to abide by the Geneva Convention of 1949 and the Declaration of Human Rights; and which further call for the achievement of a just and lasting settlement of the Arab-Israeli conflict.

3. The release of all prisoners who were arrested during the recent uprising, and foremost among them our children. Also the rescinding of all proceedings and indictments against them.

4. The cancellation of the policy of expulsion and allowing all exiled Palestinians, including the four sent yesterday into exile, to return to their homes and families. Also the release of all administrative detainees and the cancellation of the hundreds of house arrest orders. In this connection, special mention must be made of the several hundreds of applications for family reunions, which we call upon the authorities to accept forthwith.

5. The immediate lifting of the siege of all Palestinian refugee camps in the West Bank and Gaza, and the withdrawal of the Israeli army from all population centers.

6. Carrying out a formal inquiry into the behavior of soldiers and settlers in the West Bank and Gaza, as well as inside jails and detention camps, and taking due punitive measures against all those convicted of having unduly caused death or bodily harm to unarmed civilians.

7. A cessation of all settlement activity and land confiscation and the release of lands already confiscated, especially in the Gaza Strip. Also, putting an end to the harrassments and provocations of the Arab population by settlers in the West Bank and Gaza as well as in the Old City of Jerusalem. In particular, the curtailment of the provocative activities in the Old City of Jerusalem by Sharon and the ultrareligious settlers of Shuvu Banim and Ateret Cohanim.

8. Refraining from any act which might impinge on the Muslim and Christian holy sites or which might introduce changes to the status quo in the city of Jerusalem.

9. The cancellation of the VAT and all other direct Israeli taxes which are imposed on Palestinian residents in Jerusalem, the rest of the West Bank, and in Gaza; and putting an end to the harrassments caused to Palestinian business and tradesmen.

10. The cancellation of all restrictions on political freedoms, including the restrictions on meetings and conventions, also making provisions for free municipal elections under the supervision of a neutral authority.

11. The immediate release of all monies deducted from the wages of laborers from the territories who worked and still work inside the green line, which amount to several hundreds of millions of dollars. These accumulated deductions, with interest, must be returned to their rightful owners through the agency of the nationalist institutions headed by the workers' unions.

12. The removal of all restrictions on building permits and licenses for industrial projects and artesian wells as well as agricultural development programs in the occupied territories. Also rescinding all measures taken to deprive the territories of their water resources.

13. Terminating the policy of discrimination being practiced against industrial and agricultural produce from the occupied territories either by removing the restrictions on the transfer of goods to within the green line, or by placing comparable trade restrictions on the transfer of Israeli goods into the territories.

14. Removing the restrictions on political contacts between inhabitants of the occupied territories and the PLO, in such a way as to allow for the participation of Palestinians from the territories in the proceedings of the Palestine National Council, in order to ensure a direct input into the decision-making processes of the Palestinian nation by the Palestinians under occupation.

Appendix 4

THE PALESTINE INDEPENDENCE DOCUMENT
PREPARED BY FAISAL HUSSEINI
OF THE JERUSALEM ARAB STUDIES SOCIETY

The announcement in Jerusalem of the independence document will herald the establishment of an independent Palestinian state within the partition boundaries, as determined in 1947 and by the (UN) Security Council in Resolution 181. Its capital will be Jerusalem and its interim government will consist of two parts: Those who are in exile and those who reside on Palestinian soil.

The state will be headed by Yasser Arafat, chairman of the PLO executive committee. Farouk Kadoumi, who heads the PLO's political department, will serve as foreign minister in the new government. PLO executive committee members will be considered members of the new government. It will also include Messrs. George Habash, secretary general of the PFLP (Popular Front for the Liberation of Palestine) and Nayef Hawatmeh, secretary general of the DFLP (Democratic Front for the Liberation of Palestine).

In parallel, the Palestine National Council will be proclaimed the new state's parliament. It will include personalities from the occupied territories. Their names will be declared in the Declaration of Independence. PLO representations abroad will automatically be regarded as the new Palestinian state's legations.

An interim administrative body will be set up in the occupied territories. It will deal with various internal administrative matters, such as health, education, social welfare, law, police, agriculture, industry, commerce, construction, electricity, water, municipalities, press and media affairs. This is done through a hierarchy in which every department has its own internal bylaws.

The Objective

This programme aims at moving from the phase of clashes with stones on the battlefront to the stage of political initiative through a diplomatic mechanism initiated by the Palestinian side, which will provide the blessed "uprising" with renewed momentum toward an international conference.

Source: *Jerome M. Segal, College Park, MD.*

This technique will have a stronger influence on diplomatic activity than any other political initiative that could be presented by the Palestinian side. It will give the Palestinians a tremendous bargaining chip because the issue for debate both in the international and Israeli arenas will change from a demand that the PLO recognize Israel as a precondition for negotiations to a demand that the international community recognize the state established by the efforts of the Palestinian people, whose lands were occupied by the Hebrew state.

The above does not mean an end to the blessed uprising, but an escalation which lifts it to the level of the proposed national state.

Projected Scenario

Israel will find itself subjected to diplomatic pressure on the international level, especially if the declaration of the state will be accompanied by an active diplomatic campaign led by the political department in the PLO through its representatives around the world. Friendly countries will be asked to officially recognize the new Palestinian state while countries with diplomatic relations with Israel will be called on to create parallel representations in the Palestinian state, as well as having economic and trade relations with it.

Of course, the Israeli authorities are going to carry out an arrest campaign against all those who have any relationship, whether from near or far, with the draft of a Declaration of Independence. It will also put obstacles in order to stop Palestinian personalities and delegations from participating in a national conference in Jerusalem in which this independence will be declared. But the media coverage that will accompany these events will give the uprising a new face in which the characteristics of the newborn state would be reflected. This will be especially true in the eyes of the people who will see in this new state a renewed incentive to continue the resistance. They will support it in order to plant the seeds for a new infrastructure based on popular committees. Therefore, they will heed its directives and respect its guidelines as a national alternative to the occupation.

The popular committees deployed throughout the territories will gain official status as branches of the new state, helping to continue the growth and development of the state apparatus.

Regarding the Israeli position: It will be unable to fight against, strangle, or abort the "newborn." The "newborn"—the state struggling to save itself from occupation—will be accorded respect and admiration by all forces worldwide, including those that support Israel. Internally, Israel will be divided because the voices demanding recognition of the "newborn" will increase, especially since this "newborn" has come into being as the result of heroic labour pains, witnessed by everyone. This is also true because the nature of the new state will confirm that it is not aggressive, and that the Palestinian people do not desire the annihilation of the state of Israel. Rather, they wish to live peacefully as its neighbour.

The announcement of the Declaration of Independence, as outlined above, does not necessarily mean the creation of an interim Palestinian government-in-exile, as has been suggested by Arab leaders in the past. Instead, it will mean the birth of a Palestinian state in the homeland. In order to reach this objective, the Unified National Leadership of the Uprising, in Jerusalem, the capital of Palestine, will take the responsibility of carrying out this objective. Our people will thus hold the reins of the initiative even as they are setting up their state on their national land, instead of persistently demanding that other parties—especially the international conference and the United States—establish such a state.

Contents of the Declaration of Independence

The Declaration of Independence will have the following points:
—The geography of the state will be within the partition plan of 1948;
—The executive of the state will consist of:
  Mr. Yasser Arafat, president of the state;
  Mr. Farouk Kadoumi, foreign minister;
  PLO Executive Committee members—members of the new government;
  The membership will include Messrs. George Habash and Nayef Hawatmeh.
  —A general legislative body in the occupied territories made up of personalities who will be considered automatically members of the Palestine National Council. The Unified Leadership of the Uprising will nominate the following names in one of its communiques:
  (follows a list of 152 names of well-known Palestinian personalities from the West Bank and Gaza Strip, including 18 women, mayors and former mayors, heads of trade unions and professional societies, educators, doctors, artists, and community leaders)
  —An administrative board assigned from the above-mentioned legislative body will temporarily carry the affairs of the interim government inside the occupied territories. This body will consist of representatives from within the community distributed according to geographic and specialty considerations.
  —The interim government will proclaim, on behalf of the PLO, its readiness to appoint a specialized delegation whose members will be people from within and outside the occupied homeland. Its mission will be to launch negotiations toward reaching a final settlement with Israel. The negotiations will centre on the following points:
  1) The final borders between the Palestinian state and Israel;
  2) The political and practical link and ties between the two portions of the Palestinian state—Gaza and the West Bank;
  3) Issues connected to the network of (Jewish) settlements planted in the occupied territories;
  4) The nature of relations between the two countries, with special emphasis on basic necessities needed for the survival of the state, particularly the issue of water;
  5) The issue of the refugees' right of return, or their right to compensation in accordance with UN resolutions.
  The declaration of independence will be preceded by consultations with the Arab countries and friendly nations, especially with the Soviet Union. This consultation is not for the purpose of requesting permission from these countries, but in order to guarantee their needed support to this state.

The nature of the independent Palestinian state will be a republic—elected president, ministerial council made up of elected parties. The state will allow multiple political parties and religions, and the freedom of all believers to worship. It will guarantee the human, economic, and political rights of individuals and the community. It will guarantee for the citizen to live in freedom, dignity, and the pursuit of happiness. It will guarantee to him all the rights stated in the United Nations Declaration of Human Rights, including the freedoms of expression, education, and ownership. It will provide for him health, social, economic, educational and agricultural possibilities so that he can build a bright future for himself and his children.

The declaration for the creation of a Palestinian state means forcing an accomplished fact on Israel, the Arab countries, and the world community, which will have no way out of dealing with this reality created by the uprising.

All the citizens of the occupied territories will be expected to carry out the orders and instructions issued by the new state, its various executive institutions, and operational bodies as expressed through the popular committees which are subordinate to the Unified National Command. The residents will similarly be expected to surrender their Israeli identity cards and exchange them for Palestinian cards which will be issued by the interim government. These will be distributed by the popular committees. Foreign reporters, visitors and tourists will be expected to obtain travel documents from the interim government's institutions in order to enter the state.

The PNC will be called for a new session. One week before the start of the session the Unified Leadership will announce the Declaration of Independence and the Palestine National Council will discuss it and approve all of its detail.

Final note:

Following recognition of the state and the withdrawal of the Israeli army, arrangements will immediately be made for free, direct elections to form the new government and name a new President whose authority will be decided by the parliament after its first session, forming the first elected government for the new Palestinian state.

APPENDIX 5

BASSAM ABU SHARIF, "PROSPECTS OF A PALESTINIAN-ISRAELI SETTLEMENT," ALGIERS, 7 JUNE 1988

Bassam Abu Sharif, special advisor to PLO chairman Yasir Arafat, wrote a position paper, which was distributed to international media on the eve of the Emergency Arab Summit Conference held in Algiers, 7–9 June 1988. Abu Sharif's document was carried by WAFA, Washington, on 23 June 1988.

Everything that has been said about the Middle East conflict has focused on the differences between Palestinians and Israelis and ignored the points on which they are in almost total agreement.

These points are easy to overlook, hidden as they are under a seventy-year accumulation of mutual hostility and suspicion, but they exist nevertheless and in them lies the hope that the peace that has eluded this region for so long is finally within reach.

Peel off the layers of fear and mistrust that successive Israeli leaders have piled on the substantive issues and you will find that the Palestinians and Israelis are in general agreement on ends and means:

Israeli's objectives are lasting peace and security. Lasting peace and security are also the objectives of the Palestinian people. No one can understand the Jewish people's centuries of suffering more than the Palestinians. We know what it means to be stateless and the object of the fear and prejudice of the nations. Thanks to the various Israeli and other governments that have had the power to determine the course of our people's lives, we know what it feels like when human beings are considered somewhat less human than others and denied the basic rights that people around the globe take for granted. We feel that no people—neither the Jewish people nor the Palestinian people—deserves the abuse and disenfranchisement that homelessness inevitably entails. We believe that all peoples—the Jews and the Palestinians included—have the right to run their own affairs, expecting from their neighbors not only non-belligerence but the kind of political and economic cooperation without which no state can be truly secure, no matter how massive its war machine, and without which no

Source: *Journal of Palestine Studies,* No. 69, Autumn 1988, pp. 272–275.

nation can truly prosper, no matter how generous its friends in distant lands may be.

The Palestinians want that kind of lasting peace and security for themselves and the Israelis because no one can build his own future on the ruins of another's. We are confident that this desire and this realization are shared by all but an insignificant minority in Israel.

The means by which the Israelis want to achieve lasting peace and security is direct talks, with no attempt by any outside party to impose or veto a settlement.

The Palestinians agree. We see no way for any dispute to be settled without direct talks between the parties to that dispute, and we feel that any settlement that has to be imposed by an outside power is a settlement that is unacceptable to one or both of the belligerents and therefore a settlement that will not stand the test of time. The key to a Palestinian-Israeli settlement lies in talks between the Palestinians and the Israelis. The Palestinians would be deluding themselves if they thought that their problems with the Israelis can be solved in negotiations with non-Israelis, including the United States. By the same token, the Israelis— and U.S. secretary of state George Shultz, who has been shuttling to the Middle East for discussions on his peace proposals—would be deluding themselves if they thought that Israel's problems with the Palestinians can be solved in negotiations with non-Palestinians, including Jordan.

The Palestinians would like to choose their Israeli interlocutor. We have little doubt that we could reach a satisfactory settlement with the Peace Now movement in a month. We know, however, that an agreement with Peace Now would not be an agreement with Israel, and since an agreement with Israel is what we are after, we are ready to talk to Mr. Shimon Peres' Labor alignment, or to Yitzhaq Shamir's Likud block, or anyone else the Israelis choose to represent them.

The Israelis and Mr. Shultz would also prefer to deal with Palestinians of their own choosing. But it would be as futile for them as for us to talk to people who have no mandate to negotiate. If it is a settlement with the Palestinians that they seek, as we assume it is, then it is with the representatives of that people that they must negotiate, and the Palestinian people, by the only means that they have at their disposal, have chosen their representatives. Every Palestinian questioned by diplomats and newsmen of the international community has stated unequivocally that his representative is the Palestinian Liberation Organization. If that is regarded as an unreliable expression of the Palestinians' free will, then give the Palestinians the chance to express their free will in a manner that will convince all doubters: arrange for an internationally-supervised referendum in the West Bank and Gaza Strip and allow the population to choose between the PLO and any other group of Palestinians that Israel or the United States or the international community wishes to nominate. The PLO is ready to abide by the outcome and step aside for any alternative leadership should the Palestinian people choose one.

The PLO will do this because its *raison d'être* is not the undoing of Israel, but the salvation of the Palestinian people and their rights, including their right to democratic self-expression and national self-determination.

Regardless of the satanic image that the PLO's struggle for those rights has given it in the United States and Israel, the fact remains that this organization was built on democratic principles and seeks democratic objectives. If Israel and its supports in the U.S. administration can grasp that fact, the fears that prevent them from accepting the PLO as the only valid interlocutor toward any Palestinian-Israeli settlement would vanish.

Those fears, as far as I can tell from what has been written and said in Israel and the United States, center on the PLO's failure to unconditionally accept Security Council resolutions 242 and 338 and on the possibility that a Palestinian state on the West Bank and Gaza would be a radical, totalitarian threat to its neighbor.

The PLO, however, does accept resolutions 242 and 338. What prevents it from saying so unconditionally is not what is in the resolutions but what is not in them: neither resolution says anything about the national rights of the Palestinian people, including their democratic right to self-expression and their national right to self-determination. For that reason, and that reason alone, we have repeatedly said that we accept resolutions 242 and 338 in the context of the other UN resolutions, which do recognize the national rights of the Palestinian people.

As for the fear that a Palestinian state would be a threat to its neighbor, the democratic nature of the PLO—with its legislative, executive, and other popularly-based institutions—should argue against it. If that does not constitute a solid enough guarantee that the state of Palestine would be a democratic one, the Palestinians would be open to the idea of a brief, mutually-acceptable transitional period during which an international mandate would guide the occupied Palestinian territories to democratic Palestinian statehood.

Beyond that, the Palestinians would accept—indeed, insist on—international guarantees for the security of all states in the region, including Palestine and Israel. It is precisely our desire for such guarantees that motivates our demand that bilateral peace talks with Israel be conducted in the context of a UN-sponsored international conference.

The Palestinians feel that they have much more to fear from Israel, with its mighty war machine and its nuclear arsenal, than Israel has to fear from them. They would therefore welcome any reasonable measure that would promote the security of their state and its neighbors, including the deployment of a UN buffer force on the Palestinian side of the Israeli-Palestinian border.

Time, sometimes the great healer, is often the great spoiler. Many Israelis no doubt realize this and are trying to communicate it to the rest of their people. As for us, we are ready for peace now, and we can deliver it. It is our hope that the opportunity that presents itself today will not be missed.

If it is missed, we will have no choice but to continue to exercise our right to resist the occupation, our ultimate aim being a free, dignified, and secure life not only for our children but also for the children of the Israelis.

APPENDIX 6

PALESTINE NATIONAL COUNCIL, "PALESTINIAN DECLARATION OF INDEPENDENCE," ALGIERS, 15 NOVEMBER 1988

Below is the official translation of the Declaration of Independence as carried by WAFA from Algiers, 17 November 1988.

In the name of God, the Compassionate, the Merciful.

Palestine, the land of the three monotheistic faiths, is where the Palestinian Arab people was born, on which it grew, developed, and excelled. The Palestinian people was never separated from or diminished in its integral bonds with Palestine. Thus the Palestinian Arab people ensured for itself an everlasting union between itself, its land, and its history.

Resolute throughout that history, the Palestinian Arab people forged its national identity, rising even to unimagined levels in its defense as invasion, the design of others, and the appeal special to Palestine's ancient and luminous place on that eminence where powers and civilizations are joined. . . . All this intervened thereby to deprive the people of its political independence. Yet the undying connection between Palestine and its people secured for the land its character and for the people its national genius.

Nourished by an unfolding series of civilizations and cultures, inspired by a heritage rich in variety and kind, the Palestinian Arab people added to its stature by consolidating a union between itself and its patrimonial land. The call went out from temple, church, and mosque to praise the Creator, to celebrate compassion, and peace was indeed the message of Palestine. And in generation after generation, the Palestinian Arab people gave of itself unsparingly in the valiant battle for liberation and homeland. For what has been the unbroken chain of our people's rebellions but the heroic embodiment of our will for national independence? And so the people were sustained in the struggle to stay and to prevail.

When in the course of modern times a new order of values was declared with norms and values fair for all, it was the Palestinian Arab people that had

Source: *Journal of Palestine Studies*, No. 70, Winter 1988, pp. 213–216.

been excluded from the destiny of all other peoples by a hostile array of local and foreign powers. Yet again had unaided justice been revealed as insufficient to drive the world's history along its preferred course.

And it was the Palestinian people, already wounded in its body, that was submitted to yet another type of occupation over which floated the falsehood that "Palestine was a land without people." This notion was foisted upon some in the world, whereas in Article 22 of the Covenant of the League of Nations (1919) and in the Treaty of Lausanne (1923), the community of nations had recognized that all the Arab territories, including Palestine, of the formerly Ottoman provinces were to have granted to them their freedom as provisionally independent nations.

Despite the historical injustice inflicted on the Palestinian Arab people resulting in their dispersion and depriving them of their right to self-determination, following upon UN General Assembly Resolution 181 (1947), which partitioned Palestine into two states, one Arab, one Jewish, yet it is this resolution that still provides those conditions of international legitimacy that ensure the right of the Palestinian Arab people to sovereignty and national independence.

By stages, the occupation of Palestine and parts of other Arab territories by Israeli forces, the willed dispossession and expulsion from their ancestral homes of the majority of Palestine's civilian inhabitants was achieved by organized terror; those Palestinians who remained, as a vestige subjugated in its homeland, were persecuted and forced to endure the destruction of their national life.

Thus were principles of international legitimacy violated. Thus were the Charter of the United Nations and its resolutions disfigured, for they had recognized the Palestinian Arab people's national rights, including the Right of Return, the Right to Independence, the Right to Sovereignty over territory and homeland.

In Palestine and on its perimeters, in exile distant and near, the Palestinian Arab people never faltered and never abandoned its conviction in its rights of return and independence. Occupation, massacres, and dispersion achieved no gain in the unabated Palestinian consciousness of self and political identity, as Palestinians went forward with their destiny, undeterred and unbowed. And from out of the long years of trial in evermounting struggle, the Palestinian political identity emerged further consolidated and confirmed. And the collective Palestinian national will forged itself in a political embodiment, the Palestine Liberation Organization, its sole, legitimate representative, recognized by the world community as a whole, as well as by related regional and international institutions. Standing on the very rock of conviction in the Palestinian people's inalienable rights, and on the ground of Arab national consensus, and of international legitimacy, the PLO led the campaigns of its great people, molded into unity and powerful resolve, one and indivisible in the triumphs, even as it suffered massacres and confinement within and without its home. And so Palestinian resistance was clarified and raised into the forefront of Arab and world awareness, as the struggle of the Palestinian Arab people achieved unique prominence among the world's liberation movements in the modern era.

The massive national uprising, the *intifadah*, now intensifying in cumulative scope and power on occupied Palestinian territories, as well as the unflinching resistance of the refugee camps outside the homeland, have elevated consciousness of the Palestinian truth and right into still higher realms of comprehension and actuality. Now at last the curtain has been dropped around a whole epoch of prevarication and negation. The Intifadah has set siege to the mind of official Israel, which has for too long relied exclusively upon myth and terror to deny Palestinian existence altogether. Because of the Intifadah and its revolutionary irreversible impulse, the history of Palestine has therefore arrived at a decisive juncture.

Whereas the Palestinian people reaffirms most definitely its inalienable rights in the land of its patrimony:

Now by virtue of natural, historical, and legal rights and the sacrifices of successive generations who gave of themselves in defense of the freedom and independence of their homeland;

In pursuance of resolutions adopted by Arab summit conferences and relying on the authority bestowed by international legitimacy as embodied in the resolutions of the United Nations Organization since 1947;

And in exercise by the Palestinian Arab people of its rights to self-determination, political independence, and sovereignty over its territory;

The Palestine National Council, in the name of God, and in the name of the Palestinian Arab people, hereby proclaims the establishment of the State of Palestine on our Palestinian territory with its capital Jerusalem (Al-Quds Ash-Sharif).

The State of Palestine is the state of Palestinians wherever they may be. The state is for them to enjoy in it their collective national and cultural identity, theirs to pursue in it a complete equality of rights. In it will be safeguarded their political and religious convictions and their human dignity by means of a parliamentary democratic system of governance, itself based on freedom of expression and the freedom to form parties. The rights of minorities will duly be respected by the majority, as minorities must abide by decisions of the majority. Governance will be based on principles of social justice, equality and nondiscrimination in public rights on grounds of race, religion, color, or sex under the aegis of a constitution which ensures the role of law and on independent judiciary. Thus shall these principles allow no departure from Palestine's age-old spiritual and civilizational heritage of tolerance and religious co-existence.

The State of Palestine is an Arab state, an integral and indivisible part of the Arab nation, at one with that nation in heritage and civilization, with it also in its aspiration for liberation, progress, democracy, and unity. The State of Palestine affirms its obligation to abide by the Charter of the League of Arab States, whereby the coordination of the Arab states with each other shall be strengthened. It calls upon Arab compatriots to consolidate and enhance the emergence in reality of our State, to mobilize potential, and to intensify efforts whose goal is to end Israeli occupation.

The State of Palestine proclaims its commitment to the principles and purposes of the United Nations, and to the Universal Declaration of Human Rights. It proclaims its commitment as well to the principles and policies of the Non-Aligned Movement.

It further announces itself to be a peace-loving state, in adherence to the principles of peaceful co-existence. It will join with all states and peoples in order to assure a permanent peace based upon justice and the respect of rights so that humanity's potential for well-being may be assured, an earnest competition for excellence be maintained, and in which confidence in the future will eliminate fear for those who are just and for whom justice is the only recourse.

In the context of its struggle for peace in the land of love and peace, the State of Palestine calls upon the United Nations to bear special responsibility for the Palestinian Arab people and its homeland. It calls upon all peace- and freedom-loving peoples and states to assist it in the attainment of its objectives, to provide it with security, to alleviate the tragedy of its people, and to help to terminate Israel's occupation of the Palestinian territories.

The State of Palestine herewith declares that it believes in the settlement of regional and international disputes by peaceful means, in accordance with the UN Charter and resolutions. Without prejudice to its natural right to defend its territorial integrity and independence, it therefore rejects the threat or use of force, violence, and terrorism against its territorial integrity, or political independence, as it also rejects their use against the territorial integrity of other states.

Therefore, on this day unlike all others, 15 November, 1988, as we stand at the threshold of a new dawn, in all honor and modesty we humbly bow to the sacred spirits of our fallen ones, Palestinian and Arab, by the purity of whose sacrifice for the homeland our sky has been illuminated and our land given life. Our hearts are lifted up and irradiated by the light emanating from the much blessed *intifadah*, from those who have endured and have fought the fight of the camps, of dispersion, of exile, from those who have borne the standard of freedom, our children, our aged, our youth, our prisoners, detainees, and wounded, all those whose ties to our sacred soil are confirmed in camp, village, and town. We render special tribute to that brave Palestinian woman, guardian of sustenance and life, keeper of our people's perennial flame. To the souls of our sainted martyrs, to the whole of our Palestinian Arab people, to all free and honorable peoples everywhere, we pledge that our struggle shall be continued until the occupation ends, and the foundation of our sovereignty and independence shall be fortified accordingly.

Therefore, we call upon our great people to rally to the banner of Palestine, to cherish and defend it, so that it may forever be the symbol of our freedom and dignity in that homeland, which is a homeland for the free, now and always.

In the name of God, the Compassionate, the Merciful.

"Say: 'O God, Master of the Kingdom, Thou givest the Kingdom to whom Thou wilt, and seizest the Kingdom from whom Thou wilt. Thou exaltest whom Thou wilt, and Thou abasest whom Thou wilt; in Thy hand is the good; Thou art powerful over everything.'"

Sadaqa Allahu al-'Azim

APPENDIX 7

PALESTINE NATIONAL COUNCIL, "POLITICAL COMMUNIQUÉ," ALGIERS, 15 NOVEMBER 1988

The official translation of the communiqué, received from London, 22 November 1988.

In the name of God, the Compassionate, the Merciful.

In the valiant land of Algeria, hosted by its people and its President Chedli Benjedid, the Palestine National Council held its nineteenth extraordinary session— the session of the *intifadah* and independence, the session of the martyred hero Abu Jihad—in the period between 12 and 15 November 1988.

This session culminated in the announcement of the rise of the Palestinian state in our Palestinian land, the natural climax of a daring and tenacious popular struggle that started more than seventy years ago and was baptized in the immense sacrifices offered by our people in our homeland, along its borders, and in the camps and other sites of our diaspora.

The session was also distinguished by its focus on the great national Palestinian *intifadah* as one of the major milestones in the contemporary history of the Palestinian people's revolution, on a par with the legendary steadfastness of our people in their camps in our occupied land and outside it.

The primary features of our great people's *intifadah* were obvious from its inception and have become clearer in the twelve months since then during which it has continued unabated: It is a total popular revolution that embodies the consensus of an entire nation—women and men, old and young, in the camps, in the villages, and the cities—on the rejection of the occupation and on the determination to struggle until the occupation is defeated and terminated.

This glorious *intifadah* has demonstrated our people's deeply rooted national unity and their full adherence to the Palestine Liberation Organization, the sole, legitimate representative of our people, all our people, wherever they congregate— in our homeland or outside it. This was manifested by the participation of the Palestinian masses—their unions, their vocational organizations, their students,

Source: *Journal of Palestine Studies*, No. 70, Winter 1988, pp. 216–223.

their workers, their farmers, their women, their merchants, their landlords, their artisans, their academics—in the *intifadah* through its Unified National Command and the popular committees that were formed in the urban neighborhoods, the villages, and the camps.

This, our people's revolutionary furnace and their blessed *intifadah,* along with the cumulative impact of our innovative and continuous revolution inside and outside of our homeland, have destroyed the illusion our people's enemies have harbored that they can turn the occupation of Palestinian land into a permanent *fait accompli* and consign the Palestinian issue to oblivion. For our generations have been weaned on the goals and principles of the Palestinian revolution and have lived all its battles since its birth in 1965—including the heroic resistance against the Zionist invasion of 1982 and the steadfastness of the revolution's camps as they endured the siege and starvation in Lebanon. Those generations—the children of the revolution and of the Palestine Liberation Organization—rose to demonstrate the dynamism and continuity of the revolution, detonating the land under the feet of its occupiers and proving that our people's reserves of resistance are inexhaustible and their faith is too deep to uproot.

Thus did the struggle of the children of the RPG's outside our homeland and the struggle of the children of the sacred stones inside it blend into a single revolutionary melody.

Our people have stood fast against all the attempts of our enemy's authorities to end our revolution, and those authorities have tried everything at their disposal: they have used terrorism, they have imprisoned us, they have sent us into exile, they have desecrated our holy places and restricted our religious freedoms, they have demolished our homes, they have killed us indiscriminately, and premeditatedly, they have sent bands of armed settlers into our villages and camps, they have burned our crops, they have cut off our water and power supplies, they have beaten our women and children, they have used toxic gases that have caused many deaths and abortions, and they have waged an ignorance war [*sic.*] against us by closing our schools and universities.

Our people's heroic steadfastness has cost them hundreds of martyrs and tens of thousands of casualties, prisoners, and exiles. But our people's genius was always at hand, ready in their darkest hours to innovate the means and formulas of struggle that stiffened their resistance, bolstered their steadfastness, and enabled them to confront the crimes and measures of the enemy and carry on with their heroic, tenacious struggle. . . .

In all this, our people relied on the sustenance of the masses and forces of our Arab nation, which have stood by us and backed us, as demonstrated by the wide popular support for the *intifadah* and by the consensus and resolutions that emerged at the Arab summit in Algiers—all of which goes to comfirm that our people do not stand alone as they face the fascist, racist assault, and this precludes any possibility of the Israeli aggressors' isolating our people and cutting them off from the support of their Arab nation.

In addition to this Arab solidarity, our people's revolution and their blessed *intifadah* have attracted widespread worldwide solidarity, as seen in the increased understanding of the Palestinian people's issue, the growing support of our just

struggle by the peoples and states of the world, and the corresponding condemnation of Israeli occupation and the crimes it is committing, which has helped to expose Israel and increase its isolation and the isolation of its supporters.
. . .

It has thus been demonstrated that the occupation cannot continue to reap the fruits of its actions at the expense of the Palestinian people's rights without paying a price—either on the ground or in terms of international public opinion.

In addition to the rejection of the occupation and the condemnation of its repressive measures by the democratic and progressive Israeli forces, Jewish groups all over the world are no longer able to continue their defense of Israel or maintain their silence about its crimes against the Palestinian people. Many voices have risen among those groups to demand an end to these crimes and call for Israel's withdrawal from the occupied territories in order to allow the Palestinian people to exercise their right to self-determination.

The fruits that our people's revolution and their blessed *intifadah* have borne on the local, Arab, and international levels have established the soundness and realism of the Palestine Liberation Organization's national program, a program aimed at the termination of the occupation and the achievement of our people's right to return, self-determination, and statehood. Those results have also confirmed that the struggle of our people is the decisive factor in the effort to snatch our national rights from the jaws of the occupation. It is the authority of our people, as represented in the Popular Committees, that controls the situation as we challenge the authority of the occupation's crumbling agencies.
. . .

In the light of this, and toward the reinforcement of the steadfastness and blessed *intifadah* of our people, and in accordance with the will of our masses in and outside of our homeland, and in fidelity to those of our people that have been martyred, wounded, or taken captive, the Palestine National Council resolves:

First: On The Escalation and Continuity of the Intifadah

A. To provide all the means and capabilities needed to escalate our people's *intifadah* in various ways and on various levels to guarantee its continuation and intensification.

B. To support the popular institutions and organizations in the occupied Palestinian territories.

C. To bolster and develop the popular committees and other specialized popular and trade union bodies, including the attack groups and the popular army, with a view to expanding their role and increasing their effectiveness.

D. To consolidate the national unity that emerged and developed during the *intifadah.*

E. To intensify efforts on the international level for the release of detainees, the return of those expelled, and the termination of the organized, official acts of repression and terrorism against our children, our women, our men, and our institutions.

F. To call on the United Nations to place the occupied Palestinian land under international supervision for the protection of our people and the termination of the Israeli occupation.

G. To call on the Palestinian people outside our homeland to intensify and increase their support, and to expand the family-assistance program.

H. To call on the Arab nation, its people, forces, institutions, and governments, to increase their political, material, and informational support for the *intifadah*.

I. To call on all free and honorable people worldwide to stand by our people, our revolution, our *intifadah* against the Israeli occupation, the repression, and the organized, fascist official terrorism to which the occupation forces and the armed fanatic settlers are subjecting our people, our universities, our institutions, our national economy, and our Islamic and Christian holy places.

Second: In the Political Arena

Proceeding from the above, the Palestine National Council, being responsible to the Palestinian people, their national rights and their desire for peace as expressed in the Declaration of Independence issued on 15 November 1988; and in response to the humanitarian quest for international entente, nuclear disarmament, and the settlement of regional conflict by peaceful means, affirms the determination of the Palestine Liberation Organization to arrive at a comprehensive settlement of the Arab-Israeli conflict and its core, which is the question of Palestine, within the framework of the United Nations Charter, the principles and provisions of international legality, the norms of international law, and the resolutions of the United Nations . . . and the resolutions of the Arab summits, in such a manner that safeguards the Palestinian Arab people's rights to return, to self-determination, and the establishment of their independent national state on their national soil, and that institutes arrangements for the security and peace of all states in the region.

Toward the achievement of this, the Palestine National Council affirms:

1. The necessity of convening the effective international conference on the issue of the Middle East and its core, the question of Palestine, under the auspices of the United Nations and with the participation of the permanent members of the Security Council and all parties to the conflict in the region including the Palestine Liberation Organization, the sole, legitimate representative of the Palestinian people, on an equal footing, and by considering that the international peace conference be convened on the basis of United Nations Security Council resolutions 242 and 338 and the attainment of the legitimate national rights of the Palestinian people, foremost among which is the right to self-determination and in accordance with the principles and provisions of the United Nations Charter concerning the right of peoples to self-determination, and by the inadmissibility of the acquisition of the territory of others by force or military conquest, and in accordance with the relevant United Nations resolutions on the question of Palestine.

2. The withdrawal of Israel from all the Palestinian and Arab territories it occupied in 1967, including Arab Jerusalem.

3. The annullment of all measures of annexation and appropriation and the removal of settlements established by Israel in the Palestinian and Arab territories since 1967.

4. Endeavoring to place the occupied Palestinian territories, including Arab Jerusalem, under the auspices of the United Nations for a limited period in

order to protect our people and afford the appropriate atmosphere for the success of the proceeding of the international conference toward the attainment of a comprehensive political settlement and the attainment of peace and security for all on the basis of mutual acquiescence and consent, and to enable the Palestinian state to exercise its effective authority in these territories.

5. The settlement of the question of the Palestinian refugees in accordance with the relevant United Nations resolutions.

6. Guaranteeing the freedom of worship and religious practice for all faiths in the holy places in Palestine.

7. The Security Council is to formulate and guarantee arrangements for security and peace between all the states concerned in the region, including the Palestinian state.

The Palestine National Council affirms its previous resolutions concerning the distinctive relationship between the Jordanian and Palestinian peoples, and affirms that the future relationship between the two states of Palestine and Jordan should be on a confederal basis as a result [of] the free and voluntary choice of the two fraternal peoples in order to strengthen the historical bonds and the vital interests they hold in common. . . .

The Palestine National Council also addresses itself to the American people, calling on them all to strive to put an end to the American policy that denies the Palestinian people's national rights, including their sacred right to self-determination, and urging them to work toward the adoption of policies that conform with the human rights charter and the international conventions and resolutions and serve the quest for peace in the Middle East and security for all its peoples, including the Palestinian peoples. . . .

In conclusion, the Palestine National Council affirms its complete confidence that the justice of the Palestinian cause and of the demands for which the Palestinian people are struggling will continue to draw increasing support from honorable and free people around the world; and also affirms its complete confidence in victory on the road to Jerusalem, the capital of our independent Palestinian state.

APPENDIX 8

SHAMIR'S FOUR-POINT PLAN

The official Israeli Foreign Ministry formulation of the prime minister's proposal, approved by the government on May 14. Twenty ministers voted in favor of the plan and six voted against. Voting against were three Likud members—Ariel Sharon, Itzkhak Modai and David Levy—and Mafdal member Avner Shaki. Two labor members— Ezer Weitzmann and Rafi Edri—also voted against, but for opposite reasons: they said the plan hinges on PLO agreement and that therefore there should be direct Israeli-PLO talks.

1. The Camp David Partners—Reconfirmation of the Commitment to Peace

Ten years ago, the peace treaty between Israel and Egypt was concluded on the basis of the Camp David Accords. When the accords were signed, it was expected that more Arab countries would shortly join the circle of peace. This expectation was not realized.

The strength of Israeli-Egyptian relations and the cooperation between the three partners to the accords have a decisive influence on the chances for Middle East peace, and the Israeli-Egyptian treaty is the cornerstone to the building of peace in the region.

Therefore, the prime minister has called on the three countries whose leaders affixed their signature to the Camp David Accords—the US, Egypt, and Israel— to renew, 10 years later, their commitment to the agreements and to peace.

2. The Arab Countries—From a State of War to a Process of Peace

The prime minister urged the US and Egypt to call on the other Arab countries to desist from hostility toward Israel and to replace belligerency and boycott with negotiation and cooperation. Of all the Arab countries, only Egypt has recognized Israel and its right to exist. Many of these states actively participated in wars against Israel by direct involvement or indirect assistance. To this day,

Source: Israel Government Press Release, May 14, 1989.

the Arab countries are partners in an economic boycott against Israel, refuse to recognize it, and refuse to establish diplomatic relations with it.

The solution to the Arab-Israeli conflict and the building of confidence leading to a permanent settlement require a change in the attitude of the Arab countries toward Israel. Israel, therefore, calls on these states to put an end to this historic anomaly and to join direct bilateral negotiations aimed at normalization and peace.

3. A Solution to the Refugee Problem—An International Effort

The prime minister has called for an international effort, led by the US and with the significant participation of Israel, to solve the problem of the Arab refugees. The refugee problem has been perpetuated by the leaders of the Arab countries, while Israel with its meagre resources is absorbing hundreds of thousands of Jewish refugees from Arab countries. Settling the refugees must not wait for a political process or come in its stead.

The matter must be viewed as a humanitarian problem and action must be taken to ease the human distress of the refugees and to ensure for their families appropriate living quarters and self-respect.

Some 300,000 people live in refugee camps in Judea, Samaria and the Gaza District. In the 1970s, Israel unilaterally undertook the rehabilitation of residents of refugee camps in Gaza and erected 10 neighborhoods in which 11,000 families reside. This operation was carried out in partnership with the residents despite PLO objections.

The time has now come to ensure appropriate infrastructure, living quarters and services for the rest of the residents of the camps who, at the same time, are victims of the conflict, hostages to it, and an element which perpetuates its continued existence.

Good will and an international effort to allocate the necessary resources will ensure a satisfactory solution to this humanitarian effort and will help improve the political climate in the region.

4. Free Elections in Judea, Samaria and Gaza on the Road to Negotiations

In order to bring about a process of political negotiations and in order to locate legitimate representatives of the Palestinian population, the prime minister proposes that free elections be held among the Arabs of Judea, Samaria and Gaza—elections that will be free of the intimidation and terror of the PLO.

These elections will permit the development of an authentic representation that is not self-appointed from the outside. This representation will be comprised of people who will be chosen by the population in free elections and who will express, in advance, their willingness to take part in the following diplomatic process.

The aim of the elections is to bring about the establishment of a delegation that will participate in negotiations on an interim settlement, in which a self-governing administration will be set up. The interim period will serve as an essential test of cooperation and coexistence. It will be followed by negotiations on the final settlement, in which Israel will be prepared to discuss any option which will be presented.

The US administration has expressed its support for the idea, and following the prime minister's return, his proposals will be discussed here and the various questions surrounding the holding of elections will be examined. Contacts necessary for the implementation of the proposals will be maintained.

APPENDIX 9

LETTER FROM U.S. SECRETARY OF STATE GEORGE P. SHULTZ TO ISRAELI PRIME MINISTER YITZHAK SHAMIR, MARCH 4, 1988, OUTLINING U.S. PEACE PROPOSAL

I set forth below the understanding which I am convinced is necessary to achieve the prompt opening of negotiations on a comprehensive peace. This statement of understandings emerges from discussions held with you and other regional leaders. I look forward to the letter of reply of the government of Israel in confirmation of this statement.

The agreed objective is a comprehensive peace plan providing for the security of all the states in the region and for the legitimate rights of the Palestinian people.

Negotiations will start on an early date certain between Israel and each of its neighbors which is willing to do so. These negotiations could begin by May 1, 1988. Each of these negotiations will be based on United Nations Security Council Resolutions 242 and 338, in all their parts. The parties to each bilateral negotiation will determine the procedure and agenda of their negotiation. All participants in the negotiations must state their willingness to negotiate with one another.

As concerns negotiations between the Israeli delegation and the Jordanian-Palestinian delegation, negotiations will begin on arrangements for a transitional period, with the objective of completing them within six months. Seven months after transitional negotiations begin, final status negotiations will begin, with the objective of completing them within one year.

These negotiations will be based on all the provisions and principles of United Nations Security Council Resolution 242. Final status talks will start before the transitional period begins. The transitional period will begin three months after the conclusion of the transitional agreement and will last for three years. The United States will participate in both negotiations and will promote their rapid conclusion. In particular, the United States will submit a draft

Source: *Journal of Palestine Studies*, No. 68, Summer 1988, p. 191.

agreement for the parties' consideration at the outset of the negotiations on transitional arrangements.

Two weeks before the opening of negotiations, an international conference will be held. The secretary-general of the United Nations will be asked to issue invitations to the parties involved in the Arab-Israeli conflict and the five permanent members of the United Nations Security Council. All participants in the conference must accept United Nations Security Council Resolutions 242 and 338, and renounce violence and terrorism. The parties to each bilateral negotiation may refer reports on the status of their negotiations to the conference, in a manner to be agreed. The conference will not be able to impose solutions or veto agreements reached.

Palestinian representation will be within the Jordanian-Palestinian delegation. The Palestinian issue will be addressed in the negotiations between the Jordanian-Palestinian and Israeli delegations. Negotiations between the Israeli delegation and the Jordanian-Palestinian delegation will proceed independently of any other negotiations.

This statement of understandings is an integral whole. The United States understands that your acceptance is dependent on the implementation of each element in good faith.

Appendix 10

JAMES A. BAKER, ADDRESS TO
AMERICAN ISRAEL PUBLIC AFFAIRS COMMITEE,
WASHINGTON, D.C., 22 MAY 1989

There have been many analyses of the U.S.-Israeli relationship over the years and most of them begin with the fact that we share common values of freedom and democracy. That is the golden thread in the tapestry of U.S.-Israeli ties and there are other strands as well. I was proud to work in the Reagan administration that recognized the importance of U.S.-Israeli strategic cooperation and gave fiber and sinew to our strategic partnership. I'm proud also to have played a part in pioneering a historic free trade agreement with Israel which may well become a model for other nations. President Bush believes, and I believe, that on these issues, there can be only one policy and that is *continuity.* American support for Israel is the foundation of our approach to the Middle East.

Such support has become all the more important as we approach what I think is a critical juncture in the Middle East. For many years we have associated that region with either the vanished glories of ancient history or the terrible costs of modern conflict. But now the world is changing. We have seen longstanding problems in other regions begin to abate. The president spoke last week of promising and hopeful, if incomplete, developments in the Soviet Union. Everywhere there is a quickening consciousness that the globe is being transformed through the search for democracy, the spread of free enterprise, and technological progress.

The Middle East should be able to participate fully in these new developments. Often we think of the region as a place full of precious resources, such as oil and minerals. But the area's most precious resource is the lives of its peoples.

And that is the stake. Are the peoples of the Middle East going to safeguard their most precious resource? Are they going to join the rest of the changing world in the works of peace? Or is this region going to pioneer in conflict once more, through the proliferation of chemical weapons and ballistic missiles?

The people of Israel are vitally concerned with these questions. Israel is a vigorous democracy. The Israelis are among world leaders in communications,

---

Source: *Journal of Palestine Studies,* No. 72, Summer 1989, pp. 172–176.

electronics, and avionics—the new technological revolutions. And Israel understood long ago that the most important of her natural resources is the skill and
intelligence of her people.

Peace Process: Principles and Pragmatism

This is the wider context in which we and Israel must consider the peace
process. The outcome is of vital concern both to Israel's future and for our
vision of a free and peaceful world.

Not so long ago, we marked a decade of the Camp David Peace Accords.
That occasion reminded us not only of how far we have come but how much
further we must go. I want to report that we and Israel have taken some
important steps forward.

Before Prime Minister Shamir visited Washington, we had called for some
Israeli ideas on how to restart the peace process. We did so based on our
conviction that a key condition for progress was a productive U.S.-Israeli
partnership. And I believe that the best way to be productive is through
consultation rather than confrontation.

Let me assure you that we were not disappointed. The prime minister will
forgive me, I am sure, if I divulge to you a conversation at our very first meeting.

The prime minister said that, in preparing for his visit, he had studied
President Bush and me, just as he expected that we had studied him. I had
been described by the media as an ever-flexible pragmatist. The prime minister
had been described as an inflexible man of ideological principle. Well, said the
prime minister, the journalists were wrong in both cases. Yes, he said, "I am
a man of principle, but I am also a pragmatist, who knows what political
compromise means." And, he said that it was clear that I—although a pragmatist—
was also a man of principle, and that principle would guide my foreign policy
approach.

Needless to say, I didn't disagree with the prime minister. If ever an opening
statement achieved its goal of establishing a strong working relationship, this
was it. We understood each other to be pragmatists, guided by principle.

As we approach the peace process, together, we understand Israel's caution
especially when assessing Arab attitudes about peace. I don't blame Israel for
exercising this caution. Its history and geopolitical situation require it.

At the same time, caution must never become paralysis. Ten years after Camp
David, Egypt remains firmly committed to peace and Arab attitudes are changing.
Egypt's readmission into the Arab League on its own terms and with the peace
treaty intact is one sign of change. Evolving Palestinian attitudes are another.
Much more needs to be done—to be demonstrated—that such change is real.
But it cannot be ignored even now. This is surely a time when, as the prime
minister said, the right mix of principles and pragmatism is required.

U.S. Views

As we assess these changes, U.S. policies benefit from a longstanding commitment to sound principles, principles which have worked in practice to advance
the peace process.

First, the U.S. believes that the objective of the peace process is a comprehensive settlement achieved through negotiations based on United Nations Security Council resolutions 242 and 338. In our view, these negotiations must involve territory for peace, security, and recognition for Israel and all states, and Palestinian political rights.

Second, for negotiations to succeed, they must allow the parties to deal directly with each other, face-to-face. A properly structured international conference could be useful *at an appropriate time*, but only if it did not interfere with or in any way replace or be a substitute for the direct talks between the parties.

Third, the issues involved in the negotiations are far too complex, and the emotions are far too deep, to move directly to a final settlement. Accordingly, some transitional period is needed, associated in time and sequence with negotiations on final status. Such a transition will allow the parties to take the measure of each other's performance, to encourage attitudes to change, and to demonstrate that peace and coexistence is desired.

Fourth, in advance of direct negotiations, the United States and no other party, inside or outside, can or will dictate an outcome. That is why the United States does not support annexation or permanent Israeli control of the West Bank and Gaza, nor do we support the creation of an independent Palestinian state.

I would add here that we do have an idea about the reasonable middle ground to which a settlement should be directed. That is, self-government for Palestinians in the West Bank and Gaza in a manner acceptable to Palestinians, Israel, and Jordan. Such a formula provides ample scope for Palestinians to achieve their full political rights. It also provides ample protection for Israel's security as well.

Pre-Negotiations

Following these principles, we face a pragmatic issue: how to get negotiations under way. Unfortunately, the gap between the parties on key issues such as Palestinian representation and the shape of a final settlement remains very very wide. Violence has also soured the atmosphere. A quick move to negotiations is therefore unlikely. And in the absence of either a minimum of good will or any movement to close the gap, a high-visibility American initiative we think has little basis on which to stand.

If we were to stop here, the situation would be gloomy indeed. But we are not going to stop with the status quo. We are engaged and will work to help create an environment to launch and sustain negotiations. This will require tough, but necessary decisions for peace by everyone. It will also require a commitment to a process of negotiations clearly tied to the search for a permanent settlement of the conflict.

When Prime Minister Shamir visited Washington in March, he indicated that he shared our view that the status quo was unacceptable. He brought an idea for elections to—in his words—"launch a political negotiating process" which would involve transitional arrangements and final status. The prime minister made clear that all sides would be free to bring their preferred positions to the table, and that the negotiated outcome must be acceptable to all. The United States welcomed these Israeli ideas and undertook to see whether it could help in creating an atmosphere which could sustain such a process.

Just last week, the Israeli cabinet approved a more detailed version of the prime minister's proposal, indicating Israeli government positions on some, but not all, of the issues involved. The Israeli proposal is, in our view, an important and positive start down the road toward constructing workable negotiations.

The Israeli government *has* offered an initiative, and it *has* given us something with which to work. It has taken a stand on some important issues—and this deserves a constructive Palestinian and broader Arab response.

Much work needs to be done—to elicit Palestinian and Arab thinking on the key elements in the process, to flesh out some details of the Israeli proposals, and to bridge areas where viewpoints differ. Both sides must build political constituencies for peace. Each idea, proposal, or detail should be developed as a deal maker, not a deal breaker.

It may be possible to reach agreement, for example, on the standards of a workable elections process. Such elections should be free and fair, and free of interference from any quarter. Through open access to media and outside observers, the integrity of the electoral process can be affirmed. And participation in the elections should be as open as possible.

It is therefore high time for serious political dialogue between Israeli officials and Palestinians in the territories to bring about a common understanding on these and other issues. Peace, and the peace process, must be built from the "ground up." Palestinians have it within their power to help define the shape of this initiative and its essential elements. They shouldn't shy from a dialogue with Israel that can transform the current environment, and determine the ground rules for getting to, conducting, and moving beyond elections.

We should not hide from ourselves the difficulties that face even these steps at the beginning. For many Israelis, it will not be easy to enter a negotiating process whose successful outcome will in all probability involve territorial withdrawal and the emergence of a new political reality. For Palestinians, such an outcome will mean an end to the illusion of control over all of Palestine, and it will mean full recognition of Israel as a neighbor and partner in trade and human contact.

Challenges Ahead

There is no real constructive alternative to the process I have outlined. Continuation of the status quo will lead to increasing violence and worsening prospects for peace. Now is the time to move toward a serious negotiating process, to create the atmosphere for a renewed peace process. Let the Arab world take concrete steps toward accommodation with Israel—not in place of the peace process, but as a catalyst for it. End the economic boycott. Stop the challenges to Israel's standing in international organizations. Repudiate the odious line that Zionism is racism.

For Israel, now is the time to lay aside, once and for all, the unrealistic vision of a greater Israel. Israeli interests in the West Bank and Gaza—security and otherwise—can be accommodated in a settlement based on Resolution 242. Forswear annexation. Stop settlement activity. Allow schools to reopen. Reach out to the Palestinians as neighbors who deserve political rights.

For Palestinians, now is the time to speak with one voice for peace. Renounce the policy of phases in all languages, not just those addressed to the West. Practice constructive diplomacy, not attempts to distort international organizations, such as the World Health Organization. Amend the covenant. Translate the dialogue of violence in the intifadah into a dialogue of politics and diplomacy. Violence will not work. Reach out to Israelis and convince them of your peaceful intentions. You have the most to gain from doing so, and no one else can or *will* do it for you. Finally, understand that no one is going to "deliver" Israel for you.

For outside parties—in particular, the Soviet Union—now is the time to make "new thinking" a reality as it applies to the Middle East. I must say that Chairman Gorbachev and Foreign Minister Shevardnadze told me in Moscow ten days ago that Soviet policy is changing. New laws regarding emigration will soon be discussed by the Supreme Soviet. Jewish life in the Soviet Union is also looking better, with students beginning to study their heritage freely. Finally, the Soviet Union agreed with us last week Prime Minister Shamir's election proposal was worthy of consideration.

These are all positive signs.

But the Soviets must go further to demonstrate convincingly that they are serious about new thinking in the Arab-Israel conflict. Let Moscow restore diplomatic ties with Israel, for example. The Soviets should also help promote a serious peace process, not just empty slogans. It is time for the Soviet Union to behave responsibly when it comes to arms, and stop the supply of sophisticated weapons to countries like Libya.

I said at the beginning of this speech that the Middle East had approached a turning point. I believe that this region, so full of potential, will not remain immune from the changes sweeping the rest of the world. These changes begin with the quest for democracy, for individual freedom and choice. Long ago Israel chose this path. And long ago, the American people decided to walk with Israel in her quest for peace and security.

The policy I have described today reaffirms and renews that course. For our part, the United States will move ahead steadily and carefully, in a step-by-step approach designed to help the parties make the necessary decisions for peace. Perhaps Judge Learned Hand expressed it best when he said, ". . . we shall have to be content with short steps; . . . but we shall have gone forward, if we bring to our task . . . patience, understanding, sympathy, forbearance, generosity, fortitude, and above all an inflexible determination."

APPENDIX 11

STOCKHOLM STATEMENT

The text of the joint PLO-American delegation statement, presented by Swedish Foreign Minister Sten Anderson:

"The Palestinian National Council met in Algiers from November 12 to 15, 1988, and announced the declaration of independence which proclaimed the state of Palestine and issued a political statement.

"The following explanation was given by the representatives of the PLO of certain important points in the Palestinian declaration of independence and the political statement adopted by the PNC in Algiers.

"Affirming the principles incorporated in those UN resolutions which call for a two-state solution of Israel and Palestine, the PNC:

"1. Agreed to enter into peace negotiations at an international conference under the auspices of the UN with the participation of the permanent members of the Security Council and the PLO as the sole legitimate representative of the Palestinian people, on equal footing with the other parties to the conflict; such an international conference is to be held on the basis of UN resolutions 242 and 338 and the right of the Palestinian people of self-determination, without the external interference, as provided in the UN Charter, including the right to an independent state, which conference should resolve the Palestinian problem in all its aspects;

"2. Established the independent state of Palestine and accepted the existence of Israel as a state in the region;

"3. Declared its rejection and condemnation of terrorism in all its forms, including state terrorism;

"4. Called for a solution to the Palestinian refugee problem in accordance with international law and practices and relevant UN resolutions (including right of return or compensation)."

Source: Member of American-Jewish Stockholm delegation.

Appendix 12

YESH GVUL, STATEMENT REGARDING MILITARY SERVICE IN THE OCCUPIED TERRITORIES, JERUSALEM, JANUARY 1988

The following statement was signed by one hundred sixty-one Israeli army reservists and was released at a Jerusalem press conference.

The Palestinian people are rising up against the Israeli occupation in the territories. Over twenty years of occupation and repression have not stopped the Palestinian struggle for national liberation. The insurrection in the occupied territories, and its brutal repression by the army, show clearly the terrible price of the lasting occupation and the lack of a political solution. We, reserve soldiers of Zahal (the IDF), proclaim that we will no longer bear the burden of sharing responsibility for this moral and political deterioration. We hereby declare that we shall refuse to take part in the repression of the insurrection and revolt in the occupied territories.

Source: *Journal of Palestine Studies*, No. 68, Summer 1988, p. 201.

Appendix 13

TEXT OF LETTER SIGNED BY WEST BANK LEADERS REJECTING ISRAEL'S ELECTION PLAN, JERUSALEM, 27 APRIL 1989

As the Palestinian uprising enters its eighteenth month with continued vigor and self-confidence, it illustrates its aim to continue until its objectives are achieved: putting an end to the occupation, guaranteeing the right of Palestinian refugees to return, and the right of the Palestinian people to self-determination and to establish an independent Palestinian state with Jerusalem as its capital under the leadership of the PLO. While the PLO fights our political battle within the framework of the Palestine National Council resolutions from Algiers, the Israeli government finds itself more internationally isolated than ever before: Israel has been stripped of its main support and has been revealed as a terrorist state suppressing, with blood and force, a civilian population struggling with legitimate means for national independence.

Instead of responding to the Palestinians' call for peace and the demands of the uprising and to begin negotiations with the PLO within the framework of an international peace conference, which will be able to achieve a comprehensive, just peace and to give guarantees of security for all states in the region, the Israeli government offers the project of Shamir, which is nothing more than a maneuver for the media to save Israel from its international isolation.

Shamir's project stands in total contradiction to the practice of his government's policies in the occupied State of Palestine: the military forces at the disposal of Shamir are physically searching for Palestinian national leaders and political activists to imprison, exile, and, at times, kill them.

Israel is violating the human rights of the Palestinians, brutally suppressing the Palestinians in the occupied state, and blatantly ignoring their declared political points of view which clearly address the concept of Shamir's "elections." These declared points of view are the following:

1) The PLO is the sole, legitimate representative of the Palestinian people in the occupied State of Palestine and the diaspora. The Palestinians chose their representatives decades ago and have reiterated their choice through the uprising.

Source: *Journal of Palestine Studies*, No. 72, Summer 1989, pp. 155–157.

The price of declaring this choice of the PLO as our sole, legitimate representative is shown in the daily count of martyrs in the course of the uprising. Shamir's proposal ignores this fact.

2) The Palestinian people is an indivisible whole, and the PLO, as an official body and with its legitimate leadership, is the symbol of the unity and national identity of our people, both inside and outside Palestine. The attempt to select local representatives is an attempt to divide our people into "inside" and "outside" Palestinians. Shamir's project indicates his lack of seriousness: what is needed is to negotiate with the Palestinian people as a whole to solve the Palestinian question, not with any isolated fragment. Negotiations must begin with the representatives of the Palestinian people as a whole and not with the representatives of any fragment.

3) In addition to being the sole, legitimate representative of our people, the PLO is the framework of our struggle for freedom and a symbol which embodies the identity of the Palestinian people as a whole and its aspirations for return, self-determination, and an independent state. Shamir's attempt to ignore the PLO is an attempt to ignore our political legitimacy as well as our legitimate aspirations. By initiating and focusing a debate in the media and international community on the issue of representation of the population of the [occupied] territories, and bypassing the question of an entire people's search for national independence, we see that the rejection of negotiations with the PLO is a rejection of the existence of a Palestinian people searching for self-determination.

The Palestinian people's rejection of the idea of any elections held prior to the withdrawal of the Israeli army from the West Bank and Gaza Strip emanates from what has been mentioned above; it is not an indication, as some Israelis claim, of the people's rejection of democratic practices. At the Algiers PNC sessions, our people proved its love for, and practice of, democracy. The PLO in general and the uprising in particular have completed the establishment of an internal democratic structure. Our rejection of the election proposal does not indicate a rejection of elections as democratic practice, but is the rejection of a project which ignores the essence of the conflict. The elections proposed by Shamir do not constitute democratic practice within an entire political process with clearly defined principles: this isolated occurrence of elections does not illustrate how it will lead to the end of the occupation and to Palestinian national independence.

We believe real peace in the region cannot be achieved by projects that are calculated to appeal to the media, to end the uprising, and to win time. We believe that the achievement of a real solution and a lasting peace require that:

1) The Israeli government recognize the Palestinians as a people with a right to a secure life and an independent state.

2) The Israeli government recognize the necessity of negotiations with the PLO within the framework of an international conference until the establishment of a Palestinian state.

3) The United Nations administer the affairs of the occupied territories in the transitional period.

4) The international conference give suitable guarantees of security for all states in the region, according to definite principles agreed upon by all the parties.

We believe the Israeli government now bears the responsibility of taking the next step towards peace: there is, so far, a total lack of any serious response by the Israeli government to the Palestinian peace initiative taken at the PNC by the leadership of the Palestinian people—the PLO. If Israel wants to prove its seriousness, the Israeli government should respond positively to the Palestinian initiative and immediately cease its suppressive and inhuman practices in the land of our occupied state—this response is far more realistic than to propose projects which illustrate only a lack of commitment to the establishment of a lasting peace.

SELECTED BIBLIOGRAPHY

BOOKS

Al-Haq: Law in the Service of Man. *Punishing a Nation—Human Rights Violations During the Palestinian Uprising—December 1987–1988.* Ramallah, West Bank, 1988.

Aronoff, Myron J. *Israeli Visions and Divisions: Cultural Change and Political Conflict.* New Brunswick: Transaction Press, 1989.

Benvenisti, Meron. *1987 Report: Demographic, Economic, Legal, Social and Political Developments in the West Bank.* Jerusalem: West Bank Data Base Project, 1987.

_____ . *The West Bank Handbook: A Political Lexicon.* Jerusalem: Jerusalem Post, 1986.

Franks, Lynne R. *Israel and the Occupied Territories,* World Education Series. Washington, D.C.: American Association of Collegiate Registrars and Admissions Officers, 1987.

Jaffee Center for Strategic Studies. *The West Bank and Gaza: Israel's Options for Peace.* Tel-Aviv, 1989.

Krough, Peter F., and Mary C. McDavid (eds.). *Palestine Under Occupation: Prospects for the Future.* Washington, D.C.: Georgetown University, 1989.

Legum, Colin, Haim Shaked, Daniel Dishon, and Itamar Rabinovich (eds.). *Middle East Contemporary Survey,* vols. VI (1981–1982)–X (1986). Tel-Aviv: Tel-Aviv University, 1983–1988.

Lesch, Ann Moseley. *Israel's Occupation of the West Bank: The First Two Years.* Santa Monica: Rand Corporation, 1979.

_____ . *Political Perceptions of the Palestinians on the West Bank and the Gaza Strip.* Washington, D.C.: Middle East Institute, 1980.

Peretz, Don. *The West Bank: History, Politics, Society, and Economy.* Boulder, Colo.: Westview Press, 1986.

Reich, Bernard, and Gershon R. Kieval (eds.). *Israeli National Security Policy.* Westport, Conn.: Greenwood Press, 1988.

Roy, Sara. *The Gaza Strip.* Jerusalem: West Bank Data Base Project, 1986.

Shinar, Dov. *Palestinian Voices: Communication and Nation Building in the West Bank.* Boulder, Colo.: Lynne Rienner Publishers, 1987.

Shipler, David. *Arab and Jew: Wounded Spirits in a Promised Land.* New York and Toronto: Times Books, 1986.

Smooha, Sammy. *Arabs and the Jews in Israel, Vol. 1: Conflicting and Shared Attitudes in a Divided Society.* Boulder, Colo.: Westview Press, 1989.

Sullivan, Antony Thrall. *Palestinian Universities Under Occupation.* Cairo: American University in Cairo Press, 1988.

U.S. Department of State. *Country Reports on Human Rights Practices for 1988.* Washington, D.C.: U.S. Government Printing Office, 1988.

PERIODICALS AND NEWSPAPERS

Foreign Broadcast Information Service
Haaretz
Hadashot
Israel Press Briefs
Israel Press Highlights
Jerusalem Post
Jerusalem Post International Edition
Jerusalem Post Weekly
Jewish Telegraphic Agency
Journal of Palestine Studies
Los Angeles Times
Ma'ariv
Ma'ariv International Edition
Manchester Guardian Weekly
Middle East Report
Nation
New Outlook
New York Times
The Other Israel
Tikkun
USFI Field Staff Reports
Washington Report on Middle East Affairs

INDEX